"*Results* makes a solid case for organization types and the four building blocks that make up a company's DNA. Neilson and Pasternack show how business leaders can use these tools to diagnose problems and modify their company's DNA to create sustainable solutions and a healthy company."

—Chad Holliday, chairman and CEO, DuPont

"*Results* is critical for any executive. You'll learn how to figure out the DNA of your organization and then act on that knowledge. With readable tales and enlightening examples, it shows how to build on what's good and discard what's bad."

—Walter Isaacson, CEO of Aspen Institute, author of
Benjamin Franklin: An American Life

"*Results* identifies a number of all-too-common organizational pathologies that get in the way of business performance. More than that, Neilson and Pasternack provide explicit, example-filled advice on how to fix the problems and take your organization to the next level."

—Jeffrey Pfeffer, professor of organizational behavior,
Stanford Business School, coauthor of *The Knowing-Doing Gap*

Also by Bruce A. Pasternack

THE CENTERLESS CORPORATION

RESULTS

KEEP WHAT'S GOOD,

FIX WHAT'S WRONG,

AND UNLOCK

GREAT PERFORMANCE

GARY L. NEILSON &
BRUCE A. PASTERNACK

CROWN
BUSINESS
NEW YORK

Library of Congress Cataloging-in-Publication Data
Neilson, Gary L.
Results : keep what's good, fix what's wrong, and unlock great
performance / Gary L. Neilson and Bruce A. Pasternack.—1st ed.
Includes bibliographical references and index.
1. Organizational change. 2. Decision making. 3. Organizational
effectiveness. 4. Management by objectives. 5. Performance.
I. Pasternack, Bruce A. II. Title.
HD58.8.N446   2005
658.4'06—dc22   2005009527

ISBN 13: 978-1-4000-9839-2
ISBN 10: 1-4000-9839-4

Printed in the United States of America

Design by Robert Bull

10   9   8   7   6   5   4

First Edition

CONTENTS

ONE: A Tale of Two Managers   1

TWO: The Four Building Blocks: Laying the Foundation for Results   15

THREE: The Passive-Aggressive Organization:
Everyone Agrees but Nothing Changes   43

FOUR: The Fits-and-Starts Organization: Let 1,000 Flowers Bloom   71

FIVE: The Outgrown Organization: The Good Old Days Meet a Brave New World   97

SIX: The Overmanaged Organization:
"We're from Corporate and We're Here to Help"   129

SEVEN: The Just-in-Time Organization: Succeeding by the Skin of Our Teeth   153

EIGHT: The Military Precision Organization: Flying in Formation   185

NINE: The Resilient Organization: As Good as It Gets   211

TEN: Caterpillar's Journey to Resilience: The Cat That Came Back   237

The Research Behind the Book   265

Notes   281
Acknowledgments   291
Index   293

ONE

A TALE OF TWO MANAGERS

Why is it that some organizations can bob and weave and roll with the punches, consistently delivering on commitments and producing great results, while others can't seem to leave their corner of the ring without tripping on their own shoelaces? To answer that question, let's start by taking a closer look at what's going on beneath the surface.

It's late in the morning one day in early April as Judy DeGrasse and George Sullivan emerge from the quarterly management meeting deep in conversation about what the CEO, Bill Corrigan, has just said. Judy, a new account manager in *ZZ Electronics'** core media products division, is invigorated. Corrigan has just announced a major new device that promises to not only accelerate sales growth but also to catapult the company to the forefront of the industry. It will deliver greater performance at lower cost and resurrect the company's flagging brand . . . all by Christmas, when the new product is scheduled for release.

George, on the other hand, is unenthused. A director in the market research department and fifteen-year company veteran, he has seen this show before, and he knows how it will end. The top brass paint a good big picture, but they never provide the resources that the rank-and-file need to deliver on the vision—not just the bodies and the budget, but the information, the decision-making authority, and the incentives to get it done. In his gut,

*Composite company names are indicated in italics at their first mention.

George knows this will be just another failed program-of-the-month. Of course, his cynicism did not keep him from raising his hand along with everyone else when Corrigan asked them all to signal their commitment.

"You want to grab some lunch?" George asks Judy.

"Thanks, but I'd better eat at my desk today. I'll need to meet with my team this afternoon to start brainstorming. I'm not sure how we'll get this all done before the holiday shopping season hits."

"Whoa, Judy, let me give you a little advice. You've got to pace yourself or you're going to burn out. There's no way we're going to make that deadline, and there's no sense killing yourself in the attempt. Never in my fifteen years with ZZ Electronics have we turned a new product around in six months, and we're not going to start now. We just lost ten people in my unit during the last round of cutbacks, and the ones I have left are working on that market analysis project that was last week's priority number one. If anyone had bothered to ask me before this meeting, I would have told them this was a nonstarter."

"Yes, but Bill said we're going to halve the cycle time on this, and I think we can do it," persists Judy. "We've got the best engineers in the industry. So, it takes a few nights and weekends. This might just put us back on the map."

George chuckles, "Well, then go for it. I admire your spirit, Judy."

Judy returns to the office to find it empty. Her colleagues, like George, are at lunch. So Judy takes the initiative and draws up an action plan, which she e-mails to various people in the organization who will provide critical inputs. A week passes and no response. Judy hopes that their silence means they are in agreement and implementing the plan, but she harbors the suspicion that maybe George is right.

Meanwhile, the marketing department has sent out a press release and industry analysts are talking up this new product. It is better, faster, cheaper, and will be in stores everywhere in time for Christmas. The trains of internal commitment and external expectation have left the station, and they are on a collision course.

The first casualty: the CEO. When the third quarter closes at the end of September and the promised new product is not ready for shipment, ZZ Electronics' stock takes a nosedive . . . as does Bill Corrigan's credibility with the trade and financial community. The board, feeling the heat of an irate market, summarily ousts Corrigan, installing a senior director as interim head of the company. The search commences for a permanent replacement . . . and the organization hangs in limbo, not sure what the new regime will bring.

George and Judy meet at the end of the year for lunch. George is solicitous. Judy is chastened. Not only did her e-mail fall on deaf ears, but she's been reprimanded by her boss for reaching out to other parts of the organization without his express approval. Her wings have been clipped.

"You were right," she admits as she orders a glass of wine.

"No, you are," replies George, "we *should* be winning in the marketplace, not wheezing our way to the finish line. But there's something about this place that brings out the bare minimum instead of the best in people. I stopped trying to figure out why two CEOs ago."

A business is basically a collection of people working toward a common goal. The same can be said of any government or charitable enterprise. Yet, anyone who has worked in an organization of any size—private or public—has experienced firsthand the individual behaviors that can take root and either help or hinder an organization's ultimate results.[1] George's "wait and see" attitude . . . the slap on the wrist Judy receives . . . Marketing's blithe ignorance of the true status of the new product . . . these are all examples of the individual counterproductive behaviors that impede organizational performance. Yes, the external marketplace today is unquestionably more demanding, and, yes, the CEO is partly to blame when things go wrong. But the true enemy too often lies deeper within. As one middle manager we recently worked with put it, "We have inflicted more pain on ourselves than have our competitors."

If you listen closely to the lunchroom chatter at organizations like the one George and Judy work for, chances are you'll hear some of the same complaints:

- "Everyone agrees on a course of action, but nothing changes."
- "There goes another opportunity, while we wait for a decision."
- "It's a great idea; it'll never happen."
- "I'm either micromanaged or left holding the bag."
- "The businesses and functions just aren't working together to get results."
- "I don't feel motivated to go the extra mile. What's in it for me?"
- "Ready . . . aim . . . aim . . . aim . . ."
- "We have the right strategy and a clear implementation plan, but we can't seem to execute."

Why do these statements resonate with so many people at companies like ZZ Electronics? Why, in a nutshell, are there so many more Georges than Judys in so many organizations? We could throw around a lot of consulting jargon and show you a series of complex charts, but the reason is too simple for such devices. People at work—whether they're top executives, senior managers, middle managers, or business professionals—are products of their environment . . . and most organizations are inherently unhealthy.

THE POWER OF THE INDIVIDUAL

But the damage is not permanent. It's reversible. And that's the message of this book. It's within your power to make your organization healthy. By focusing on the building blocks of how your organization works—or doesn't—you can keep what's good, fix what's wrong, and unlock performance to produce great results. The self-defeating behaviors you witness every day are not external factors beyond your control. They are the direct result of your actions and decisions . . . and those of every other person working within your organization. The key to unlocking superior results is aligning those thousands of daily actions and decisions with the strategic objectives of the enterprise.

This goal—getting everyone in your organization from the top to the bottom aligned to achieve great results—is not wishful thinking. It starts with a little self-analysis. First, however, you need to determine whether you are a George or a Judy. The Georges dismiss the possibility of organizational transformation as so much science fiction. Judys celebrate the ability of optimistic individuals to change the world.

Some organizational fixes require leadership from the top, and we'll discuss these, but, in our experience, there are more opportunities for people in the middle of the organization to make a real impact than is commonly addressed or even perceived by the individuals themselves. Not only can middle managers make a difference, but no significant change is possible without their commitment and follow-through. As our opening story illustrates, top management's directives mean very little unless they are translated into individual behavior changes further down in the organization.

The key to inspiring such pervasive change is developing a common view on what works (and should be kept) and what is wrong and how to fix it. That's where this book comes in. It provides individual managers at every level with an objective perspective on their organization, one they could not otherwise acquire from the inside. Furthermore, it quickly moves beyond a diagnosis to a set of specific remedies designed to generate results. By taking an online self-assessment survey of nineteen short questions, you can generate an instant snapshot of your organization—what it looks like, how it tends to behave, and, most important, where the dysfunctions are and how to fix them.

What you do with that information is your choice. You can resolve to change your own behavior and, by so doing, inspire change in others. You can get your whole organization to take the survey and evaluate results and potential remedies together. Or you can dismiss the results as provocative, but not worth acting on. In short, you can break the cycle or remain its complicit victim.

ORGANIZATIONAL DNA

So, how do you build a better organization? How do you reverse entropy and restore an organization to robust health and profitability? How do you change a George into a Judy? The first step is figuring out what sort of organization you live in. What are its unique traits and attributes? What is its "DNA"?

The DNA metaphor is useful in understanding the idiosyncratic characteristics of an organization. Like the DNA of living organisms, the DNA of living organizations consists of four basic building blocks, which combine and recombine to express distinct identities, or personalities (see Figure 1.1). These organizational building blocks—decision rights, information, motivators, and structure—largely determine how a firm looks and behaves, both internally and externally. The good news is that—unlike human DNA—organizational DNA can be modified.

FIGURE 1.1—THE FOUR BUILDING BLOCKS OF ORGANIZATIONAL DNA

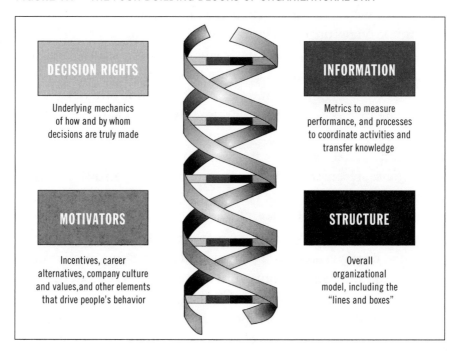

DECISION RIGHTS

Underlying mechanics of how and by whom decisions are truly made

INFORMATION

Metrics to measure performance, and processes to coordinate activities and transfer knowledge

MOTIVATORS

Incentives, career alternatives, company culture and values, and other elements that drive people's behavior

STRUCTURE

Overall organizational model, including the "lines and boxes"

An organization's DNA strongly influences—and, in some ways, even determines—each individual employee's behavior. It explains why the Georges in your organization behave as they do. It accounts for your behavior as well. Which customers do you call on? Which e-mails do you leave unanswered? What determines whether you offer a customer a discount to increase volume or hold the line to protect margins? How do you share information with someone in another business unit or region? These daily decisions—often made far from the executive suite—determine an organization's ultimate success or failure.

The next chapter examines each of the organizational DNA building blocks and how they combine in different patterns to influence both functional and dysfunctional behavior. We also suggest, through real-world case examples, how you can adjust and integrate your organization's decision rights, information, motivators, and structure to drive improved performance.

THE SEVEN ORGANIZATIONAL TYPES

Based on the nature of each of these four DNA building blocks and the degree of coherence between and among them, most organizations fall into one of seven broad types—four unhealthy, and three healthy:[2]

Passive-Aggressive

"Everyone agrees, but nothing changes."

This is the seething, smiley-face organization. Building consensus to make major changes is not a problem; implementing these changes, however, is next to impossible. Entrenched, underground resistance from field operations routinely defeats corporate initiatives, as line employees assume "this too shall pass." Confronted with an apathetic organization, senior management laments the futility of "nailing Jell-O to the wall."

Fits-and-Starts

"Let 1,000 flowers bloom."

This organization lures intellect and initiative—smart people with an entrepreneurial bent, but they often do not pull in the same direction at the same time. It's a no-holds-barred environment where you can take an idea and run with it. But, in the absence of strong direction from the top and a solid foundation of common values below, these initiatives either clash and burn or simply peter out. The result is an overextended organization on the verge of spinning out of control.

Outgrown

"The good old days meet a brave new world."

This organization is literally bursting at the seams, having expanded beyond its original organizational model. Because power is closely held at the top, the Outgrown organization tends to react slowly to market developments and often finds it cannot get out of its own way. If you're in the middle of this organization, you might well see opportunities for positive change, but it's just too hard to run these ideas up the flagpole. The legacy of top-down direction and decision-making is too well entrenched.

Overmanaged

"We're from corporate, and we're here to help."

Burdened with multiple layers of management, this organization is a case study in "analysis paralysis." More consumed with the trees than the forest, managers spend their time checking subordinates' work rather than scanning the horizon for new opportunities or threats. Frequently bureaucratic and highly political, this organization frustrates self-starters and results-oriented individuals.

Just-in-Time

"Succeeding by the skin of our teeth"

Although not always proactive in preparing for change, this type of organization has demonstrated an ability to "turn on a dime" when necessary, without losing sight of the big picture. Just-in-Time organizations have a "can-do" attitude that infuses the office and inspires creative outbursts, frequently real breakthroughs, but it can also burn out the best and brightest bulbs. In the absence of consistent, disciplined structures and processes, this organization's home runs often become "one-hit wonders," rather than a reliable source of competitive advantage, leaving this firm scrambling to stay healthy.

Military Precision

"Flying in formation"

Everyone knows his role and implements it diligently in this organization, creating the overall effect of fluid and consistent execution. The Military Precision organization is hierarchical and operates under a highly controlled management model that allows it to efficiently execute large volumes of similar transactions. It can conceive and execute brilliant strategies—often repeatedly—because it has drilled the organization and run it through every scenario in the manual. However, it does not typically deal well with events not planned for in the playbook.

Resilient

"As good as it gets"

This is the organization that inspires both awe and envy . . . because everything seems to come so easily to it: profits, talent, respect. Like the popular kid in high school who got all As and lettered in track, the Resilient organization seems destined for greatness; it fires on all cylinders. Resilient organizations are flexible, forward looking, and fun, and they attract team players. While it may hit a bump in the road—as all companies do—the Resilient organization bounces back immediately, having learned from the experience. The Resilient organization is the healthiest of all the profiles, precisely because it doesn't believe its own press; rather, it is always scanning the horizon for the next competitive battle or market innovation.

FIND OUT WHERE YOU STAND . . . OR SIT

So, which of these organizations do you work for? A quick visit to www.orgdna.com will answer that question. There you will find the *Org DNA Profiler*[SM], an online, self-assessment survey consisting of nineteen short questions.[3] Individuals at all levels in an organization can take this quick survey and not only instantly identify their organization's type but also understand what's working and what's not. You can then diagnose the root causes of your organization's dysfunctional traits and behaviors. Based on that feedback alone, you can begin to make changes.[4]

GENE THERAPY

Most organizations are also-rans. They go through the motions, but they fail to operate at peak performance because of internal obstacles. The building blocks of the organization's DNA—decision rights, information, motivators, and structure—are faulty or misaligned, frustrating the best efforts of its people . . . and the ultimate success of the company.

When an organization's DNA is poorly configured, it exhibits unhealthy symptoms and counterproductive behaviors. Even Resilient companies demonstrate dysfunctional behaviors from time to time; their challenge is to stay vigilant and healthy. The first step in fixing problems is to identify and isolate them. That is the purpose of the *Org DNA Profiler*^{SM}. Using a DNA-based framework, the tool allows you to step back twenty paces and gain some perspective on what is working and what isn't inside your organization.

But generating a profile is not the point. It is one thing to know you are overweight and have high cholesterol, but quite another to convert that diagnosis into remedial action such as an improved diet or more exercise. The *Org DNA Profiler*^{SM} was designed to focus managers on the root causes of their organizational problems. It is up to management to translate these findings into sustainable solutions. The aim of this book is to show you how.

THE ROAD TO RESILIENCE

What kind of organization is yours? Is it Passive-Aggressive? Just-in-Time? Fits-and-Starts?[5] What occurs easily in your organization? What is like pulling teeth? How do people behave, and why? And how could you help make it all work better?

According to our research, most organizations are perceived as unhealthy (see Figure 1.2). But even healthy organizations have issues and behaviors they'd do well to address. Achieving and maintaining good organizational health is a journey, and consistently successful companies are always recognizing the emerging signs of dysfunction and embarking on a new leg of this journey.

Chapters 3 through 9 focus on this perpetual quest by looking at each organizational type in turn. Each chapter will feature the real-life story of a company that recognized the unhealthy symptoms of that particular "type" in its own organization . . . and did something about it. In fact, all of these featured companies, without exception, are today highly successful and healthy enterprises. Since implementing their organizational changes—in some cases, more than ten years ago—all have produced a total return to shareholders that significantly exceeds that of the S&P 500. They have either achieved resilience or are well on their way.

FIGURE 1.2—MOST ORGANIZATIONS PERCEIVED AS UNHEALTHY:
    ORG DNA PROFILER^SM RESULTS

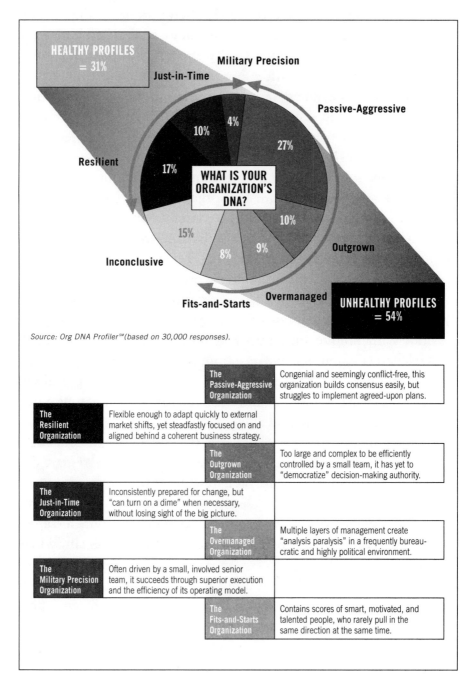

Source: Org DNA Profiler^SM(based on 30,000 responses).

		The Passive-Aggressive Organization	Congenial and seemingly conflict-free, this organization builds consensus easily, but struggles to implement agreed-upon plans.
The Resilient Organization	Flexible enough to adapt quickly to external market shifts, yet steadfastly focused on and aligned behind a coherent business strategy.		
		The Outgrown Organization	Too large and complex to be efficiently controlled by a small team, it has yet to "democratize" decision-making authority.
The Just-in-Time Organization	Inconsistently prepared for change, but "can turn on a dime" when necessary, without losing sight of the big picture.		
		The Overmanaged Organization	Multiple layers of management create "analysis paralysis" in a frequently bureaucratic and highly political environment.
The Military Precision Organization	Often driven by a small, involved senior team, it succeeds through superior execution and the efficiency of its operating model.		
		The Fits-and-Starts Organization	Contains scores of smart, motivated, and talented people, who rarely pull in the same direction at the same time.

And that transition to organizational health carries with it tangible bottom-line benefits. In fact, our research confirms that organizational health correlates strongly with profitability.[6]

In addition to the featured "journey" story, each chapter provides a detailed discussion of the specific characteristics of that organization profile and the potential fixes for the problems associated with it. In the case of unhealthy types, we talk in terms of "symptoms" and "remedies." For healthy types, it's "traits" and "treatments." We illustrate these characteristics with examples and anecdotes from companies we have interviewed or worked with, and with illustrative composite stories we have written based on our fifty-plus years of organizational consulting experience. These illustrative stories zero in on what it feels like to be a middle manager in one of these organizations.

We recommend that you read all seven DNA-type chapters, as there are valuable insights for any organization in each, but readers who skip straight to the chapter most relevant to their organization will find plenty of value as well. Our aim is to arm you not only with unique insights on what's holding your organization back but also an actionable strategy for overcoming or circumventing these obstacles. After reading this book, you should have the knowledge and tools you need to set your organization firmly on the Road to Resilience.

It's important to remember that there is no one-size-fits-all formula. The first step is understanding your "type" and then developing unique solutions based on your unique problems and issues. While it's tempting to think of a great company as a role model and implement whatever they seem to be doing, this is a trap to be avoided. Your situation is different. Your solutions should be as well.

TWO

THE FOUR BUILDING BLOCKS:
Laying the Foundation for Results

Barbara Jackson had seen this movie before. Just back from a tedious meeting, she checked her e-mail, and there was a company-wide announcement from the CEO talking about challenging times and the need for change. She had been with *National Telco* for five years now as director of Sales Planning. Before that she had worked for a wireless competitor, and before that, a short-lived dot-com. She knew what a restructuring memo looked like. There it was in the last paragraph: "To improve our service to customers, we will be reorganizing the company around customer segments, rather than product lines. Effective January 1, our core businesses will no longer be Wireless and Wireline, but rather Consumer, Small Business, and Enterprise. We will be back in touch over the next several weeks with further information about your new role in the company."

Barbara was well versed in what would be coming next: a lot of internally focused meetings on reporting changes and a lot of jockeying for position . . . but, ultimately, no real change in how work got done and no discernible impact on results. This was her fourth "restructuring"; she knew the drill. They all started the same way with an uplifting memo from the CEO promising a brighter future. Then months of confusion and job dislocation would follow . . . maybe a move to a different floor and a new boss . . . then nothing. She and her colleagues would settle into the new routine, which would mimic the old: interminable meetings with different topics, but the same underlying themes—how to push more product, cut costs, work together as a team. In the end, the restructuring would amount to little more than rearranging deck chairs on the *Titanic*.

When an organization fails to produce desired results, the usual solution is a "restructuring"; the company alters who is in charge, who reports to whom, which names go in which boxes, and so on. But this is, at best, only a partial answer; structural fixes by themselves are usually ineffective. Our purpose in this chapter is to broaden your perspective to include all *four* of the building blocks of organizational DNA—decision rights, information, motivators, *and* structure. Only in combination do these building blocks become the key to unlocking great performance.

Underlying the quest for a results-driven enterprise is one central question: How does a business modify its very makeup—the elements of its organizational DNA—to execute the strategy, whatever the strategy is, and successfully adapt when circumstances change?

- "Our industry is undergoing tremendous upheaval, but our people either don't recognize it or won't do anything about it."
- "The merger is supposed to be behind us, yet even Wall Street can see that we're still acting like separate organizations."
- "The Internet usurped our place in the value chain. What happened?"

To address such external changes and discontinuities, you must first understand and remedy the internal constraints that keep organizations from adapting successfully. They're familiar to anyone who has worked in any organization, large or small. Someone hijacks a meeting to advance his own agenda, rather than the firm's. Corporate staffers—overburdened or too far from the action to have the right information—inject delay or unnecessary cost into business unit programs and processes. Organizational units argue about who "owns" what decisions, rather than working together to achieve common goals. Individually, these traits and behaviors are irksome; collectively, they can spell the difference between success and failure. Yet few organizations have discovered the right formula to fix these common problems. Many of us, sadly, are living inside a Dilbert cartoon.

The first step to breaking out of this vicious and debilitating cycle is to recognize the powerful role the individual plays in any organization. Organizations are not monolithic entities; they are collections of individuals who usually act in their own self-interest. They make thousands of decisions and tradeoffs every day influenced by their access to information, the incentives that motivate them, and the consequences that result from their actions. To generate consistently superior results, organizations need to unlock the trapped potential of their own employees by aligning individual actions with the actions of others and the interests of the firm as a whole . . . every day . . . at every level.

So, to use Barbara as an example, she is likely going to make decisions over the next several weeks to preserve her position and domain in the new order. If those decisions coincide with the interests of the customer, then everyone is happy. But that is by no means a guarantee. Barbara is focused on her own agenda; she's not necessarily thinking about whether a bundled calling package is a better deal for the consumer.

The right people—imbued with the right values, armed with the right information, and motivated by the right incentives—are the driving force behind a winning organization. The fundamental challenge is to align these building blocks so the individual's self-interest coincides with the company's agenda. We mention values here, because they are the sine qua non of any successful organization.

Achieving organizational alignment takes different forms from company to company. There is no right answer or universal prescription. The only imperative is that the four building blocks of Organizational DNA—decision rights, information, motivators, and structure—work together rather than at cross purposes to solve the organizational puzzle, as illustrated in Figure 2.1.

FIGURE 2.1—ALIGNING ORGANIZATIONAL DNA BUILDING BLOCKS

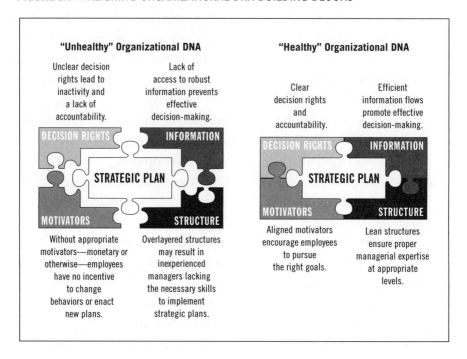

The combinations of and interactions among these four building blocks define the unique traits of each of the seven types of organizations we describe in this book. For example, let's look at the Military Precision organization. Here you have a highly disciplined and tightly controlled operating model, in which decision rights are centralized at corporate headquarters and delegated, on a limited basis, to field operations. The reason the Military Precision model is healthy and so effective for certain types of organizations (e.g., those that handle large volumes of similar transactions) is that its information and motivators are aligned with these decision rights; they reinforce this crisp, tightly delegated operating model. Mission-critical information is centralized, so it's available to decision-makers at the top, who provide it to front-line managers as needed. Motivators reinforce efficient and disciplined behaviors.

Fits-and-Starts organizations, on the other hand, are unhealthy because their building blocks are fundamentally misaligned. The organization is highly decentralized in terms of decision rights, and yet relevant information is hoarded at headquarters, so regional managers are flying blind in making decisions that optimize the interests of the organization as a whole. They are not ill intentioned, just poorly informed. Motivators fail to compensate for this lack of information.

In general, when building blocks fit together well (i.e., they are aligned and complementary), organizations produce results. They deliver on their commitments to customers, shareholders, and employees. However, if any of the four building blocks is out of place in the organizational puzzle, the company will not achieve its full potential. The challenge for managers charged with delivering results then is to determine what changes to the existing organizational DNA are necessary to align the building blocks and create the conditions for optimal performance.

In the case of the Fits-and-Starts organization, the remedies depend on where you sit. If you are a senior executive, you likely can make rather sweeping changes at the top; you can centralize control over disparate operations by taking back decision rights that now reside in the field managers' hands. Or you can implement an IT program to move more information out to the field where it is needed. Either way, decision rights and information can be reunited.

So, what if you're a middle manager on those front lines? What can you do to remedy a Fits-and-Starts organization? A lot, as it turns out. You already have the decision rights in this decentralized operating model; you just need to get better informed. Make it your business to establish relationships with other operating units and corporate staff. Get a copy of the company's strategic plan, and set up a team to determine how your division can help the company achieve its overall objectives. Your example may light the way for others.

But remember, in introducing change, you must be mindful of the unintended consequences that can ripple across an organization once any element of its DNA is altered. Whether you seek to enhance the performance of your company, your small business, or your project team, you need to understand the magnitude of the change effort required. Steps taken to modify any or all of the four building blocks of your organization's DNA must be coherent, co-ordinated, and clear. Initiatives that address only structure or information, in isolation, will not gain any traction. To understand how the four building blocks are presently configured in your organization, ask the following questions:

- **Decision Rights**. Who decides what? How many people are involved in the decision process? Where does one person's decision-making authority end and another's begin?
- **Information**. How is performance measured? How are activities co-ordinated and knowledge transferred? How are expectations and progress communicated? Who knows what? Who needs to know what? How does information get from the people who have it to the people who require it?
- **Motivators**. What objectives, incentives, and career alternatives do people have? How are they rewarded, financially and nonfinancially, for what they achieve? What are they encouraged to care about, by whatever means, explicit or implicit? Are their goals aligned with the organization's goals?
- **Structure**. What does the organizational hierarchy look like? How are the lines and boxes in the organization chart connected? How many are in the hierarchy, and how many direct reports does each layer have?

Notice that structure is last. There are situations where it acts as the chief impediment to an organization's effectiveness and therefore must be addressed first, but it's not the "secret sauce" of organizational success. A restructuring, in the absence of aligned changes to the other building blocks, rarely produces sustained positive results.

Look at how Barbara and her colleagues at National Telco react to the news of their restructuring. Rather than spurring productivity or motivating a greater effort, this announcement precipitates an outbreak of office politics as managers scramble for position. Consider what might have happened if the CEO had reorganized the company around the customer by changing decision rights, information, and motivators? What if he had announced that effective January 1, bonuses would constitute up to 20 percent of managerial compensation and that they would be tied to total customer satisfaction (i.e., with all the services customers purchase from National Telco, whether wireless or wireline). What if the CEO delegated full authority over pricing decisions to the operating heads of the Wireless and Wireline businesses, and began measuring those units on total customer profitability? What if the back offices for each of these products were merged so that the customer experienced seamless service, and all units had access to the others' information? These are the changes that would motivate positive behavioral change. These are the changes that would align individual self-interest with the company's goals. And these are the changes that would drive improved results.

Moreover, these are the sorts of changes that can be made at any level within a company. While they cannot change the bonus structure for the whole company or merge back offices, middle managers can make meaningful changes to the decision rights, information, and motivators in their part of the company . . . and instigate substantial and positive change.

WHO GETS TO DECIDE WHAT?: DECISION RIGHTS

"We have to assemble ten executives in a room to make routine business decisions."

To change the way your organization works, you must first understand who does what, how, and why. This investigation takes you quickly past the lines and boxes of the organization chart into the underlying mechanics of how decisions are truly made.

An organization's overall performance is simply the sum total of all the actions and decisions that people inside it take every day. At some fundamental level, everyone is constantly making decisions and managing trade-offs, whether it's how to price a customer quote, which engineering projects to fund given a limited budget, or what phone calls or e-mails to return first. These are not big, board-room issues; they are the mundane action items that incrementally drive the business forward. How well and how efficiently individuals in a firm make these decisions largely determines the organization's success in the marketplace.

When companies stumble or fail to execute, corporate leaders too quickly jump to the conclusion that decision-makers in the problem areas have acted irrationally, or worse, subversively. Rarely is that the case. Instead, if you assume that people—your fellow workers and managers—are rational actors whose choices reflect sensible decisions in the context of what each knows, sees, and cares about, then the true breakdowns in the decision-making apparatus and logic begin to reveal themselves. While decisions and choices may seem wrongheaded or random to others, they almost always make perfect sense to the individual decision-maker, who usually wants to do the right thing for the company, given the information and incentives she has.

The key to improving performance then is not to blame the decision-makers, but rather to understand what organizational building blocks encourage individuals to make suboptimal, even counterproductive, decisions or trade-offs from the firm's perspective, and then change those building blocks to encourage decision-making more aligned with the overall strategy and performance objectives of the company.

At automotive parts manufacturer *ACW Auto*, it wasn't clear whether Manufacturing or Strategic Planning had the ultimate decision rights for new capacity planning (i.e., building new plants and lines). Since these important decisions "fell between the cracks," no one paid much attention to them . . . except Sales, when it was too late.

That's what happened last year when David James, director of Sales, got a call from one of ACW's largest customers, *Rapid Fire Motors*, pulling their business from the company. Rapid Fire had placed an unusually large order for locking mechanisms and wiper assemblies some four months earlier and had just received the shipment—two weeks late. To add insult to injury, at least half the parts required rework. Rapid Fire had already put their contract with ACW—which expired the following month—up for bid.

David was irate. He dialed Amit Jain, head of Manufacturing, and gave him an earful. When he paused for breath, Amit politely informed him that it was not Manufacturing's problem. They had been operating at capacity for six months now, and so had to outsource that oversized order to a number of outside suppliers (which, incidentally, had cost ACW 15 percent more than it would have cost to produce the parts in-house, eliminating any profit). If David had a problem, he should take it up with Carol Mapother, head of Strategic Planning and the person he presumed was in charge of capacity investments.

Carol deftly sidestepped any blame as well. Hired a year earlier, she had been specifically charged with shepherding the financial budgeting process, and had been focused exclusively on that exercise for the past eight months. Besides, she'd been on board only twelve months, and everyone knew that adding new capacity required at least fifteen months' lead time.

Bottom line: no one "owned" the decision rights for long-term capacity planning at ACW, a gap that had gone unnoticed because the company had been so focused on driving down costs in compliance with automakers' demands. Now capacity constraints were apparent and costing the company both customers and profits.

If the decision rights for planning new capacity had rested squarely with, say, Manufacturing in the first place, the company would have recognized far earlier the need to invest in additional lines. A plan would have been developed, updated periodically, and implemented, eliminating the need for emergency measures. Failing to clarify decision rights is arguably worse than assigning them to the wrong decision-maker.

Who gets to make what decisions at your company? And what information, constraints, tools, and incentives affect the way they

evaluate those decisions? Understanding why and where the existing set of decision rights (many of which are tacit and informal,
rather than consciously designed) affect decision-making is the
core insight required to redesign your organizational model.

Decision rights determine how well organizations work . . .
how quickly the right new products/services get to market . . .
how much the organization spends to get results. Therefore, it's
the first building block that dysfunctional organizations should
address; it's the cornerstone of effective organizational renovation.

Decision rights determine who is responsible for what choices
and is the most significant factor in influencing how individuals
spend their time. For example, if Carol at ACW knew that she was
responsible for making long-term capacity decisions, she would
have performed her job differently. She would have solicited more
information from the business units, validated her assumptions
with relevant functional experts in manufacturing and marketing,
and perhaps delegated more decision-making in her own unit. She
would have brought a different agenda to management meetings
and would have measured her own performance and that of her
team differently. She would have spent more time on the plant
floor. In hundreds of subtle ways, her behavior would have
changed. That's why decision rights need to be specified before
you can begin to make sense of any organization chart. As form
follows function, so structure follows decision rights. Assigning
Carol the decision rights for capacity planning affects her day-to-
day role more than who she reports to.

When people running organizations fail to lay out clear and unequivocal decision rights, they pay a steep price. Poorly articulated
decision rights are more than a time sink; they are the leading
cause of substandard performance—frankly, of nonperformance.

If yours is an organization where newly promoted executives
still do their old jobs and second-guess their subordinates or where
unauthorized channels or "black market" workarounds crop up to
circumvent "official" decision-making protocols, then you know
what badly centralized decision rights feel like. You live in an en-

vironment of missed opportunities, stalled momentum, and thinly veiled frustration.

On the other hand, if yours is an organization where everyone has the wheel, where field operations are so autonomous that they ignore or confound one another and defeat corporate attempts to impose coordination, you are suffering the opposite problem . . . badly decentralized decision rights.

Again, ACW Auto is a good example of badly decentralized decision rights. In its never-ending effort to cut costs in line with customer demands, the head office had imposed a "hiring freeze" via internal memo. Each of the division heads posted the memo prominently on their break-room bulletin boards, and then promptly forgot about it. Amit Jain reasoned that the plants were operating at full capacity, so surely this freeze did not apply to his operations. David James was looking to cover more of the East Coast so he needed to hire salespeople. Carol Mapother circumvented the hiring freeze by outsourcing work to consultants; they weren't being added to the company payroll, so she felt she was in compliance. Six months after the hiring freeze was implemented, the company was employing 125 more people . . . and the organization had learned an important lesson: you can ignore memos from headquarters . . .

. . . as long as you make a big show of "doing the right thing." For example, at ACW, as at many companies today, the importance of pushing accountability down to lower levels in the organization was widely touted, but managers' actions didn't always live up to the rhetoric. Head of manufacturing Amit Jain bragged about how his plant managers had full accountability for every line item in their budget, including wages, materials, travel, training, and temporary help. Rather than giving them accountability for the entire budget, however, and the discretion to spend money where they deemed appropriate, he monitored each individual expenditure. His plant managers had very little discretion to substitute spending in one category with spending in another—that is, to make meaningful managerial decisions about how the end objective was to be achieved. So, the notion of pushing accountability down was largely a farce.

When the company, as a whole, moved to a different model in which decision rights were explicitly spelled out, plant managers were, for the first time, given true responsibility for their overall budgets and could make the necessary trade-offs among expense items. As a result, they took greater ownership for their plant's and the overall company's results. One plant manager, for example, spent more money training his workforce to spot recycling opportunities, significantly reducing materials costs. This best practice was quickly transferred to the other plants.

In a system where clarity and accountability prevail—where decision rights are clearly assigned and understood—everybody has a good idea of what decisions and actions are their responsibility. There are no missed handoffs or dropped balls, as at ACW when capacity planning went unaddressed. Whoever owns the decision knows it and sees it through to completion. Because accountability is so clearly and sensibly allocated, decisions are made quickly and well. There's no need for second-guessing or blame shifting. Effective decision rights, in short, have a positive multiplier effect.

WHAT DO I NEED TO KNOW?: INFORMATION

"I don't have the information I need to do my job."

Almost everyone has been in a situation where, despite having the best of intentions, he or she simply did not have the right information to make an effective decision. The key to organizational success is identifying the critical information required to make correct decisions and ensuring that this information is in decision-makers' hands, if and when they need it.

Information is the lifeblood of any organization. Its contribution to high performance and competitive advantage is widely acknowledged. In fact, studies confirm that companies focused on managing and enhancing internal information flows generate superior shareholder returns.[1] Business units communicate with each other; overall goals and management strengths are widely shared; and best practices are deployed across disparate locations.

This prescription may sound simple, but arming the right people with the right information—all the time—is among the most challenging of management tasks.

Inflated costs are a strong signal that there is a problem in any company. In a commodity business, however, it is nothing short of a death knell. As he read through a benchmarking analysis comparing his company's cost structure to that of its competitors, Will Kawena, VP of Agriculture at *Crystalline Sugar*, knew his company was just steps from the grave.

A midsized sugar grower and processor, Crystalline cultivated about nine thousand acres of sugarcane on the islands of Hawaii. The land was divided into nine large farms, each run by a manager who was given an annual budget and yield target for his acreage. The farm managers all reported to Will, who reported to the CEO.

The annual yield targets were calculated by Crystalline's VP of Planning and Research, Wally Harvell. A PhD in Ag Sciences, Wally had compiled one of the most impressive datasets in the industry—gigabytes of historical productivity data on every acre Crystalline had ever cultivated in the past thirty years. Wally could tell you which cane varieties were planted in what fields; how many times and on what dates each field was fertilized, cultivated, and harvested; and the sugar yield of each field every year. By running all of these historical data through a proprietary model that he had developed, Wally was able to come up with yield targets for each of the nine farms. Over the years, his model had grown mind-numbingly complex; in fact, Wally was the only person on earth who understood how exactly it worked. Yet the results were the same each year from the farm managers' perspective; they would joke with one another when they received their targets: "Hmm, last year plus a little. What a surprise."

In an effort to meet these ever-increasing yield targets, the farm managers would use a little more fertilizer or cultivate a bit more intensively every year. Consequently, their budget requests would increase incrementally each year. After thirty years of this routine, the consequences were apparent. The benchmarking study in front of Will Kawena showed that Crystalline's costs had grown steadily higher than the competition's; in some categories such as agricultural equipment, Crystalline's costs were 20 percent higher than the industry average.

Will would always note as he drove down the rural routes of Hawaii's sugarcane country that he could instantly tell where a Crystalline field ended and an independent farmer's field began; the independent farmer's field always had more weeds and older tractors in it. It was actually a point of pride among Crystalline farmers that they had the cleanest fields and the best equipment of any farmer in the county. Will knew his farm managers weren't overly concerned with costs; as long as they didn't overspend their budgets, they felt they were running a tight ship. Still, when it came time to buy a tractor, they almost always bought new ones rather than used (as long as they had the budget to cover it). But with the yield targets increasing every year, Will didn't see how his farmers could be expected to get by on a smaller budget.

Information, as we define it, is all the data, metrics, knowledge, and coordinating mechanisms resident in various corners of the organization. Good information is targeted, accurate, and available to those who need it. It's information that produces results.

To judge whether your information is "good," ask yourself the following questions:

- If one of your key customers was not satisfied, how and when would you find out about it? When they took their business to your competitor? Or would you have enough lead time to do something about it?

- If someone on the assembly line had a million-dollar cost-saving idea, how would she communicate it so that it reached someone with the authority to implement it? What incentive would she have to share it?
- If an engineer in R&D began working on a project that had been tried and scrapped two years earlier, at what point in the development process would he learn about the earlier work?
- If your Wally Harvell disappeared overnight, what would become of all that institutional knowledge he had amassed? Would it leave the company with him?

Poor information is the organizational equivalent of junk food. It clogs communications arteries, bloats the system with empty calories, and fools the body into thinking it's nourished, when, in fact, it may well be on the verge of crisis. At Crystalline Sugar, farm managers were content knowing that they were operating within their prescribed budgets. They had no idea that the company's costs were way out of line. Wally's computer models and gigabytes of data gave the false impression that Crystalline had this farming business down to a science, when, in fact, their costs were considerably higher than those of the less sophisticated family farms right next door.

In our experience, problems with information span the gamut. Even within one particular company, you can be either glutted or starved for the right data depending on where you sit. People like Wally at Crystalline Sugar are swimming in information, while the farm managers are in the dark about competitive costs. Whether it's from information glut or starvation, however, the organization suffers. It suffers from poor prioritization, stalled decision-making, and the inability to transfer best practices. In the worst-case scenarios, uninformed boards and senior officers end up under investigation. Inadequate governance and lax controls are, at their core, an information failure in the organization. If the CEO doesn't know what's going on, he can't know what's going wrong in the organization, and that's a problem, even if it doesn't lead to an indictment.

The effects of bad information on the other DNA building blocks—particularly decision rights and motivators—are obvious. Without accurate and available information, decision-makers cannot make quick, smart moves in the marketplace, and employees don't receive the recognition—either positive or negative—that their actions merit.

In response to the cost benchmarking study's wake-up call, Will Kawena convened a task force of farm managers and functional heads, including information guru Wally Harvell. Together, they developed a new business model for Crystalline Sugar in which each farm became an independent profit center. To ensure their success in this new structure, farm managers were equipped with new information—specifically their farm's P&L, which reflected, among many other things, the cost of the equipment they used. Farm managers were paid bonuses based on the profitability, not the yield, of their farms. Immediately, their behavior changed. They started buying used equipment instead of new. They began querying Wally's data to better understand what had worked in the past and what hadn't. They began talking to other farmers and to one another, sharing cultivation tips and techniques. Within a few months, costs had declined substantially, and the company's share price jumped 48 percent within a year.

Better information did more than keep down costs; it helped allocate scarce resources more efficiently . . . specifically mill capacity. Fields ready for harvest had a peak yield window of only fifteen days or so, and the crop had to be milled within twenty-four hours of harvest. Wally Harvell had long been responsible for designing the harvest plan for all nine thousand acres, determining which fields to harvest in what order so that the mill had a constant supply of ripe, freshly harvested cane. Wally would design the plan months in advance, and then tweak it continually as the season approached and local rainfall or temperatures fluctuated. Invariably, starting in October every year, Wally's phone would start ringing nonstop as farm managers whose fields were ripening a little too fast or too slow sought to reschedule their harvest dates. While Wally tried to stay on top of the ripening process across all nine thousand acres, there was only so much he could do; by about November 1, he was usually reallocating harvest dates to the farm managers who screamed the loudest.

In the new model, Wally was no longer in the middle. He and his team created an online market for mill time; farm managers were each allocated a certain number of credits they could use to bid for mill time. If a manager saw that his highest-yielding acreage was ready to harvest and couldn't wait because rain was forecasted, he could bid more for mill time. Alternatively, if his crop could wait, he could save credits and buy less expensive mill days later in the season. This market mechanism allocated scarce mill resources much more efficiently and equitably than Wally ever could. It effectively put the decision rights on mill scheduling in the hands of those with the best information, the farmer in the field observing the sky and testing the ripeness of his crop hour by hour, acre by acre.

HOW DO YOU GET AHEAD AROUND HERE?: MOTIVATORS

"We paid bonuses, but no one seems to behave any differently."

Motivators include more than money; they also encompass all of the objectives, incentives, and career opportunities that prompt people to care and achieve. These rewards, both financial and non-financial, can encourage individuals to align their goals with those of the firm and pursue them in earnest . . . or they can, however inadvertently, stimulate counterproductive behaviors by driving a wedge between self-interest and the good of the firm.

★   ★   ★

It was 6:00 p.m. Friday night, and Terry Howard, Northeast district manager for *Security First Insurance,* had just arrived home from Logan airport after a week in Puerto Rico at the annual agent award conference. Even before she called out to her husband, she rifled through the mail until she found what she was looking for: her annual bonus check. She opened the envelope immediately, looked at the amount, and calculated what percentage of her salary it represented: 19 percent. She let out an audible sigh of relief; she was within the "band"—the standard bonus range for people at her level in the company.

At Security First, everyone above manager level received an annual bonus three months after the fiscal year closed, and it was well understood—even before the checks arrived—what the amount was likely to be. The Corporate Leadership Team (CLT) would meet behind closed doors and come up with a bonus band for each level based on company-wide results; senior vice presidents typically made as much as 40 percent of their salaries, VPs up to 30 percent, and managers like Terry as much as 20 percent. While this information was never promulgated, the grapevine got word within a day of that closed-door session and spread the news. At 19 percent, Terry knew she had made out well. Now the next question was "Why?"

Terry knew her district's performance was—by any measure—mediocre last year. She had responsibility for the most affluent market in the country; the demographic profile of the Northeast made her peers salivate. Yet she had grown premium revenues by only some 6 percent. By contrast, her colleague Rudd Connors in the Southwest district had grown his district's business some 26 percent. But the bonus payouts at Security First barely took these salient performance distinctions into account; there was very little variance within bonus bands. If the company had a good year, managers could expect between 15 and 20 percent of their salaries in bonus, no matter what their individual or business unit contribution to total revenues was. In other words, everyone at the same level got basically the same bonus. What variation did occur was attributable to factors like seniority that were outside an individual's control. As it turned out, Terry had ten years' seniority over Rudd so her bonus was actually quite a bit larger than his; even she privately conceded that was unfair, but what was she going to do about it?

Terry grabbed some champagne from the fridge and some glasses from the china cabinet and joined her husband in the living room to celebrate her bonus . . . then moan about the corporate politics at work. In Security First's "employment for life" culture, politics was a high art. People focused more energy on getting promoted (and moving into the next bonus band) than on doing an extraordinary job in their current positions. Why bother putting in the extra effort if it wasn't going to be rewarded? You quickly learned at Security First to put off today what could be done by your successor . . . when you were promoted in 2.5 years. So unglamorous chores such as cost-cutting and employee development fell by the wayside, while superiors' pet projects received undue attention.

Terry had to admit she was sick of it, but it wasn't bad money for a job that got her home in time for *Jeopardy* every night.

Once people are equipped with appropriate decision rights and adequate information, motivators are what prompt them to take the actions necessary to move the organization forward. An exhortation to follow the vision and pursue the strategy—to run faster, row harder, whatever the chosen metaphor—is only so much air if the organization's objectives and incentives send contradictory signals. To be effective, motivators need to be aligned not only with the other building blocks, but also with the performance goals of the enterprise.

At Security First, the main motivators hinged more on "time served" and "having an in with the boss" than on an individual's contribution to the organization's results. Rudd Connors overdelivered last year, but you wouldn't know it by looking at his compensation; he actually made less than his more senior colleagues, though his district's performance, by every measure, was far superior. There was no cork-popping in the Connors' house.

Based in Phoenix, Rudd rarely had the opportunity to lunch with the head of Individual Insurance, Suhail Nasser, as Terry Howard did every month, nor could he serve on a corporate task force—another way to secure valuable "face time" with the higher-ups, since Security First was headquartered in New York. The brass paperweight that proclaimed "#1 District" and the conference in Puerto Rico were hardly adequate acknowledgment of the extraordinary efforts he had put forth in his two years with the company. The financial planning seminars he designed for retirees had created such a "buzz" in Arizona and New Mexico that they were now "invitation-only." And he had taken it upon himself to visit all five districts around the country to train other managers' agents in how to present the material. He wouldn't make that mistake again. He was only helping his peers look good. The Southwest district had single-handedly pulled up the company's performance numbers the past two years, disguising a multitude of "sins" elsewhere in the company . . . particularly in the Northeast district.

Motivators need to provide decision-makers like Rudd Connors with clear direction and compelling reasons to continue to act in the firm's best interest and must extend beyond financial incentives to include nonfinancial rewards, including promotions, development opportunities, recognition, and perks, among others (see Figure 2.2). Moreover, motivators should reward the individual, not the job.

In Rudd's case, there are any number of ways Security First could motivate him to even higher levels of performance. If he seems to have attached himself to money as the measure of his success, it's in part because that's what the organization taught him to do. In two years, Rudd has yet to receive a formal performance review or an invitation to corporate headquarters. His com-

FIGURE 2.2—MOTIVATORS ENCOMPASS ALL LEVERS, NOT JUST FINANCIAL

	Lever	Description	Examples
PERFORMANCE	Compensation	• Increased remuneration for meeting or exceeding defined performance goals	• Performance bonuses • Stock options • Faster vesting of options
	Recognition	• Public celebration of accomplishment in meeting or exceeding execution goals	• Awards • Articles in internal and external publications
PEOPLE	Promotion	• Increased authority and/or autonomy to reward and encourage specific behaviors	• Added responsibility • Consultation and inclusion in senior management decision-making processes
	Attention	• Increased interface/interaction with senior managers on a one-to-one basis or in groups	• One-on-one or group meetings with management • Coaching by seniors

　■ Primarily financial in nature　　　　□ Primarily nonfinancial in nature

pensation is all he has to go on in figuring out what the company thinks of him.

Let's imagine a different environment, a more motivating one for Rudd. In this new meritocracy, Rudd's standout performance is apparent to the Corporate Leadership Team as soon as the quarterly district performance numbers come in. Rudd is flagged as a high-potential executive and is offered special benefits (e.g., executive MBA, lunch with the CEO). He is assigned a senior executive mentor who sits down with him once a quarter and charts a career development course with him that will take him through all the company's major lines of business over the next five to ten years. He is invited to serve on a high-profile corporate task force and has frequent visits from his boss, Suhail Nasser. Finally, he is awarded a top-tier bonus in the new incentive compensation scheme based not on level but performance tier.

Some of these motivators would require corporate-level approval. Some of these, however, require little more than a bit of time and attention on the part of Rudd's boss. Every manager possesses the ability to motivate. It's as simple as scheduling regular performance appraisals and providing candid, constructive feedback. It's as easy as setting clear performance expectations and acknowledging a job well done.

Surprisingly few organizations motivate their people well, and the effects of demotivation are crippling over time. Without effective motivators, people do one of three things: they coast (like Terry), collecting bonus checks that even she admits are ill deserved; they downshift and deliver less; or they leave. It's a lose-lose-lose situation. Recognizing that their individual contributions are not being measured and rewarded on a consistent or rational basis, people resign themselves to punching a clock and delivering the bare minimum. Star talent gives up and leaves to pursue more promising or remunerative opportunities elsewhere, leaving less productive colleagues to plod along.

At its best, unmotivated employees and managers demonstrate apathy and mediocrity; at worst, a brewing resentment. The moral of this story is that morale matters, and morale improves markedly in the presence of honest, consistent, and results-based motivators.

WHERE DO I FIT IN?: STRUCTURE

"Here's our org chart, but let me tell you how it really works around here."

Structure is the most visible and obvious of the four organizational DNA building blocks, and it's where most organizational change programs start (remember National Telco?). Why? Because organization structure is "transactable"; you can move lines and boxes around and easily demonstrate what has changed in a single snapshot.

Organizational charts communicate—at a glance—the locus of political power in the firm to insiders (i.e., who got demoted/promoted, who has the most direct reports). But, by themselves, they tell outsiders precious little about how the organization actually works.

Structure is not the starting point; it's the logical outcome of the choices made regarding the other three building blocks. While important and potentially crippling if designed poorly, structure is the capstone, not the cornerstone of most reorganization efforts.

Structure, in principle, should follow strategy. For example, if a company's strategy is oriented around customer segments, then its structure should reinforce that orientation. In practice, however, a company's organizational structure and strategic intent are often mismatched.

Consider the case of *Pro-Line Supplies,* a Pittsburgh-based medical equipment manufacturer bent on improving its customer responsiveness in the fast-changing health-care marketplace. Susan Jacobson, the president and chief operating officer of Pro-Line, was nervous. She was meeting with Carl Martino, head of Purchasing for Gamma Health, a leading national hospital chain and physicians' network, and she was worried Pro-Line was going to lose their business. In the past year, her company had lost three major accounts to smaller, nimbler, local suppliers, and she could not afford to lose Gamma. She had called this lunch to impress upon Carl that she stood ready to get him whatever he needed.

They had just ordered when Carl said to Susan, "You know, there is something I'd like to get some clarity on. I'm wondering which of our hospitals did the most business with you last year. Can you get me that rundown?" Susan spilled the water she was drinking as she exhaled with relief. "Sure, I'll have that to you by tomorrow, Carl."

As soon as she got back into the office, she called the company controller, Chuck Matthews, and asked him to get monthly sales figures for Gamma Health broken down by hospital for the last three years . . . and the odyssey of a simple data request began. Starting at the top of the organization chart with Susan, the query finally wended its way to Mark Yenko, an analyst in the Operations Analysis unit four levels below. Of course, by the time Susan's simple request reached him, it was far from simple. Every person who had touched it added more and more detail to the query, so that they could understand the issue as well or better than their boss. Chuck, the controller, asked to see the data for five years instead of three. The head of Sales wanted the figures broken down by region as well. Each of the product managers involved asked to see it broken down by product line, and Mark's boss, the director of Operations Analysis, asked that the data be graphed. By the time the request reached the Mark's desk, it had become a two-day-long project, rather than a simple thirty-minute task.

What's worse, as the data request made its way through each layer, it lost most of its clarity or context, so Mark had no understanding of why the data was needed in the first place or how it would be used. Like a corporate version of the child's game Telephone, the message got more garbled with every link in the chain, so that by the time it reached him, its intent was lost. Scrambling to comply with a "top priority" project that was being demanded immediately by multiple parties, Mark had no time to follow up and clarify the original request. He just shook his head and generated a hundred-page report, only ten lines of which were relevant to Susan and, more important, the customer. Even worse, the two and a half days it took to generate this report seriously compromised Susan's credibility with Carl Martino and damaged Pro-Line's relationship with Gamma Health.

Pro-Line's problem is its elaborate hierarchy. A 150-year-old company, it's been handing out ritual promotions every two to three years since its inception. To accommodate all of these promoted people, it created layers and layers of unnecessary middle management and inadvertently fostered a culture where people "politicked" their way to the top. Junior managers spent inordinate amounts of time assembling data and anticipating every conceivable question a superior might ask in a meeting. This is how you displayed your star potential and got promoted. Not surprisingly, the focus of attention in the organization has slowly shifted away from the decision itself and the quality of the results to the thoroughness of the analysis applied. The ultimate result of this "hourglass" organization structure is bottlenecked decision-making, bureaucratic buildup, and, in Pro-Line's case, lost business.

Another structural problem is the proliferation of "shadow staff," people performing tasks surreptitiously that duplicate those performed "officially" elsewhere in the organization. Typically, shadow staff spring up in business units and perform work that should be performed by a corporate support function, such as HR, finance, or IT. Dissatisfied with the quality or cost of these corporate support services, business units circumvent corporate and "grow their own" support.

The fix is *not* to eliminate these shadow staff, but rather figure out why they came to be. If you don't address the organizational issues that caused the business units to grow their own staff in the first place, these positions will just grow back.

These are just a couple of the more prominent structural flaws we've seen in organizations. The list is long. But, as we've stressed, structure alone is not the cancer that brings down an organization, nor is it the cure.

Certainly there are structures that tend to work more effectively than others, but there is no one ideal structure. Many consistently successful organizations avoid an over-reliance on structure; there are fewer boundaries and more cross-functional teaming. People operate "outside of the box." Some winning companies organize by product line; others by function or geography. What works is what best accommodates the most appropriate decision rights, information, and motivators. Typically, that argues for fewer layers and wider spans, but that prescription is not universal. Too often, companies make the mistake of overhauling the org chart when their business falters . . . instead of looking more closely at the people who populate the organization and motivating them to make the right decisions based on the best information.

THE FOUR BUILDING BLOCKS: INTEGRATION IS EVERYTHING

Although we have illustrated the four building blocks of organizational DNA separately to emphasize their distinct characteristics, they clearly are intertwined, as several of these stories suggest. Decision rights are of little help without access to relevant and accurate information, and individuals may not be inclined to make optimal decisions unless motivators encourage the right behaviors and objectives.

In short, people have to have the information to make a decision, the incentives to make the right one, and the authority to act. An effective organizational structure facilitates the appropriate alignment of these three other building blocks. No building block stands alone; it's how they combine to create an organization that matters.

And it is the way the building blocks interact—or don't—that determines an organization's performance profile, and whether or not it produces results. Based on our experience working with companies and our research on how well or badly the four DNA building blocks are aligned in these companies, we have identified seven principal types of organizations: Passive-Aggressive, Fits-and-Starts, Outgrown, Overmanaged, Just-in-Time, Military Precision, and Resilient.

Obviously, most large organizations are far too complex to fit squarely into only one type, but in any organization one type typically predominates. By the same token, you cannot characterize the building blocks as either black or white. There's rarely a case, for example, where all the important decision rights in a business are either centralized or decentralized.

Like archeologists who determine the history and behaviors of a society by the layers they uncover, managers and consultants alike have typically looked first at structure—the levels in the hierarchy—to posit a view on how institutions operate. Structure can tell you a lot—whether the organization is rife with ritual promotions, shadow staff, micromanaged subordinates—but is only one determinant of organizational health. It can exert a strongly helpful or hindering effect on the other three building blocks, but it cannot trump them.

Most organizations have not been built by master designers; they have evolved over time in response to the competitive marketplace and other, often arbitrary, forces. The loss of a key division manager, for example, might prompt a company to fold that entire division into another unit. A merger might result in strangely "spliced" information systems. These quick fixes tend to persist over time, and subsequent organizational changes are layered upon them, until after a few years, the resulting organization becomes an incoherent collection of expedient solutions that have no real rational basis. In these cases, a periodic fresh look into how the organization really operates and why can lead to important insights into what must be changed to unleash the firm's potential.

Improving or fixing the DNA of a business means weaving intelligence, decision-making capabilities, and a collective focus on common goals widely and deeply into the fabric of the organization so that each person and unit is working smartly—and working together. It's one thing to get senior executives on the same page. It's another thing entirely to influence every level of an organization all the way down to the loading dock. What every employee does every day, aggregated across the company, determines results.

Yet in our experience, most management teams do not fully appreciate the role the four building blocks of organizational DNA play in improving performance. Nor do managers grasp the difficulty of their organizational challenges. Many leaders inherit organizational models, and lack the time or resources to develop a detailed perspective on how they really work. They may be frustrated by an inability to realize their objectives, but rarely do they identify the inherent assumptions, trade-offs, and motivations at work in their organizations as root causes.

Any attempt to address a business weakness or strategic opportunity must explicitly address the underlying organizational reasons the current strategy is not working. The attempt cannot begin, as many traditional approaches do, with the conclusion that the problem lies in the strategy itself, and immediately concentrate on refining the aspirations or vision for the company. That difference in starting point, coupled with the recognition that the task is difficult, represents an opportunity to create an enduring competitive advantage over rivals, and leads to a fundamentally different way of thinking, not just about organizational issues, but about strategy. The most resilient and consistently successful companies have discovered that the devil is in the details of organization. For them, organizing for results has truly become a competitive edge.

THREE

THE PASSIVE-AGGRESSIVE
ORGANIZATION
Everyone Agrees but Nothing Changes

So congenial as to seem conflict free, this is the seething, smiley-face organization. Building consensus to make major changes is not a problem; implementing these changes, however, is next to impossible. Entrenched, underground resistance from field operations routinely defeats corporate initiatives. Lacking the authority, information, and incentives needed to undertake meaningful change, line employees tend to ignore mandates from headquarters, assuming "this too shall pass." Confronted with an apathetic organization, senior management laments the futility of "nailing Jell-O to the wall."

Passive-Aggressive organizations tend to strive for the mean. Mediocrity is not only quietly accepted, it's often promoted. Decision-making authority is murky at best, and, once made, decisions are often second-guessed. The herd mentality runs rampant, trampling innovation and ownership, and information is locked down, inaccessible to those who most need it. Ironically, this profile fits many Fortune 500 companies. Having secured a large and defensible market position, they are now fiddling while Rome slowly burns.

Let's revisit ZZ Electronics and George Sullivan, the dispirited director of Market Research. If you'll recall from Chapter 1, George was the somewhat jaded fifteen-year veteran who counseled his enthusiastic, young colleague, Judy, to cool her ardor about the new media player launch, because the company was not going to get its act together in time to meet the deadline. As it turns out, George was unfortunately right; the company did not launch the new product in time for Christmas, and the CEO, Bill Corrigan, lost his job.

A week after Corrigan's ouster, George is in the regularly scheduled monthly Marketing meeting with his peers from Market Management, Advertising, Promotions, and Channel Relations as well as his boss, Roger Marcinno, VP of Marketing. Also present are the HR and Finance leads assigned to support Marketing and a staff member from the Sales department. Absent is anyone from Product Development, as it didn't occur to Roger or anyone else in Marketing to invite them.

The monthly meeting is a marathon session that generally consumes the entire workday, during which each of the Marketing heads updates the team on what they're up to. This particular meeting was off to a slow start as managers swapped stories they'd heard about Corrigan's final days and the new interim CEO's reputation. It was essentially idle chatter, since no one believed anything would really change. It was just a matter of gaming the new system to figure out how to survive any possible layoffs.

At about 9:30, almost thirty minutes after the scheduled start time, Roger asks everyone to sit down. There was a standing agenda; everyone had an hour to discuss their plans. On the table for discussion was the "new" media player that had failed to make it to market by Christmas. How was Marketing going to support the new launch date, which had been pushed off to next Christmas according to the last conversation Roger had had with Conrad Hobbs, the head of Product Development? Now that Corrigan had gone, so had his sense of urgency.

During his presentation, George walked through the market research he was putting together to test reactions to the prototype. There would be five focus groups held in each of four cities—New York, Miami, Los Angeles, and Chicago—in early May. That was almost six months out, a more typical pace for ZZ Electronics than the expedited schedule that Corrigan had tried to impose on the organization. George outlined the objectives, timing, and costs of the market research plan. ZZ would retain a market research firm to set up the focus groups, retain facilitators, and write up key findings. The cost would be about $75,000.

As he could have predicted, Sarah Tillman from Market Management, the unit responsible for competitive analysis of market trends, was the first to raise her hand when he completed his presentation. In between unctuous words of praise, she asked a series of seemingly innocuous questions meant to expose his lack of preparation and to position herself as more "in the know": "George, this sounds like an ambitious schedule, do you already have facilities and focus group leaders retained? . . . I take it that you've already cleared this with Product Development? . . . Listen, we've done a lot of analysis on those four cities, would you like me to have one of my staff help you put these groups together?"

George fielded each of her questions with an exhaustive and gracious reply . . . the intent of which was to shut her down and reinforce the boundaries. "Good question, Sarah, we've already done our homework and reached out to the firms that will be helping us, but I appreciate your offer."

After the discussion, Roger essentially gave the go-ahead, but, as always, it was a conditional green light. He suggested to George that he write up his proposal and circulate it to the group for their review and comment. This begged the question, "Then what was this meeting about?" . . . but George had seen this request coming. At ZZ Electronics, you documented everything; a verbal approval was meaningless, you had to get it in writing. The meeting adjourned at 5 p.m., and George headed right to the parking lot to drive home for dinner with his family.

ZZ Electronics exhibits all the signs of a Passive-Aggressive organization, including decision shopping, accountability avoidance, stifled information flows, and consensus-driven inertia. As with many Passive-Aggressive companies, ZZ Electronics has lapsed into complacency; it is resting on past laurels. Its managers now ride out market disappointments and turnover at the top by doing just enough to stay off the radar screen.

The Passive-Aggressive organization is the most common organizational profile among the seven we've identified.[1] This reality is rather sobering as Passive-Aggressive behavior is inherently unhealthy; if left unchecked, it spreads like a cancer, slowly and surreptitiously.

The Passive-Aggressive profile can be a hard one to pin down as the dysfunctions it describes are so widespread and insidious. All of the DNA building blocks in the organization are in some way compromised or out of synch. Decision rights, information, motivators, and structure all work against each other and the organization's strategic goals. Authority and accountability are unclear or fleeting, prompting rampant second-guessing, and information is often inaccessible to those who need it.[2] Structure is an impediment to smooth execution, and motivators are ineffective in stopping the spread of frustration and, ultimately, cynicism.

PASSIVE-AGGRESSIVE: THE SYMPTOMS

Passive-Aggressive companies suffer a variety of symptoms. At first, these indicators are almost imperceptible, but what begins as water-cooler grumblings inexorably escalates in severity and frequency.

Smiles Mask Internal Dissent

When we first met George and Judy, they were coming out of a management meeting held by the CEO, in which they joined their colleagues in committing to launch a groundbreaking product by Christmas . . . and then watched (in Judy's case, with great frustration) as nothing got done. That experience is universal at the Passive-Aggressive firm; it's as if everyone jotted down in their daily planner: "Attend a meeting where I will nod and do nothing." The Passive-Aggressive organization is extremely resistant to change, not because its people are subversive or ill intentioned, but because it's easier not to object. The silent majority go along for the ride, even though they know the initiative is doomed to failure. For many managers, long experience in a large, highly politicized organization has taught them to think small. They've seen too many "high priority" initiatives come and go to invest heavily in the next one. They bide their time, barely registering strategic edicts from the top. This pervasive lack of ownership and accountability explains why the Passive-Aggressive organization is so poor at dealing with discontinuous change in its competitive environment.[3]

When George got into work at ZZ Electronics the next morning, he called Randy Williams into his office. Randy was the manager in his department tasked with getting the focus groups organized, but more important, Randy was the first stop on George's "gripe grapevine." Randy asked how the meeting went, and George filled him in on Sarah's "underhanded" attempt to make him look bad. They both agreed that Sarah was making a play for their department. At the airline where Sarah worked prior to coming to ZZ Electronics, Market Research reported to Market Management. George and Randy were convinced that Sarah was working behind the scenes to take over their group.

George then told Randy that Roger, as expected, had asked for a formal focus group plan that could be circulated to the Marketing team for comment and review. Since the focus groups were scheduled for early May and it was now late November, George suggested that they should get something out to the team by mid-February. Backing into that date, they determined the vendor should get them something by the first week in January, so they would have time to tweak it.

The vendor delivered a plan on schedule, and Randy stripped out the vendor logo, reformatted the document, adjusted some details, and gave it to George two weeks later. It sat in George's inbox for another week. Then he spent another week reviewing it and forwarded it to the Marketing meeting participants. (There was no sense in submitting it to the team early, as it would have bumped up the plan discussion by a month and possibly expedited the whole focus group schedule. George's motto was "Don't borrow trouble.")

George asked for feedback from the group by the end of February. That gave them two weeks to review the plan and offer comments. When the deadline hit on the twenty-eighth, George had received one e-mail . . . from the Sales liaison who attended the meetings. He said the plan looked good. Knowing, based on his long experience at ZZ, that silence was not golden . . . and did not denote consent, George recirculated the plan, asking for feedback before the monthly meeting scheduled for the following Friday. A few more e-mails trickled in essentially supporting the plan. Then Sarah weighed in with a four-page list of comments and questions. She even went so far as to sketch out the focus group discussion document. What she didn't do was indicate whether she "approved" the plan or not.

Sarah's note, which arrived the night before the meeting, effectively knocked discussion of the plan off the docket. Now, George and Randy had to go back to the vendor to answer Sarah's nitpicky questions and address her comments. Sarah had accomplished her goal, to make George look unprepared in front of Roger and the rest of their peers. George was steaming.

When John Thompson left a twenty-eight-year career with IBM in 1999 to join Symantec Corporation, a Silicon Valley–based software vendor, as chairman, president, and chief executive officer, he quickly came face-to-face with passive-aggressive resistance from the company's internal fiefdoms. He describes a simple example from his early days with the company:[4]

"We have a product called PC Anywhere, and back in 1999, PC Anywhere came in this enormous box with a little disk and a big cable," recalls Thompson. "During a review that I was conducting on costs, I asked, 'Why is this cable in this box?' The answer was,

'Well, you know, a lot of customers need that cable to connect systems so they can pass files back and forth using PC Anywhere.' I asked, 'How many of our customers buy multiple copies?'

'Oh, most of them.'

'We ship them a cable every time?'

'Yeah.'

'What do they do with all the extra cables?'

'I guess they just throw them away.'

'How much does that cost us?'"

It turns out that including this large cable in the box was costing Symantec nearly $5 per box. So, Thompson proposed removing the cable, shipping a smaller box, and providing the cable free-of-charge to any customer that requested it. The management team readily agreed.

A few weeks later, Thompson learns that PC Anywhere is still shipping with the cable. At the next executive staff meeting, he asks, "What is the status for pulling the cable from the PC Anywhere box?"

The business unit executive in charge of that product opened his mouth and said, "Well, we've decided to do something different." Thompson fired back, "We don't make a decision but once. And we made a decision two weeks ago on this issue. Why couldn't you communicate it and get it implemented in your organization? Go back and get it fixed. We're not shipping cables anymore. And if you can't communicate that, I will."

Thompson recalls the organization's reaction. "That was the shot heard around the world. There was this epiphany, 'Wow, this guy's serious.'

"But the point to be made was this: once we've decided—if you've got a disagreement or a point of view, bring it up when we're going through the discussion. Don't hold back and give me this smiley kind of benign agreement when, in fact, your later actions say 'No, I don't agree.' This was a classic example of the organization rearing up and saying, 'We've decided we don't like that decision, and we're going to go do something else. That's the moment of truth. At that point, you have to step in and say, 'No, you're not. You're going to do what we agreed to do . . . now.'"

Shopping for Decisions

Decision rights were ill defined at Symantec, as is the case in most Passive-Aggressive organizations; it is unclear who has the final say on decisions large and small, from whether a cable ships in a box to what new product to launch or market to enter. Line managers regularly second-guess decisions that come down from headquarters, because there are no sanctions or incentives in place to motivate their compliance (until someone like John Thompson steps in to clarify things). On the other hand, senior managers habitually micromanage their subordinates. It's a constant contest of wills, where politics and personality trump process and protocol. A decision is rarely made and executed; instead it's thrown like chum into a sea full of sharks, who either digest it or chew it up and spit it out. Whichever is the case, the result is the same: stymied decision-making, delayed execution, disappointed customers, lost sales . . . or, in the case of Symantec, unnecessary costs. Critical initiatives hang in limbo as their sponsor—provided there is someone with enough energy and idealism to act as the sponsor—shops for a desirable ruling . . . or for someone with enough clout to overturn an undesirable one.

So endemic was the frequently revisited decision, that the CEO of a medical equipment company we've worked with coined a phrase for it: the "hallway decision flip." In his first few months in office, senior managers used to buttonhole him after a meeting in which a decision had been made to argue against implementing it. In the hallway or after hours, they would accost him with a new piece of data or a chart illustrating the folly of the decision. These backdoor appeals only reinforced the internal walls that had been erected across the organization and stalled the implementation of critical decisions.

The Bermuda Triangle of Information Flow

Information is hard currency in every organization, but in the Passive-Aggressive organization, managers tend to hoard this wealth instead of sharing it. As a result, line managers and senior executives are rarely "on the same page" when it comes to setting priorities or evaluating performance; frankly, they're usually looking at different data. Consequently, the organization's moves in the marketplace often appear inconsistent or contradictory.[5] Line managers make suboptimal choices about such important issues as hiring personnel, marketing products, or investing capital, because they do not understand the true bottom-line impact to the company of their decisions. And headquarters flies blind as it is not apprised of important information—both competitive and internal. Divisions, functions, and regions operate at cross-purposes, since information does not flow across any more than it flows up or down. Of course, this all presumes that critical information exists in the first place, which is not always the case. Oftentimes, it is "lost" in the void between competing IT systems.

We're now well into March, and George is having lunch in the ZZ Electronics cafeteria with a group of friends from around the company. George regales the group with his impersonation of Sarah Tillman and how she is trying to "kill his career with kindness." But he's confident he'll regain the upper hand with Roger when the focus groups go off without a hitch in May. At this point in the conversation, Grace Li, an engineer from Product Development, clears her throat and interjects, "George, I hate to tell you this, but we're months behind schedule on the prototype for that new media player. We've been trying to shrink the size of the unit without compromising the sound quality, and we've realized that we have to redesign the whole electronic circuitry. We're not going to have it ready for market testing until June at the earliest."

At this point, Dante Rinaldi, one of Sarah Tillman's direct reports in Market Management, confesses, "Phew, because, to be frank, we haven't even begun the competitive analysis or consumer positioning report on this new player. We're behind schedule. But you didn't hear it from me." George excuses himself from the lunch table.

On the way back to his office, he gets increasingly upset. In his efforts to game Sarah, he took his eye off Product Development. He'd been around this track enough to know how this process worked. He had let others paint a target on his back.

But he still had time. To repair the damage, he had to quickly set up a paper trail. First, he had to reach out in writing to Conrad Hobbs, head of Product Development, to "reconfirm" the schedule they had discussed for the prototype. He couldn't let on that he knew anything was awry, since that would expose Grace and, more important, reveal that he'd taken his eye off the ball. He'd handle Sarah later. For now, he had to reschedule the focus groups from May to July without making it a big deal. He knew that the vendor had already made commitments and this was going to cost Market Research a pretty penny, but first things first.

In preparation for the April marketing meeting, George sent out his preread the day before. He kept his update short. He put the July dates in the schedule for the focus groups, but didn't address the reasons for the change. His boss, Roger, seized on it immediately and sent an e-mail to George that evening asking why the focus groups were being delayed.

Mixed-Message Motivators

Nothing much moves in the Passive-Aggressive organization, including people. Promotions come slower than in most organizations, but they *do* come . . . regardless of how you're performing.[6] The organization's failure to distinguish exceptional from poor performance breeds complacency and frustrates strong performers, who tend to leave for more merit-based opportunities. Incentives are not effectively aligned with the best interests of the enterprise, and the appraisal process is almost wholly ineffective, since the vast majority of employees receive either #1 or #2 bonus rankings.

Given these misaligned motivators, Passive-Aggressive firms can find it exceedingly difficult to attract and retain talent.

"I found when I got here," says Symantec's John Thompson, "that the business units were not motivated to work together. In fact, the development teams were fundamentally pitted against one another in a battle for resources. It used to be that if you got to be a VP in this company, you got a BMW, so the leadership team had this entitlement mentality. If you wanted somebody to do something for you, the answer was, 'Well, what are you going to give me to do it?' It was this *Let's Make a Deal* internal barter system."

Symantec's stock had underperformed most other Silicon Valley stocks in the late Nineties, but the executive team did not feel the pain. Their compensation and reward system was heavily skewed toward cash, with a very small equity component. Nor were senior managers particularly motivated to improve their unit's performance. Most of their overall compensation was based upon the financial performance of the company as a whole. As Thompson says, "If the stock didn't do well, they didn't care. If the stock did well, they got a little bit of extra bump, but they had their car, and if the company hit its quarterly numbers, they got their bonus checks like clockwork. My reaction was, 'How do you encourage an executive management team to think long-term when their bonuses hinge on quarterly results?'"

The Defensive Memo

The most popular acronym in the Passive-Aggressive lexicon is CYA ("Cover Your Ass"). Indeed, it could serve as the mission statement for many of these companies. Managers communicate by documenting, and they document to defend their turf, deflect blame, and rationalize their actions . . . or lack thereof. The defensive memo abounds in the Passive-Aggressive organization. Instead of meeting with customers or developing new products,

ZZ ELECTRONICS
INTERNAL MEMO

To: Roger Marcinno
        Vice President, Marketing
From: George Sullivan
        Director, Market Research
Date: April 1, 2005
SUBJ: DELAYED FOCUS GROUPS

I received your e-mail regarding the missed launch date for the new media player focus groups. The purpose of this memo is to address your stated concerns and draw your attention to the issues that resulted in the delay.

As you know, we had scheduled these focus groups for the first two weeks of May in New York, Miami, Chicago, and Los Angeles. Our plan called for five focus groups in each city to test reactions to the new media player. It became clear as May drew near, however, that Product Development was not ready with the prototype, and Market Management had not yet put together the competitive analysis and consumer positioning report.

As you'll recall, I presented our market research plan last November. We outlined a very aggressive schedule, which was predicated on Product Development having the prototype ready by now and Market Management completing their consumer positioning assessment no later than mid-March. Unfortunately, neither Product Development nor Market Management met their deadlines. It appears that the issues that disrupted last year's headphone line launch are still unresolved . . . despite assurances to the contrary.

We called off the focus groups, costing our department considerable time and money. Invitations had been printed and were ready to be mailed. Facilitators were under contract, and facilities were on hold. We stand ready to reinitiate our plan when the other departmetns deliver on their commitments.

I would suggest that we schedule a meeting with Product Development and Market Management in the next two weeks to ascertain when their deliverables will be forthcoming. I look forward to getting this launch back on track.

George Sullivan

managers spend their time and the company's resources justifying their failures or, more often, their inaction.

NEW HORIZONS MEDICAL SYSTEM: WHEN "YES" MEANS "NO"

When Larry Schmidt joined New Horizons Medical System as senior vice president of Human Resources a few years ago, he was immediately reminded of the time he had spent in Japan earlier in his career.[7] "In Japan, there are eight ways to say 'no' in a business meeting, and all of them begin with a nod of the head, 'yes,'" recalls Larry. "That's what it was like in our management meetings, lots of what we called 'the New Horizons nod,' but little in the way of follow-through. People, it turns out, had no intention of implementing what they had just agreed to do."

Well known for the quality of its patient care, New Horizons had always projected confidence and professionalism to the outside world. Internally, however, the reality was quite different. Despite employees' fervent belief in the system's mission and values, the organization seethed with conflicting agendas and deep-seated discontent. So dire was its internal dysfunction, the system had nearly broken up a few years before. According to Wall Street, the individual medical centers and physicians' groups were worth more as separate businesses than as part of the New Horizons extended enterprise, and they knew it. In fact, the physicians had tried to secede from the company . . . but the legal hurdles were just too high. So they stayed . . . and fumed.

"There was an atmosphere of distrust between the physicians and virtually everyone else," recalls Dr. Genevieve Poissant. "Not only was there no trust, but there was open hostility." People questioned colleagues' motives, and as one executive put it, "waited for you to screw up, so they could pounce on you and overturn a decision."

As its senior leaders assembled for a meeting in 2003, it struck many of them that the greatest impediment to New Horizons' achieving its aspirations was its own organization. All four of its

DNA building blocks were compromised and misaligned. Its structure and governance model were highly complex, leading to confusion regarding roles and responsibilities. As a result, decision rights were ill defined, leading to frequent turf wars. Information stalled as it inched through the enterprise. Finally, motivators were not aligned with the system's strategy and were applied inconsistently.

Structure: Scattered, Not Synergistic

As far as structure goes, New Horizons Medical System was an amalgam of assets and activities. It was essentially three organizations in one: (1) ten medical centers that operate as distinct, vertically integrated systems; (2) New Horizons Select Coverage, an insurance carrier that insured high-risk populations; and (3) six physician groups scattered throughout the Northeast. To make matters even more complex, they had just completed the acquisition of a Pennsylvania Medical Center, and were in the midst of a contentious integration effort that only exacerbated their organizational problems.

While all of these operations enjoyed the benefits of the New Horizons brand, they were not behaving as parts of the same whole in early 2000; in fact, many operations seemed to work at cross-purposes. While each unit took pride in its own performance and the reputation of the System for quality care, employees washed their hands of the gaps and shortfalls in the overall operating model, claiming "that's someone else's problem." As one executive put it, "We act like a federation of fiefdoms, not a unified and synergistic organization."

Decision Rights: Underground Turf Wars

Decision rights and accountabilities were particularly vague, which many insiders maintained was intentional, "so no one has to deal with the issues." In most functional areas and between headquarters and the various facilities, it was unclear who made decisions and how progress was measured in terms of strategic objectives, capital allocation, transfer of knowledge, IT investment, and other system-wide operating issues. To get anything done, you had to "shop around" for a decision-maker. An inside executive at the time lamented, "There is nobody senior enough to drive change, and nobody too junior to stop it. We are really tough until the first sign of conflict, and then we agree to make the decision next year. How much more study, thought, agony, delay, and procrastination is enough?" Even when decisions were made, it was unclear who was monitoring their execution.

As an example, as part of the postmerger integration work after the Pennsylvania Medical Center was acquired, the company decided to invest $50 million in consolidating the two patient record systems. Despite commitments from both sides and the selection of an IT services company to manage the project, the project stalled as no one made a decision on key design principles or what data would be included in the shared data base.

Silo walls were built to last at New Horizons. Rather than share information or trust another unit to provide a service for you, the general attitude was "build it, make it, run it yourself," which resulted in significant duplication of effort and many lost cost-saving opportunities. Defending one's turf was a priority and a key driver on the management agenda. In essence, New Horizons functioned as little more than an umbrella over expensive islands of excellence.

Information: Surfeit of Systems

When Jeff Ball arrived as chairman and CEO of New Horizons Medical System in early 2003, he couldn't even get an accurate count of how many people worked for the organization. "We had dozens of HR systems," Ball recalls, "so when I asked how many employees we had, no one could actually give me an accurate answer. The first official tally turned out to be twenty percent short of the actual number. They actually had people count, just for the heck of it, all the paychecks at every place the paychecks were issued, just to get a sense."

Access to timely, accurate, and consistent information was a huge problem for New Horizons. With more than two hundred separate IT systems and no central planning function, managers would cross their fingers and "hope the numbers work out." As one executive in the head office conceded, "We can't measure the profitability of any of our medical centers or by type of patients." Nor could New Horizons' functional divisions or medical centers benchmark their results against one another or the outside world; financial data did not allow for apples-to-apples comparisons.

Best practices in one medical center were not transferred to others; the "not invented here" syndrome ran rampant. If one area developed an effective employee orientation and training program, it was reluctant to share it, and the other centers were uninterested in adopting it. If one medical center developed a more efficient way to admit a patient, it was guarded like a trade secret. "We preferred to reinvent the wheel," admitted one senior manager.

Motivators: Mixed Messages

Internal surveys and patient feedback highlighted the fact that the experience of patients and others who come in contact with New Horizons Medical System was largely determined by the quality and training of its employees, and there was room for improvement in several areas. For example, too much staff time was spent on administration and not enough on patient care; best practices were not widely shared, and decision rights were unclear.

In short, the organization was demotivated. Physicians and nurses spent more time on administrative headaches than attending to patients. Moreover, because New Horizons was also an insurer, its people got mixed messages: satisfy patients, but don't spend too much time with them. Doctors and nurses felt pulled in opposite directions.

Meanwhile, Back in the Marketplace . . .

These internal dramas played out against a background of dramatic changes in the health-care arena. Struggling under the weight of increasing premiums, many employers were shifting the cost burden of health insurance onto their employees. To mitigate the pain, they were beginning to introduce choice—a range of benefit designs, including high-deductible plans to lower individual premiums. This shift posed both opportunities and challenges for New Horizons. Some integrated health-care providers were losing their healthiest (i.e., most profitable) members, who were smart enough to shop around for the best coverage at the lowest price. But New Horizons was not prepared to compete in this arena of empowered and cost-conscious health-care consumers. "We can't afford the luxury of each person deciding what to do and how to do it," said one manager at this juncture. "We need to bite the bullet and change our behavior." If not, New Horizons would not only miss the wave, it could potentially get caught in its fatal undertow.

Healing Hands: Placating Passive-Aggression

Recognizing these dramatic market changes and the internal impediments to a swift and effective response, as well as the opportunity for change as a consequence of its recent merger, the System's leadership formed a temporary working team from all parts of the enterprise to tackle organizational issues, including decision rights, information, motivators, and structure. This team was called Healing Hands.

The Healing Hands task force studied every aspect of New Horizons' organizational model, including the respective roles and responsibilities of the headquarters office, the medical centers, and functional services (e.g., human resources, IT, finance, public relations). Working teams reviewed how decisions were made, how accountability was measured, how information flowed, and how work was structured. Discussions were honest, open, and deep reaching, and gave people hope that, as one task force member put it, "We were tackling organizational and behavioral issues at last." After several months of study, the working group issued a set of sweeping recommendations.

Decision Rights: Charting a Road Map

With the Healing Hands task force recommendations in hand, the senior management team pored over the allocation of roughly one hundred different decision rights, specifying who could propose, validate, and decide various actions and who was responsible for executing them. These decision rights covered everything from the strategic direction of the enterprise (e.g., capital allocation) to adoption of medical best practices to functional operations (e.g., human resources, IT, finance, purchasing). The management team also resolved how best to communicate decisions once made, so there was no room for misinterpretation or blame-shifting.

To capture these new decision rights and information flows in the context of New Horizons' strategy, the team developed the "New Horizons Road Map" outlining every major strategic goal and how the organization intended to achieve it by 2006. This plan not only specified each step, but who was accountable for taking it and how performance would be measured. As Ball explains it, "This road map identifies the interrelationship and migration of various strategic initiatives. We update these regularly, and they are a critical tool that we use with the board and with the staff. Each senior team member has very detailed plans for exactly which goals will be met and when, and we roll these out deep into the organization. Each month, our management team reviews progress against the goals. When a problem arises, the executive in charge identifies it immediately, so the team can work collaboratively to solve it then and there. The focus isn't on shifting blame anymore, but rather on 'How do we fix this and get back on track?'"

Information: At Doctors' Fingertips

Not only did the company establish the "New Horizons Road Map" milestones to gauge progress against strategic objectives, but it also overhauled the systems that support the doctors and administrators in the field. They now have far more information on their desktops about patients, treatment options, and likely outcomes.

Motivators: Focusing on Patients

Based on the Healing Hands group's recommendations, teams were formed to look at various gaps in the New Horizons operating model. Under the direction of Larry Schmidt, an HR working group—composed of individuals from across the organization including physicians, nurses, technicians, finance professionals, and IT experts—redesigned the entire HR process. In particular, they designed a compensation structure that keeps doctors focused on patients, and a streamlined billing process. The newly designed model has significantly increased organizational effectiveness and employee satisfaction, while reducing administrative costs.

Structure: Shaking Things Up

When he arrived at New Horizons in 2003, CEO Jeff Ball moved quickly to assemble his team. Within weeks, he had changed the roles of some key executives, brought in leaders from outside, and asked others to leave, because he felt they would not support his plan. One of the most important priorities for an "outsider" CEO is to determine which managers are capable of and prepared to change and which ones are likely to subvert the change agenda.

New Horizons Medical System: Postcript

In the past few years, New Horizons has addressed both its external market pressures and its internal dysfunctions by committing to a "game changing" course of action. It has designed and rolled out more flexible products and is supporting them with a substantial investment in integrated IT systems. Meanwhile, Jeff Ball has recruited top-notch operators from across the industry to champion change and drive the organization, as a whole, to the next level of performance.

In 2004, the administrative and medical leadership from all of the various operations—medical centers, physician groups, insurance—came together to sign the "New Horizons Road Map," committing themselves to a detailed, five-year agenda for change in terms of access, quality of care, administrative costs, and value to patients.

While it will take continued investment and commitment to achieve its objectives, New Horizons is on the Road to Resilience. It now has clear decision rights, more useful metrics, better knowledge-transfer processes, and a clear road map to measure progress against its objectives.

PASSIVE-AGGRESSIVE: THE REMEDIES

So, how do you "cure" the Passive-Aggressive organization? One thing is clear: you cannot stop at cosmetic changes. You have to get into the very marrow of the Passive-Aggressive company and transform its underlying DNA. Only then are you likely to see clear and continuing results.

Leave No Building Block Unturned

Passive-Aggressive cultures, by definition, resist change and are, therefore, uniquely difficult to fix. Tackling the project building block by building block is a futile exercise with negligible impact, since they are all dysfunctional. To make changes stick, companies need to tackle all four building blocks at once—decision rights, information, motivators, and structure. Remedies must be holistic and sweeping. While the action plan itself may be built on a series of small steps that build on one another, the intent and outcome of this organizational redesign should be nothing short of transformational.

John Thompson overhauled the Symantec organization when he arrived as CEO in 1999. He spun off several businesses and product lines, changed the management team, revised all the incentive systems, and, as he says, "changed almost everything about the company." He describes the discovery process as opening a Pandora's box. "You'd open something up, and see something you didn't like, and you'd either close the lid again, because you didn't have time to deal with it right then . . . or you'd just dive in and start hacking away.

"We chopped up all of the old signal paths. It's like what goes on in Florida when the hurricanes hit one after another. The power lines are down; they're just crackling there on the ground. And somebody's got to reconnect them. We decided to seize the opportunity to reconnect them a different way."

The result has been nothing short of astonishing. In five short years, Symantec's revenues have grown from $632 million to $1.87 billion and the company has successfully shifted its market focus from consumer software publishing to Internet security solutions for individuals and enterprises, a niche that it now dominates. Today, Symantec is expanding into the broader information management market and is focused on helping customers ensure that their information is both available to a variety of audiences and secure. Under Thompson's leadership, the company has integrated more than twenty acquisitions so successfully that it is today regarded by *Fortune* magazine as one of the top companies to work for in the United States.

Bring in New Blood

To instigate the overhaul required to redirect the Passive-Aggressive organization, the impetus must often come from the outside. That said, outsiders suffer certain handicaps in leading companies through big changes. They lack the support network that a company veteran has spent years cultivating, and can easily alienate middle management . . . thus intensifying the roots of passive-aggressive resistance. Those who are successful retain enough of the old guard in the senior ranks to enlist the loyalty of the organization, while purging those who will never get on board. Alternatively, the "outsider" is, in fact, an insider, a change agent from within the organization. Whether the new leadership team is homegrown or recruited from the outside, they need to cultivate the trust and grudging respect of the rank and file. They do that by acting swiftly and decisively. In fact, in interviews conducted with chief executives hired from the outside, almost all of them admit that the one thing they would have done differently is make quicker decisions about who to keep and who to let go.

John Thompson says of Symantec: "This was a company that had lost its way, and it needed somebody who was not connected to the people or processes or strategy to ask the tough questions and be prepared to act on the answers. The company's former CEO, Gordon Eubanks, did a terrific job of building the company from nothing. This was a company that had gone from a standing start to $632 million in roughly fifteen years. And that's what I saw from the East Coast when I was deciding whether to take this job. The raw material, the raw attributes were there. I just brought a different set of eyes, a different set of lenses, through which to view the likely evolution of this company."

What happens to a company like Symantec is a guy like John Thompson comes in, takes inventory, and seizes the reins. He makes a series of wholesale changes to the organization's DNA, lets the company enjoy the taste of success again, and then starts letting out the reins a bit. It's a balancing act determining how much control to give back to the organization, because old behaviors can lay dormant for years. "That passive-aggressive gene is still sitting there, waiting to be awakened," says John Thompson.

Make Decisions . . . and Make 'Em Stick

One of the hallmarks of the Passive-Aggressive organization is the inability to take decisive action. Even when decisions are made, they are certain to be second-guessed, vetoed, or ignored, and only rarely implemented. So, one of the first priorities in rendering a Passive-Aggressive organization more effective is to allocate and clarify decision rights. These "rights" should be delegated to those equipped with the pertinent information and most able to effect the desired outcome (which often means front-line, customer-facing employees). It is not sufficient, however, to make up a grid assigning decisions and leave it there; Passive-Aggressive organizations need to institutionalize accountability for those decisions, tying appraisals and incentives into successful execution. Moreover, senior management needs to take steps to streamline the decision-making process, removing obstacles such as second-guessing and naming process owners to shepherd the execution of decisions.

"We had many people who could say 'no' but few people who could say 'yes' and make it stick," notes John Thompson. One of the first things he did when he arrived at Symantec was wrest veto authority from the all-powerful regional and product heads. "Back then, the product manager was king. A Level 10 product manager could tell the CEO what he or she was going to do," recalls Thompson. "And the regional managers were even more autonomous. They dictated to the development teams what they would or would not sell." Regions were known to redesign packaging and sit on inventory they were disinclined to sell.

"We had to regain control of who was responsible for making what decisions," says Thompson. "So, we told the regions, 'Your job is execution. You're going to do what you're told to do. You're not a business unit. You are the sales engine of the company. Your job is to sell what we build, not to decide whether or not you want to sell it and then design your own company campaign around it.'

And we told the business units that they needed to think more about the customers they served. So we restructured the company around customer groups: consumer and enterprise."

Spread the Word . . . and Data

Effective decision-making is predicated on timely and efficient access to relevant, accurate information; that is not a hallmark of the Passive-Aggressive organization. So, as decision rights are being articulated and assigned, information flows need to be systematically rerouted across the organization. Management needs to set up systems to "arm" decision makers with easy access to key information. That means streamlining the reporting process to ensure that top management is close to the pulse of the market and customers. It also means facilitating the flow of data to the right middle managers, those in the best position to use it to serve customers. Passive-Aggressive firms need to pay particular attention to breaking down the functional and regional silos *across* the organization and instituting suitable incentives to encourage efficient sharing of information horizontally as well as vertically. Finally, top management needs to install mechanisms to ensure that all information going to the market is consistent and clear. Metrics need not be numerous, but they should furnish visibility on the impact of decisions and progress against objectives. Metrics also need to provide advance warning if plans or programs are not likely to be achieved. Put simply, you need to measure the right things, and measure them right.

In late June, as George Sullivan is gearing up for the rescheduled focus groups, he runs into Judy DeGrasse at a management off-site retreat and they catch up over dinner. Judy is bursting with enthusiasm, which strikes George as strange given how disheartened she'd been the year before when the original launch date for the new media player had collapsed. Judy, as you might remember, had been an account manager in the Media Products Division.

Since then, however, Judy had been promoted into a sales management position and had been identified as a high-potential executive candidate through a program instituted by the new CEO, Toshi Yamamoto. She had twelve people reporting to her and had created a performance model within her group that was being widely emulated throughout the Sales organization. In fact, she was scheduled to give a presentation the following day to the senior management team about her winning model.

George went back to his hotel room that night inspired by Judy's example. Buried below his seeming cynicism, George still remembered the ambition and energy he had brought to his first job at ZZ Electronics, sixteen years before. For the first time in a long time, he allowed himself to consider the possibility that he could change his corner of the organization, as Judy had done. He decided to give it a try.

In preparation for the July Marketing meeting, George reached across silo walls to solicit input from Product Development and Manufacturing. He put together a one-page summary spreadsheet of the status of all ongoing market research projects. No more subterfuge and hidden agendas; he was going to volunteer everything that he knew and see what came of it. Instead of dodging calls from Finance, he set up a meeting with his team and the Finance support group to build a comprehensive report on the budget requirements, timing, and risk assessment of all current and projected new products. No one asked this of him; it was not technically in his job description, and it would probably result in more work for his group . . . but it's what an effective market research group does. And George was ready to be effective.

So, rather than leave them in the dark as usual, George invited representatives from Product Development, Manufacturing, and the market research vendor conducting the focus groups to attend his portion of July's Marketing meeting. George knew that getting everyone in the same room was the key to expediting this program; issues could be addressed and surfaced at once. The discussion that followed his presentation on the new media player market research plan was the most engaged and productive that he could remember in all his years with ZZ.

But the capstone was when Sarah Tillman came up to him afterward and commended him on the effectiveness of his approach. He also received a thank-you note from the vendor and follow-up e-mails from his colleagues in Product Development and Manufacturing in which they actually sounded excited about the new media player launch and asked to see the focus group report as soon as it came in. Suddenly this was not just another drill to put out yet another product. You could sense people imagining how it would impact the consumer. George sat back, satisfied not only that the company was going to make the deadline this time, but also that he was making a difference.

Ring in the Bell Curve

Passive-Aggressive companies are conspicuously bad at communicating what is expected of employees and where performance falls short. Subpar performers, consequently, never "get the hint." If an individual is to align his behaviors to the overall purpose of the organization, senior management needs to set and communicate rigorous expectations when it comes to employee performance and tie compensation and rewards directly to these criteria. In short, they need to grade on a bell curve. Top performers—both in terms of quantitative results and adherence to values—should be apprised of their superior performance and be rewarded for it with more than token bonuses. They should enjoy other incentives, both financial and nonfinancial. Meanwhile, poor performers should be made aware of their marginal status and provided the opportunity to improve or leave. The organization should tie compensation and appraisal systems to decision rights and critical metrics (e.g., impact on operations, budget accountability, quality, customer impact) and make these links explicit and public. Basically, Passive-Aggressive companies need to become less bureaucratic and more of a meritocracy.

* * *

"We have a stock option plan that is broad based, but not universal," says Symantec CEO John Thompson. "One of the things we recognized early on was—if we were going to grow at the rate that we were growing—we had to be more selective in who we gave options to, so as not to dilute the value of our stock. And so the first thing we did was identify a range of employees who were valuable to the company but didn't need equity to come to work and focused their compensation around cash bonuses. Then we increased the equity we gave to the engineers and other people that were critical to our long-term success."

In addition, Symantec introduced a number of other changes to its compensation schemes to align employees with the goals of the enterprise. It reduced the cash component of senior management compensation and significantly increased the equity element. VPs no longer got a BMW; instead they got a car allowance and an annualized incentive plan that effectively separated the wheat from the chaff.

"We changed the alignment throughout the organization," says Thompson. "Now, everyone gets paid based upon revenue production as well as profit generation. From an employee working in the mailroom to my office, we all worry about and get paid based on two things—how fast did we grow revenue and how well did we improve the bottom line? When we shifted the focus from profit only to profit and revenue growth, there were a lot of people wondering, 'Why do I want to worry about that?' My view was, 'Most of you don't have anything to do with profit. But *all* of you have something to do with revenue, so let's rebalance our incentives to reflect that reality.'"

Almost all Symantec employees participate in the employee stock purchase plan, through which they can buy Symantec stock at a discount. "And that's as it should be," adds Thompson. "What assets does a software company have? We have a bunch of computers and some buildings, but the principal assets are the thousands of people who come to work here every day. If you can't get good internal alignment in a software company, you're not going to build good products; you're not going to deliver good service. Attitudes show through pretty quickly."

The Passive-Aggressive organization's plight is an intriguing one. Externally, it appears to be all smiles, but internally, it's riddled with dysfunction. It's only a matter of time before the diseased elements overwhelm the healthy ones and drive the organization over the brink. While the task of transforming a Passive-Aggressive organization may seem monumental, it is possible and, more importantly, crucial to a company's continued relevance and competitive success. Our experience suggests that applying these remedies consistently and collectively can result in clearer accountability, properly directed information flows, balanced performance measurement systems, and, most importantly, enhanced execution and results.

FOUR

THE FITS-AND-STARTS ORGANIZATION
Let 1,000 Flowers Bloom

Scores of smart, motivated, and talented people work in the Fits-and-Starts organization, but they usually do not pull in the same direction at the same time. When they do, brilliant, breakout strategic moves can be the result. Typically, though, they lack the discipline and coordination to repeat these successes on a consistent basis. The Fits-and-Starts organization lures intellect and initiative—smart people with an entrepreneurial bent; it's a no-holds-barred environment where you can take an idea and run with it. But, in the absence of strong direction from the top and a solid foundation of common values below, these initiatives either crash and burn or simply peter out. The result is an overextended organization on the verge of spinning out of control.

The Fits-and-Starts organization is profoundly uncoordinated. Its movements in the marketplace are spasmodic and its messages conflicting, because of the inherent contradictions between and among its core building blocks. For example, while decision rights are highly decentralized, the information required to make the best decisions for the company is often available only at headquarters, if at all. Decision-makers at every level fly blind, and the organization, as a whole, fails to prosecute its strategic agenda.

Linda Simon was eighteen months into her job at *Advantage*

Advertising and was beginning to question whether she made the right career move. Brought in as managing partner by CEO Ray Cortes, Linda had nineteen years' experience in the advertising business, first as an account executive at a major New York ad agency and later as chief marketing officer of the nation's largest toy retailer, *Top Tier Toys*. After all those years in big company environments, she was ready for a change and had initially been enticed by the creative energy and freedom that infused the air at Advantage. She had worked with Ray for years as a client when she was at Top Tier Toys, and before that at the ad agency where she had worked. Ray had been her mentor. In fact, she had been largely responsible for moving the Top Tier account to Advantage when Ray founded Advantage eight years earlier. Shortly after that, she took a job with a large packaged goods company and had lost touch with Ray. When he had called her two years ago to offer her a partnership at his agency, she jumped at the opportunity to leave the stable, corporate life behind and take an equity stake in a dynamic advertising business run by someone of Ray's caliber.

Ray had specifically recruited Linda for her client expertise. She knew what it was like to be on the customer side of the table—what criteria they used in picking an agency, what caught their eye and interest. And Advantage was sorely in need of that insight. Despite Ray's unerring advertising instincts and considerable charisma—and the abundance of creative talent that he had attracted to the agency—Advantage was not winning accounts at the rate required to sustain its sprawling operations. With offices in Dallas, Atlanta, Detroit, and Los Angeles and a staff of 75 people, Advantage was chasing even small accounts just to make ends meet.

Within a month of her arrival, Linda learned the uncomfortable truth. When Linda first saw the books, she was struck by the agency's waning profitability and its unhealthy dependence on one major client, Top Tier. In fact, Top Tier represented 40 percent of Advantage's $100 million in media billings. Ray had arguably overpaid for small agencies in Atlanta and Los Angeles just to be able to support the Top Tier account. The Detroit office was an at-

tempt to diversify the agency's client base and was focused on the
auto industry. While a step in the right direction, it had yet to
break even. After running the numbers by client instead of by
office, something that no one had thought to do before, she determined that there were maybe a dozen other modestly profitable
accounts and four accounts that were losing money for the agency;
in fact they had always been unprofitable.

As she participated in client pitches, she became even more
alarmed. Several months into her tenure, she participated in a
presentation to a prospective client, *Wax-On Products,* a company
that sold automotive waxes and cleaning solutions. They had put
their $5 million account up for review after sales had begun to fall
off, and Advantage was one of three finalists competing for the account. Linda had seen the pitch document and reviewed the research that Advantage's team had put together on the plane to
Detroit; it was a really strong submission. The advertising concept
was compelling and specifically addressed a proven customer
need. It reflected strong knowledge of the automotive sundries industry. She felt Advantage had this one in the bag.

That is, until the presenting team assembled at the hotel the
next morning. Scheduled to meet at 7:30 to review the materials
and coordinate roles, Linda was the only one in the hotel restau-
rant at the appointed hour. The three junior professionals responsible for conducting the research and preparing the pitch arrived
breathless fifteen minutes late, having spent all night at Kinko's
babysitting document production. Ray Cortes and Rob Knox, the
partner in charge of the Detroit office, arrived at 8 a.m., with
apologies for getting stuck on another client call. They then enter-
tained the group with an engrossing account of the call, complete
with impersonations of the client in question. By the time they
turned to the Wax-On pitch, it was already 8:30, and it was time to
get in the cars to head to the client for the 9:00 a.m. presentation.

Rob suggested to Serina Hayes, the manager in charge of putting the pitch together, that she take the lead in presenting. Serina
was dumbfounded but clearly thrilled . . . until Rob added jok-
ingly, "Ray and I really haven't had a chance to go through this

latest version of the presentation." What Rob did not add—and should have—is the fact that he had dined with the chief marketing officer of Wax-On the previous week. They had spent much of the dinner sharing funny focus group stories and agreeing that too many companies had become overly dependent on this dated research technique.

By the time the cars wended their way through Detroit rush-hour traffic, the Advantage team was late for their 9:00 slot, and the agency scheduled to go after them had already arrived. They were engaged in an animated conversation with the Wax-On executive team handling the review. Looking at the crisp, professional attire of the competing agency's team, Linda took quick note of her own team's motley attire. She and the junior managers were wearing suits. Ray and Rob were business casual. So were the Wax-On executives, but they were the client. Linda registered Ray and Rob's informality—and the lack of a uniform dress code on the part of the team—as the client would, a sign of sloppiness . . . and another strike against Advantage.

And they hadn't even opened their mouths.

As the presentation got underway, however, Advantage began to recover some lost ground. Serina's command of the material and the team's understanding of Wax-On's market were masterful. The creative concepts were inspired and on target. And Ray and Rob interjected frequently with pithy, witty, expert commentary. Linda could see client heads nodding. They were back on track.

After Serina presented, Wax-On's chief marketing officer asked a question that should have been a layup: "How important do you think focus groups are to the research phase of this campaign?" An emboldened Serina jumped right in and explained that focus groups were an indispensable part of the research program, a fundamental first step. Rob quickly stepped in front of Serina and refuted everything she had just said, offering that focus groups were dinosaurs and were less and less important in terms of understanding customer behavior. In fact, Advantage viewed them as a last resort after ethnographic research and mall intercepts.

Ray concluded the pitch with his standard close, the "Trust Advantage" speech, complete with slides on what Advantage had done for Top Tier Toys. The figures on the slide were three years old.

A week later, Rob heard from the chief marketing officer of Wax-On, who relayed their decision to go with the other agency. She volunteered that Advantage had presented better creative and a more astute understanding of the automotive sundries business; on a person-for-person basis, Advantage had the advantage. But her fellow Wax-On executives were uncomfortable entrusting their brand image to an agency that could not seem to coordinate its own message. She noted how Rob and Serina had presented opposite viewpoints and how the overall program seemed a bunch of components, not a coherent whole. When Rob relayed this news to the rest of the team, Linda was not surprised.

Most ominous of all, the Top Tier Toys account was up for review, and she'd heard from a former colleague that there was no guarantee Advantage's contract would be renewed.

Advantage Advertising is typical of Fits-and-Starts firms. Endowed with lots of entrepreneurial energy and raw talent, it is largely bereft of coordination and discipline. For all of its creative genius and market intelligence, Advantage loses more "bake-offs" than it wins. How could that be? The partners from the various offices cannot seem to coordinate their efforts and present a coherent, compelling message to the client.

Fits-and-Starts companies often flourish for years, but their management model fails to mature as they expand in scale and scope, often through acquisition. While these organizations are rich in talent and resources, they don't have the management skills necessary to integrate and harness them effectively. When their competitive market changes, they're often caught flatfooted, and the best they can do, in the absence of a clear vision and robust management processes, is exhort people to "work harder." This rallying cry inevitably sets in motion a variety of new initiatives, which promptly fail as there is still no strong central direction or coordinated follow-through.

FITS-AND-STARTS: THE SYMPTOMS

In Fits-and-Starts organizations, the decision rights and information building blocks are fundamentally misaligned. Decision-makers throughout the enterprise feel free to act—a sign of initiative that is usually hailed as healthy—but, in this case, the decision-makers are cut off from the information needed to make sound decisions. Their actions do not demonstrate a common purpose or overall sense of direction, leading to incoherent market movements. Fits-and-Starts organizations often manifest the following unhealthy symptoms.

Win Some, Lose More

Every so often, a breakthrough new product or marketing campaign hits big at a Fits-and-Starts firm, and the company cashes in on its "lottery" winnings, but there is no consistency, no predictability to these windfalls. Indeed, there is no guarantee that there will ever be one. Having taken decentralized decision-making to an extreme, the Fits-and-Starts philosophy seems to be "Let 1,000 flowers bloom," a reference to Chairman Mao's rejoinder during China's Cultural Revolution. The result is that resources are quickly dissipated, and the company fails to execute consistently. Its results show peaks and valleys.

Because of the random big wins, management finds it hard to understand when and why the organization loses. And Fits-and-Starts organizations *do* lose . . . much of the time. Why? Because the organization lacks the discipline to perform consistently. Autonomous decision-makers in the field don't have the right information or clear incentives to pull in one, coherent direction.[1] Because there is no overriding vision or sense of direction, Fits-

and-Starts organizations lurch from success to failure, frustrating managers and front-line employees alike.

Asleep at the Switch

Unlike Overmanaged and Outgrown organizations, Fits-and-Starts organizations are fundamentally *de*centralized. The corporate culture is "persuade and cajole" rather than "command and control," and entrepreneurial personalities are cultivated rather than quashed. The problem is these rogue intellects are largely left to their own devices, as corporate takes a hands-off approach to managing their progress.[2] Top executives in Fits-and-Starts companies are not firmly in control; they are either too weak or too disengaged to instill deep values or steer a clear course. Without these leadership tools, headquarters is unable to rein in the excesses of the organization.

One high-flying, Silicon Valley, high-tech company epitomized this behavior. Senior management's job at this company was to get out of the scientists' and engineers' way. It was the scientists and engineers who created value . . . and who got the private offices. As long as the executive team kept the talent happy and well fed, then the firm would stay ahead of the technology curve and remain the vendor of choice for its deep-pocketed customers.

Or so they thought. The truth was—in the absence of firm direction from the top—the organization was working at cross-purposes. Business development was a haphazard array of loosely supervised, often conflicting, interesting ideas. Multiple marketing and sales teams pursued individual programs without coordinating—or even communicating—their efforts. Externally, customers were buffeted by the mixed signals.

Amidst the din, there *were* voices of reason. In addition to its top-notch engineers, the firm had some very savvy business people who understood, for example, that the company needed to develop applications for the ubiquitous Microsoft Windows platform. Still, no one was charged with systematically assessing the market and identifying the areas of greatest profit potential. No one was empowered to drive the company toward these bright opportunities. Worse yet, no one was looking at costs. In fact, the company was spending to support more than twenty separate offices in Silicon Valley and the development of a showpiece new headquarters building.

Then the bottom fell out. The market started to tighten in the mid- to late 1990s just as competitors began to move into the company's space. Unprepared for the worst, the organization fell into an inexorable downward spiral. Unaccustomed to tight operating budgets, the company could not cauterize the wounds it developed; no one had the authority or organizational clout to kill products, exit product lines, or slash operating expenses. One former executive described the company as "an organization with a control panel that had no wires connected to its back." Even as the company was sinking, its longtime CEO continued to say that its technology and people were the best in the industry. But the black hole had opened. The CEO left the firm. Several months later, his replacement quit.

Internal Strife Leads to Market Confusion

Because the decision-making reins are effectively in the business units' hands, separate agendas multiply and corporate loses control. Businesses pursue their own best interests rather than those of the whole firm, leading to suboptimal decisions and poor corporate performance. Even worse, some decisions don't get made at all—or are hopelessly delayed—as divisions duke it out or play hot potato. Unless headquarters can reassert its decision rights, it cannot resolve these conflicts and keep divisions on the same page. The overall organization becomes disjointed, incoherent, and, ultimately, sends contradictory or inadvertent messages to the marketplace.[3]

Information Quagmire

Ideas flourish, but information languishes in the Fits-and-Starts organization. It travels neither up nor down nor sideways.[4] Corporate is cut off from field market intelligence by its laissez-faire attitude and the autonomy asserted by its field operations, and middle managers are in the dark about how their decisions impact the bottom line of the enterprise. Information does not get lost in the layers, as it does in Overmanaged organizations; it never gets relayed. Unfortunately, for these organizations, ignorance is not bliss. Senior executives are unable to adapt strategy to changing market conditions, and line managers make suboptimal choices, because they lack full information about the rest of the company. They cannot effectively coordinate resources, leverage best practices, or even align their efforts with the company's overall strategy. The consequences of this information quagmire are stronger silos, increasing inefficiencies, and ever more duplication of effort.

Random Rewards

If decisions and information are not coordinated, you can imagine what the compensation and incentive schemes look like at Fits-and-Starts companies . . . all over the map. Each business unit and functional leader handcrafts his or her own set of financial and nonfinancial rewards. These inevitably misaligned motivators naturally give rise to intraorganizational conflicts, as the office grapevine (the only working information channel in the firm) circulates word of the "spectacular" differences in compensation and perks between regions or divisions that perform essentially the same work. Suddenly, the smart, talented employees of Fits-and-Starts organizations start updating their résumés on company time.

Scant attention is paid to career development at Fits-and-Starts companies. Performance evaluations are not consistent across divisions and are hard to compare as the company lacks any well-defined or uniform performance measures. Weak and inconsistently applied appraisals lead to irregular promotion practices. The link between performance and promotion is often tenuous.[5] Rather than train and develop exceptionally talented employees, resource-constrained Fits-and-Starts organizations promote them . . . then promote them again. Without the necessary skills and experience, the emerging stars of the business burn out as they take on more and more managerial responsibility. No one is shepherding them through the organization, making sure they rotate through various functions and line operations. The end result is that they flourish, but ultimately fail completely. Consequently, Fits-and-Starts organizations are at risk of losing their greatest assets: their people.

QUEST DIAGNOSTICS: THE QUEST FOR COHERENCE

Ken Freeman had his work cut out for him. A twenty-year veteran of Corning Incorporated and proven turnaround executive, Freeman was tapped in May of 1995 to fix Corning Clinical Labs, the glass giant's "broken" clinical testing business. Freeman's bosses offered him a "round-trip ticket" to go to Teterboro, New Jersey, and serve as temporary CEO of the ailing subsidiary. They figured it would take him about a year to "tweak" the controls and get the business back into shape . . . maybe eighteen months.

Freeman's first day at Corning Clinical Labs was enlightening. "I walked down the long corridor from the entrance, past the cafeteria toward the office area. And I'm a reasonably friendly person, so I was smiling and saying 'hello.' A lot of people walked by; several thousand people worked there. Yet virtually no one acknowledged me, much less said 'hello' or smiled back. They looked at the floor, looked out the window, anything they could to avoid connecting. That was my first big clue that perhaps this company needed more than a little tweaking."[6]

Freeman was right. Corning Clinical Labs was struggling with a number of pressing issues that were impeding its performance. For one, the business had been wolfing down acquisitions of competing labs. In the eighteen-month period before Freeman arrived,

Corning Clinical had completed three major acquisitions . . . on top of the nearly five hundred small labs it had absorbed during the 1980s and '90s. Little attention had been paid to integration. To use Freeman's words, Corning Clinical's approach to acquisitions in those days was, "Buy it, get it done, smash it together."

The result was a company that had "no identity." Freeman recalls going to Baltimore one of his first days on the job and asking employees, "What company do you work for?" Some said Met-Path. Some said Maryland Medical. These were the companies they had worked for *before* they were acquired. Years after the ink was dry, many employees continued to identify with their old employer, not Corning.

There were no employee-satisfaction surveys. There were no customer-satisfaction measures. There were only limited productivity metrics in place in the laboratories. As Freeman says, "It was really processing and performing the tests and reporting. There were no significant metrics beyond the most blatantly obvious. They weren't getting at process variables, those things you can adjust to actually improve performance like turnaround time."

Corning Clinical Labs was little more than a loose federation of acquired businesses, where talent ran high but almost never in the same direction. Each lab was run as a separate fiefdom under the watchful eye of a lab director who knew a lot about diagnostic testing, but little about running a business. Old company alliances continued to flourish, while the company as a whole floundered. Those decisions that did come down from corporate were either second-guessed or ignored altogether.

"It was hard to find anything that worked," says Freeman. "The lab businesses had been run very autonomously, and they had gotten into some bad habits, partly because they felt they could get away with it. Historically, the power in the company rested with the general managers in each lab. They had the sales, they had the operations, they had the medicine, they had everything. They were the kings and queens of Corning Clinical," notes Freeman.

"It was a company wholly focused on the bottom line. The prior administration would basically say, 'Look, if you give me twenty percent operating margins and are achieving your budget, you won't hear from me.' And a lot of the company wasn't heard from and wasn't hearing from management.

"Lab directors made expedient decisions about everything, including what industry regulations to follow. Their view was 'There's fifty thousand pages of rules from Medicare regarding reimbursement; they can't expect us to play by that.' The result: a company that was facing huge fines for charges of Medicare fraud and abuse . . . not to mention tens of millions of dollars in write-offs."

Parent company Corning quickly realized it wanted nothing to do with this renegade operation and began shopping Corning Clinical around. Ultimately, Corning decided to spin the company off to its shareholders by the end of 1996. "We were tossed away for garbage," observes Freeman, who gave up his round-trip ticket to lead the spun-off company. He found himself starting a new career "in an industry in deep trouble, a company in deep trouble, with owners that didn't want us, customers that didn't want to deal with us, employees that didn't want to be with us . . . and regulators who were convinced we were crooks."

In these less than auspicious circumstances, Quest Diagnostics was born at the beginning of 1997. Many on Wall Street believed that the new company wouldn't last a year. "No one wanted to be in this business," Freeman recalls. "I had people at Corning saying, "'Why, Freeman, would you ever go into the lab business? What did you do wrong?'"

Freeman was undeterred, and he saw the birth of Quest Diagnostics as the opportunity to recast the unhealthy Corning Clinical's DNA. With the help of Surya Mohapatra, PhD, a health-care industry veteran he recruited in early 1999 to be president and chief operating officer, he set out to change no less than everything about the company with the brilliantly immodest goal of becoming the leading company in the laboratory testing industry. His immediate focus: execution and results. Freeman puts it succinctly, "Strategy is interesting, but execution gets results."

Quest Diagnostics emerged from the ashes of a classic Fits-and-Starts company, a motley assortment of independent laboratories.

Loosely managed and poorly supervised, the company was rife with counterproductive and often suspect practices that were costing its parent not only financial but reputational capital.

Populated with thousands of bright, talented scientists and technicians armed with lots of ideas and initiative, the company had everything going for it but a solid sense of direction. As a result, Corning Clinical had dissipated its energies, exhausted its goodwill in the marketplace, and, ultimately, invited the scrutiny of the government.

Stop the Bleeding: Common Focus

To fix Corning Clinical and chart a new course for Quest Diagnostics, Freeman rallied his top team—the seventy senior-most people in the new company—and made the case for change using a values-based "focus document" that outlined eight critical success factors (see Figure 4.1).

FIGURE 4.1—QUEST DIAGNOSTICS' ROAD MAP TO RECOVERY

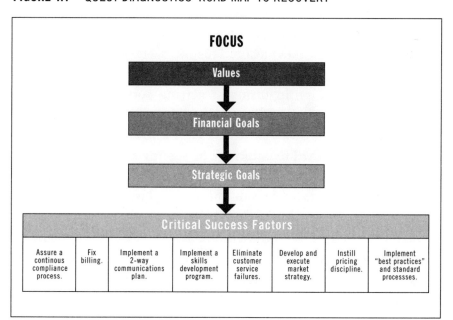

Needless to say, achieving these ambitious objectives provoked a lot of discomfort. As information systems started to become standardized, for example, local labs often lost the customization that they had painstakingly built into their proprietary systems. Such changes were difficult for people working in lab environments, where the best interests of the corporation seemed very distant from the day-to-day requirements of the job. Consequently, Freeman spent a lot of time walking the talk, going to town meetings and labs, and introducing his change agenda face-to-face.

As Freeman puts it, "If you really want to change the DNA of an organization—and I mean really change it—you have to start by laying out some really clear ground rules. It's such an important time for leadership. The CEO has to step up and say, 'Look, I'm a new guy in town, and here's what I stand for. And I realize it may not be what you stood for before, but we're going to live by these values around here, and here's what they are. And by the way, you're going to hear this message from me until I die.'

"You have to reinforce that message and those values every single day, because behavior doesn't change with a 'one time only' program. You've got to repeat yourself forever, and you've got to make sure when employees see you, they say, 'Here comes the guy in the blue shirt again. I just know he's going to talk about the values. I know he's going to talk about the importance of behaviors and results, in terms of getting performance out of the company. I know he's going to tell me he respects me. I know he's going to tell me he values what I do. I know he's going to survey me to find out how I feel. I know he's going to be accessible . . . in and out of the office.' That's what leading is . . . being consistent, clear, and in their face with the principles you want people to follow."

Once everyone was on the same page, so to speak, Freeman and his team rolled up their sleeves and began the hard work of fixing the organization's DNA—all four building blocks—so Quest Diagnostics could execute against each of its eight objectives.

Decision Rights (1): Corporate Reasserts Control

It was clear that the first step to restoring the fortunes of the company was regaining some central control of its disparate operations. Often, unhealthy companies find they need to delegate decision-making authority further down into the organization. However, Fits-and-Starts organizations generally need to tighten the reins—at least temporarily—and that's precisely what Freeman did. He centralized and consolidated decision-making authority in the hands of a small senior team.

Observes Freeman: "It's interesting. Decision rights go both ways. Upon arrival at Corning Clinical, since it was a turnaround situation, so the decision rights became very clear, I said, 'I'm going to make them.' You have no choice but to take the lead and force the change required, and then gain engagement later as performance improves." Senior management quickly stepped in and assumed responsibility for every major decision the company made—as well as quite a number of the minor ones.

Lab managers, who had previously been answerable to no one as long as they generated their target operating margins, bristled at the "usurping" of their authority, but there was no arguing with the results. A company that lost $626 million in 1996, the year after Freeman arrived, was generating $162 million in net profits by 2001. In that same timeframe, Quest Diagnostics' stock increased a staggering 914 percent.

Information: Prying Open the Black Box

"We had to invest in information," sums up Freeman. "We had to pile lots of money into IT." Getting billing coordinated across the company was an immediate priority; billing had become by the mid-1990s the "black box" that senior management dared not open. "Each unit had its own billing manager and did its own billing. The billing managers didn't talk to each other, and there were no billing best practices nor common metrics. So if we asked

'What's your DSO (days sales outstanding)?'" recalls Freeman, "one would say fifty, the other would say ninety, and they'd be accounting differently . . . which is a scary thing in any company. So we had to get consistent definitions and metrics in place."

"Day one, we simply dictated to the billing function, 'Look, here are your metrics. I don't care what you measured yesterday. Here are the metrics we're going to start reporting. And we're going to have billing calls each month with the billing managers from each of the business units on the phone, so they can compare notes.' That's how we began that process of driving by the standard metrics and comparing between units and forcing communications."

Motivators: Goal Sharing

Freeman and Mohapatra did more than put an expanded network of metrics in place at Quest Diagnostics, they created targets and paid people for hitting them. The company introduced a program called Goal Sharing that allowed employees to earn between 0 and 6 percent of their yearly pay for achieving various goals—both financial and nonfinancial (e.g., customer satisfaction, turnaround times, client service quality). To encourage resistant employees to commit to Quest Diagnostics rather than just their individual lab, the firm tied 25 percent of the payout to company-wide performance objectives.

The day the company was spun off in 1997, each employee received twenty-five shares of newly minted Quest Diagnostics stock. "Not enough to put the kids through school," Freeman notes, but enough to focus employees' attention on the task ahead.

Not all motivators are measured in dollars and cents. Freeman describes Quest Diagnostics employees' greatest motivator as "the emotional tug of what they are doing in the lab. People know—particularly if they're touching a specimen—that that represents somebody's life. It's not like flipping hamburgers, right? Somebody is waiting for an answer out there, and it might be their parents. It could be their kids . . . or a relative. That's powerful."

Decision Rights (2): Propose, Validate, Decide, Execute

Once Quest Diagnostics was on the right course, it consolidated its leadership position in the medical-testing industry by acquiring one of its two main competitors, SmithKline Beecham Clinical Laboratories. With this acquisition and its successful integration, Quest Diagnostics entered a new chapter of its existence. The company had proven that it could effectively implement dramatic organizational change and react swiftly to market developments. The company also now had a deep and committed management team. It was time to loosen the reins and redistribute decision-making authority.

Surya Mohapatra, who became chairman and CEO of the company in 2004, describes the early decision-making approach as "making the rounds."[7] Reluctant decision-makers would "debate, decide, debate, disagree . . ." Now, the decision-making process is spelled out for all to see: Propose, Validate, Decide, and Execute (see Figure 4.2). An individual proposes a decision, gathers input

FIGURE 4.2—SINGLE-POINT DECISION-MAKING: PROPOSE, VALIDATE, DECIDE, EXECUTE

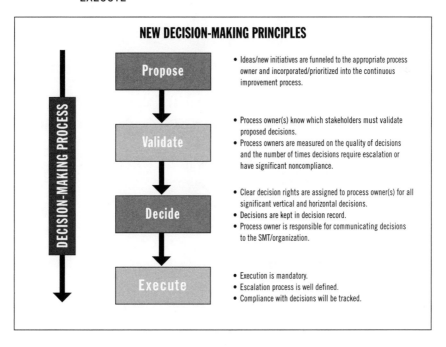

(including criticism) from the appropriate subject matter experts, then takes the proposal to senior management for a decision. Once the decision is made, execution is *mandatory* and closely tracked.

Mohapatra offers a real-world example: "Take the lab at Teterboro. Teterboro is now processing sixty thousand samples a night. The good news is we're doing sixty thousand samples. The bad news is, what if something goes wrong? So who is going to propose the decision that we really need to divide this lab into two labs? In this case, it was me.

"But my proposing it doesn't make it so, and this is where people miss the art in this new decision-making design. My idea proceeds to the validation phase, which I often describe as a "fierce conversation." Who are the people in validation? The people who have the greatest stake in that decision—among them the regional vice president, the sales vice president, and the laboratory manager, parties who may or may not be inclined to support my proposal. People tend to confuse proposal with validation—they really want to skip to step three, 'decide.' And that's a problem, because you cannot decide without input from appropriate and interested parties. You cannot decide unless you validate. That means you intentionally have to create a group of people with both positive and negative opinions."

Once a decision has been made, it's assigned to a "process owner." The role of this process owner is to drive decisions *horizontally* . . . across the functional groups and business units. By giving these people cross-functional and cross-team responsibilities, Quest Diagnostics not only drives decision-making but develops individuals skilled in lateral collaboration, fluent in end-to-end processes, and shrewd enough to help make trade-off decisions for the company. Process owners also develop a sense of accountability as they know they are responsible for the successful execution of decisions in their sphere of influence.

Structure: Reinforced Horizontally and Vertically

Finally, Mohapatra has streamlined the organization by eliminating two layers of management. The new organization chart has only four management layers, including the CEO. In place of the four decision-making bodies that existed before, Quest Diagnostics now has a single decision-making body composed of the Senior Management Team and fifteen horizontal-process owners, who "own" processes that cut across functional and business unit lines. Another key structural change is the creation of a new Front Line Forum, made up of individuals literally on the front line of customer contact who can bring the customer's experience to relevant decisions.

Quest Diagnostics: Postscript

From its inauspicious beginnings as Corning Clinical Labs, through its dramatic turnaround, to its rise to industry leadership, Quest Diagnostics has charted a remarkable journey. Together Ken Freeman and Surya Mohapatra have led a team that successfully transformed a dysfunctional collection of Fits-and-Starts labs into a Resilient and winning organization. In the five years ended 2004, Quest Diagnostics generated a return to shareholders of 530 percent.

Today, Quest Diagnostics is at the top of its industry with over $5 billion in annual revenues and a national network of laboratories and patient service centers that touch 140 million patients a year. The company is the undisputed leader in the diagnostic testing industry with 12 percent market share and 38,000 dedicated employees. Nearly a decade after arriving for a short stint, Freeman formally passed first the CEO baton and then in 2004 the chairman title to his handpicked successor, Surya Mohapatra.

Mohapatra has already put his stamp on the organization with a vision that has three central thrusts: "relentless focus on the patient, growth, and people." Rather than relax and enjoy Quest Diagnostics' remarkable success, he has set the organization's sights on the "challenging future" rather than the "glorious past."

Says Mohapatra, "We have two thousand patient service centers. I call them McQuest's. And they have to offer the same experience—every time—to the forty million people a year who walk through their doors. We receive half a million patient samples a night. That means half a million families are waiting the next day to know whether their loved ones are ill or well. That's a tremendous social responsibility; we cannot afford to make a single mistake." In fact, from an organizational perspective, as Mohapatra is fond of pointing out, Quest Diagnostics is at once a retail company, a logistics concern, a bank, and a medical provider. One thing it definitely is not anymore is a Fits-and-Starts organization. It has achieved good health and is today a Resilient organization.

FITS-AND-STARTS: THE REMEDIES

If these symptoms sound all too familiar, we have good news . . . and bad news. The good news is that most Fits-and-Starts organizations are blessed with talent and can rally the intellect and initiative needed to generate consistent wins. The bad news is that it won't happen without the direct and rigorous intervention of the organization's Senior Management Team, who may well need to centralize control for a period of time to turn around performance.

Executives Should Decide Rather Than Preside

Letting lower-level talent run with a good idea makes sense within parameters. Fits-and-Starts companies have misplaced the parameters; senior managers have become bystanders, and they need to play a more active role in monitoring activities, mediating disputes, and allocating resources. Many highly successful start-ups stumble in making this transition. Given the wealth of talent in the organization, it's tempting to let it operate unfettered, but without firm direction from above and a common foundation of company values below, business units will make choices that maximize their own interests, rather than those of the enterprise.

Unlike other, unhealthy profiles that need to delegate decision-making authority further *down* into the organization, Fits-and-Starts organizations generally need to consolidate authority at the top, at least temporarily. In extreme cases, the CEO of a Fits-and-Starts company will step in and centralize decision-making to regain control and access to critical information and stop the bleeding. He or she will personally sign off on big and small decisions alike until the organization is back on solid ground.

Remember Linda at Advantage Advertising? She had the experience and clout to point out and rectify some of the mistakes she saw made before and during the Wax-On presentation, yet she did nothing. She had been specifically recruited to furnish a client's perspective and help the firm "pump up" its pitching, and yet she remained a bystander. She did not step away from the sidelines to drill the team beforehand, or at least postmortem their performance.

She could have assembled the team prior to the day of the presentation to block out logistics, debrief one another on client research and/or conversations, agree on a consistent "look" not only for the presentation and leave-behinds but for the team as a whole. She could have called up to Rob and Ray's hotel rooms to expedite their trip down to meet with the team . . . or insisted that they depart for the client site earlier, so as not to be late.

These are minor fixes that most likely would have resulted in their winning this $5 million account. A major fix would have been to present her client profitability analysis to Ray. The irrefutable logic of results would have prompted him to either renegotiate contract terms with money-losing clients or walk away.

Develop a Standard MO

To address the incoherence and lack of coordination characteristic of Fits-and-Starts organizations, firms need to establish a consistent modus operandi, or operating model. Company leaders need to create and institutionalize a standard set of expectations as well as standard operating systems and processes. For example, Advantage Advertising would have been well served to set up standard procedures for responding to client requests-for-proposal (RFPs) and account reviews or a standard way of calculating return on investment. Moreover, Fits-and-Starts firms need to ensure that these standards are documented and communicated effectively to all employees. Then, to ensure that employees actually adopt the new processes, incentives must encourage and reward performance throughout the process.

To establish a better sense of common purpose and coherence, Linda might have approached Ray with the idea of engaging all the agency's employees in defining Advantage's vision and values. Asking questions like "What is our differentiating advantage?" and "Which customers do we want to serve?" would go a long way in refining the firm's focus.

Building on this base, Advantage could then forge a closer knit culture with a common language and shared expectations. In the absence of this unifying framework, it is hard for Advantage to capitalize on its tremendous talent and resources. Teamwork, service excellence, and accountability are three obvious values or goals that come to mind.

Since Advantage is clearly an environment that cultivates initiative, Linda should seize it to begin to establish consistent policies and best practices across the firm's disparate organizations. As the firm's managing partner—its chief operating officer, in effect, she should be identifying teams of professionals across offices to develop company-wide processes for marketing, selling, and client service activities. In addition, she should begin to institutionalize the notion—indeed, the expectation—of teaming across boundaries to provide the best the firm has to offer.

Assign Unambiguous Accountability

As decision rights are not clearly understood in Fits-and-Starts organizations, and managers who are promoted often tend to do their old jobs rather than stepping up to their new responsibilities, there is a screaming need for clarity on decision rights throughout the organization. Employees at all levels need to understand what they are accountable for, and what they are accountable for needs to support the overall objectives and performance of the enterprise. Goals and responsibilities need to be clearly communicated and understood and reinforced by appropriate motivators, both financial and nonfinancial.

Having been brought in to help improve Advantage Advertising's customer orientation and focus, Linda is in an excellent position to clarify accountabilities within the firm. She can, for example, suggest that the agency designate client service directors for select national accounts. These individuals would manage the relationship, act as the client liaison, and would be responsible for all media planning, strategy, and execution. Most important, they would be accountable for the profitability of the account. These directors would "own" their accounts. No dropped balls or missed handoffs.

To reinforce accountability and "professionalize" the career development track at Advantage—which heretofore hinged on Ray's opinion of an individual and his decision on what bonus to give him or her—Linda could help Ray introduce formal and consistent performance reviews, particularly for senior professionals. A performance "contract" would be developed at the beginning of the year and reviewed by Ray and the whole senior group. When it came time for promotions and bonuses, actual results could be assessed against these agreed-to targets.

Set Up Clear Signposts

The Fits-and-Starts organization, more than any other, is in need of a clear vision and focused goals to rally employees and guide their progress. Because of the business units' tendency to pursue individual agendas and maximize divisional rather than corporate returns, senior management needs to spend extra time and effort not only developing but communicating strategic plans and the road map for how to execute them. The corporate center needs to be rigorous in specifying and closely supervising a range of key measures, rather than letting each unit define its own metrics. Every employee in the field should know where the organization is headed and what is expected of him or her. Moreover, the Fits-and-Starts organization needs to have robust information systems in place to keep employees across the organization apprised at all times of any change in direction, the rationale behind it, and how it affects their actions.

If there were clear and quantifiable business objectives at Advantage Advertising, Linda had yet to locate them. Early on, she should have hammered out with Ray some specific objectives in terms of profit and diversification, for example setting revenue and profit targets for the next three years, or deciding how much of the total Top Tier would represent.

Another priority would be coordinating the efforts of Advantage's four far-flung offices. As it was, each office was pursuing the same nationwide accounts, developing their own marketing materials, pursuing their own individual agenda. The agency as a whole needed to impose order on these mixed signals and set up signposts.

It was clear—even given her short tenure with the firm—that certain offices excelled in certain aspects of the advertising business. L.A. consistently produced award-winning creative work. Detroit had deep research capabilities, and Atlanta had won many clients with its relationship management skills. Why not set up these offices as centers of excellence within the firm and rotate employees from other offices through each center to spread best practices and round out employees' skill base? National teams could be developed to set standards in each key area and metrics could be aligned with these standards.

To capture information on best practices, Linda resolved that every client pitch would be followed by a debriefing on why Advantage was chosen or why they lost the opportunity.

Reward Collective Endeavor

One of the greatest challenges confronting the Fits-and-Starts organization is how to coordinate the disparate activities of individual business units, such that they optimize company-wide performance. Again, this remedy requires stronger engagement at the top of the corporate hierarchy . . . and far greater communication across the organization. To drive collective behavior, it's often necessary to establish cross-company rewards and institute incentives that foster coordination and collaboration across diverse functions or divisions. By linking appraisals and rewards to these team behaviors, the organization sends important signals to people—not just "do this and we'll pay you" but "this is what we encourage and support as an institution."

Linda could have taken some action to reward collective behavior. Her analysis already showed that some of the most profitable customers were the ones that were served by multiple offices. These customers had caught on to the fact that each Advantage office offered distinct strengths, so they reached for where the expertise was. To flourish, Advantage needed to do that "integration" work for the client by drawing on the best of all of its offices in delivering its products. To encourage that collective effort, Linda should consider tying bonus incentives to firm-wide performance, not just individual or office performance. Promotion reviews and appraisals should include criteria on how well an employee identifies and shares best practices with others, in their own office as well as across offices.

The Road to Recovery for a Fits-and-Starts organization is long and arduous. To pretend otherwise and implement solutions at the edges is to doom any turnaround effort to failure. Senior management must have the clout and the commitment to seize the reins of the organization and establish common, consistent processes and systems. Business units need to cede control—until the company's course can be corrected—and conform to Corporate's efforts to align, once again, the organization's decision rights, information flows, motivators, and structure. Once that alignment is reestablished, however, the Fits-and-Starts organization can and will flourish.

FIVE

THE OUTGROWN ORGANIZATION
The Good Old Days Meet
a Brave New World

The Outgrown organization is literally bursting at the seams, having expanded beyond its original organizational model. Too large and complex to be controlled effectively anymore by a small team of senior executives, it has yet to "democratize" decision-making authority. Consequently, much of the organization's potential remains untapped. Because power is closely held at the top, the Outgrown organization tends to react slowly to market developments and often finds it cannot get out of its own way. If you're in the middle of this organization, you might well see opportunities for positive change, but it's just too hard to run these ideas up the flagpole. The legacy of top-down direction and decision-making is too well entrenched, and old habits die hard.

This model worked very well when the organization was smaller and less complex, but now it is stunting growth of the organization and the career development of its best and brightest. Ironically, this unhealthy type is a natural outcome of early success, and an easy trap for high-growth companies to fall into. It's worth paying attention to its symptoms, so you know what temptations to avoid.

At $60 billion-plus in annual net sales, Cargill Incorporated is, quite possibly, the largest privately held company in the world.

Now a leading processor, marketer, and distributor of agricultural, food, industrial, and financial products, Cargill is best known for its roots in grain trading. W.W. Cargill started the company in 1865 with a single grain storage warehouse in Conover, Iowa, and he, his brothers, and the MacMillan family steadily expanded the business over the next century into a premier food and agriculture company and one of the world's leading commodity trading operations.[1]

To this day, the Cargill and MacMillan families retain roughly 89 percent of the equity in the corporation and are active members of the board. Until quite recently, they ran the company, serving in the CEO capacity for all but 26 years of the company's 140-year history. But much has changed since W.W. Cargill first arrived on the edge of America's frontier after the Civil War. Periodically over the years, the firm has outgrown its organizational model and had to make adjustments. Here we describe the most recent example of how Cargill acknowledged and addressed signs of "outgrowth."

"As we surveyed the world of Cargill in 1998, we could see that the ground was fundamentally shifting under our feet," recalls Jim Haymaker, vice president of Strategy and Business Development.[2] "It was very clear that our largest customers—packaged-goods manufacturers, retailers, and major food service companies—were becoming even larger and consolidating their power. Grain-related farm policy in the U.S. was shifting toward more protectionism, and there was a certain amount of tumult in the world . . . skirmishes here and there that you could see escalating. Monsanto and DuPont were attempting to change the agricultural and food system with their development of genetically modified organisms. And the Silicon Valley, 'New Economy' phenomenon was in full flower. Small, agile competitors were feeding around the edges of our market position. It looked like scale, sheer scale, was less powerful as a stand-alone business model than it had been previously."

Cargill had spent decades building an organization that ran long global-supply chains, where the handoffs in those supply chains and the efficiencies of those handoffs were critically important. That was an argument for scale and breadth. Cargill lived on the scale and efficiency of its processing of commodities, products with low levels of differentiation. And it particularly thrived in logistics and managing price risk across that system. Now, technology of the sort that drove other high-tech, fast-cycle industries all of a sudden appeared in its backyard.

While people throughout the company could see these threats brewing, Cargill's organizational DNA, at the time, hindered its ability to respond quickly and decisively. Jim Haymaker sums up the situation: "What kind of organization was Cargill back then? First and foremost, private. And I start there, because I think it colors much of the culture. Cargill was a company where the long service model prevailed, where you came and stayed for a career. Former CEO Whitney MacMillan worked very hard at communicating a couple priorities. One was maintaining and nurturing Cargill's reputation for honest dealing. The other was creating the kind of family environment that—even though we were from many different cultures and countries and backgrounds—made everyone feel part of the Cargill family."

This paternalistic management model had worked for Cargill—in fact, very effectively—for almost a century and a half. It bred incredible company loyalty and instilled in employees a strong sense of ethics. "But, as we surveyed the landscape in 1998, there was the realization that we had become an inward-looking firm," recalls Haymaker. "And our traditional strengths were beginning to falter as new models of entrepreneurship, extreme agility, and rapid strategy cycling came to the fore."

At the time, Cargill was organized around a three-dimensional matrix. Throughout the organization, there were overlapping units defined by geography, product lines, and functions. Multiple reporting dimensions required individual managers to include as many as three different parties in making important decisions: the regions in which they operated (e.g., Latin America, Asia), the functions they performed (e.g., Finance, Legal), and the product lines they represented (e.g., cocoa, dry corn milling). This structure slowed decision-making and impeded the firm's agility. Too many people were accountable for various initiatives.

Moreover, the senior levels of the corporation were spending too much of their time managing individual businesses, rather than governing an increasingly complex enterprise. Notes Haymaker, "There was a dawning recognition that we needed more decision-making authority closer to the front lines than the traditional hierarchical organization allowed for, at least the way we ran ours."

Cargill was progressively outgrowing its once highly successful operating model. Dramatic changes in the competitive environment and the looming threat of new technologies conspired with the company's own rapid global expansion to undermine the informal, collegial, and fiercely private management approach that had always characterized the firm.

While the values of family and integrity were as important as ever to the agribusiness giant's identity, a broader set of core values and principles was needed to guide decision-making and corporate governance. The company needed to be more explicit in its expectations and rigorous in its processes; it needed to institutionalize a new set of management systems and processes so it could delegate more decision-making, require more accountability, and unleash the latent entrepreneurialism within the organization. And it needed a structure that would accommodate greater flexibility and transparency.

So, in the summer of 1998—at the prompting of Cargill's board—then CEO Ernie Micek assembled the Strategic Intent Team. Their task: to take a "blank slate" look at the future—looking out twelve years to 2010—and prepare Cargill for it.

Cargill in the late 1990s was not yet an Outgrown organization, but it manifested some—not all—of the incipient symptoms. Fortunately, it was self-aware enough to diagnose these symptoms early, before they could spread and hinder results.

Outgrown organizations have, typically, developed beyond their initial—and once successful—organization model. Often, they are family businesses and start-ups that have expanded beyond their comfort zone or are poorly integrated mergers of a number of firms with different organizational personalities.

In the early years, or "garage stage," it was well understood who did what and who was accountable. The model worked well, but it could take a successful organization only so far. As the enterprise grows, the organizational constraints become apparent and show signs of stress. While everyone can see the problems, no one wants to be the one to tell the powers that be (and everyone knows who the "powers that be" are).

Outgrown organizations tend to operate from the top down; most decisions are made by a small group of very senior managers. But much of the information relevant to those decisions resides elsewhere in the organization, often in the field. Since much of that information never makes its way to the decision-makers at the top, decisions are not as informed as they should be, and often just plain poor. Meanwhile, the workforce becomes increasingly frustrated every time it receives a decision from headquarters that fails to meet customers' needs or solve the business units' problems.

OUTGROWN: THE SYMPTOMS

The symptoms of an Outgrown organization are unmistakable. Just look for an organization straining at the bit, and you'll likely find a company that has outgrown its organizational model. Some of the telltale signs include the following:

Remote Controls That Don't Work

The centralized, top-down management structure of the Outgrown organization is not solely to blame for its inability to get things done—after all, healthy Military Precision organizations thrive with a command-and-control management model. Rather, it's the combination of centralized management and *de*centralized information that impedes the organization. Critical customer information and insight does not move up the organization to where decisions are made.[3] Instead, it languishes in stores, sales organizations, or customer service centers where it is of little use.[4] The result is predictable. The organization is slow to respond to competitive developments. When it does, it does so reactively, often missing critical opportunities.[5] In the early days of the company, the top team could shout across the room or walk the halls to gain intelligence, often a very fond memory for these executives. They are reluctant to let it go, and, in fact, continue to visit field operations and customers to keep that spirit of intimacy alive. But they just don't have the capacity to manage the enterprise in that manner anymore. The organization is operating in too many geographic areas serving too many customers with too many different products, services, and technologies.

For 130 years, Cargill flourished as a family-run private enterprise. "In the old days, you could convene a board meeting in five minutes," recalls Jim Haymaker. There were no outside directors. The executive team and founding-family board members all worked in the firm's headquarters building, so everyone could be assembled in short order. The environment was collegial, and the body of knowledge needed to make critical decisions resided for the most part in the room.

However, as Cargill expanded its operations globally, it grew too complex to manage in this familial manner. As product lines proliferated, so did the systems and business models needed to support them. "Already we were seeing siloism and the rapid spread of disparate systems in the company," notes Haymaker. Customer needs, meanwhile, were becoming increasingly sophisticated. For example, customers who purchased animal feed from Cargill now wanted information about the nutritional benefits of these products.

The implications in terms of governance were becoming clear. To achieve the crisp execution and enhanced flexibility increasingly needed at the customer interface, Cargill could no longer operate as a centrally run, distantly managed concern. The board and senior management could not expect to participate in every decision. It was time to delegate more authority.

When David Murray stepped into the CEO role at Commonwealth Bank of Australia in 1992, he was taking over a classic Outgrown organization. The bank had just been partly privatized, but, for all intents and purposes, it was still a government-run enterprise. It had been, and still was, heavily unionized with a culture based on seniority. Its processes were, in some areas, up to fifteen years behind market practice.

"Nobody in this organization ever did anything unless the managing director said so," recalls Murray. "The bank had lived for eighty years successfully. It was protected by its government ownership in a highly regulated market, which had only opened up to competitive forces ten years before, so it had a strong culture of loyalty and pride. In the field, people lived in their own world where Commonwealth Bank would always be the market leader.

"There was no real organizational model or design, and *talk* about a highly political environment: our internal social processes were handed down by an Act of Parliament. If you live under an Act of Parliament—where the staffing arrangements are all written down (that is, rules based), and there are appeal processes for promotions and discipline, and the workforce is heavily unionized—you get an organization of people just trying to do their best, but there really isn't a system, including leadership, that's driving the firm along."[6]

Branch employees performed their prescribed duties, day in and day out. Whatever intelligence they might gather or portfolio gaps they might spot stayed with them as there were no formal or informal mechanisms for elevating information to the top of the organization, where decisions were made. As a result, those running the bank in Sydney had little perspective on overall sales patterns or trends.

"There was a joke in the head office that if you wanted to go to Queensland or Victoria to visit the state manager, you should get a visa, because you were entering foreign territory," says Murray. Information did not travel up *or* across the organization; it had nowhere to go and no way to get there. There were no daily or weekly reports on sales or service issues, or training on cross-selling, for example. Employees' duties were carefully circumscribed, and overstepping those bounds was not encouraged.

The Founder's Fingerprints

The Outgrown organization is run from the top, often by larger-than-life founders or family members and their protégés. Not surprisingly, their sweat equity tends to be valued more highly than any other "shares" in the enterprise. These individuals are inextricably linked with the company's image and reputation. Everyone inside and outside the organization watches their every move and waits for their ultimate verdict on issues both large and small, hence the often tortoiselike pace of execution and the pervasive sense that actions are audited and decisions second-guessed.[7] Outgrown organizations generally don't have layers and layers of decision-makers, so it's crystal clear who makes the decisions; he or she is semideified. Deep in the organization, people talk about what "Sam" or "Michael" or "Bill" believe. There may be fifty thousand people in the company and three hundred "Bills," but everyone knows who *the* Bill is.

Throughout the 1980s and into the 1990s, Bill Gates personally oversaw every inch of Microsoft. He not only charted the company's course, but he coordinated and controlled the company's myriad projects and programs. On a biweekly basis, he would pore over one hundred status reports from dozens of teams in between hosting now-famous Bill Meetings, at which he would interrogate employees on their progress and plans. So daunting were these Bill Meetings that teams would rehearse their presentations with someone playing the role of Bill Gates. According to one software developer, "The objective became to get Bill to like your product."[8]

Laura Ashley's floral-print frocks and chintz-covered home furnishings evoked romantic notions of the English countryside, an aspiration that resonated with customers for decades. Together with her husband, Bernard, she created a vertically integrated miniempire to further her vision. What began with a single silk-screen press in their London flat in 1953 grew to become a major specialty retailer with more than five hundred stores worldwide. Until her death in 1985, Laura Ashley held staunchly to her traditional British values and to the reins of her company, reacting to the permissive attitudes and miniskirts of the 1960s with ankle-length dresses sporting a "made in Wales" tag.[9] While other apparel makers moved manufacturing operations offshore to save money, she refused to close her factories in the U.K.[10] When women's fashion moved toward tailored, professional attire, she stuck with the "landed gentry" look. Bernard carried on her legacy and retained nearly two-thirds of the company's stock when it went public in 1985. His battles with the professional management brought in to revive the company's fortunes in the 1990s were epic, resulting in a revolving door at the top of the organization that ushered in—and out—five successive CEOs between 1991 and 1998.[11] As one departing company executive said of Bernard Ashley, "He still regards it as his business."[12]

Proliferating Workarounds

As isolated executives craft company policies in the executive office, managers in the field devise ways to circumvent them until, ultimately, exceptions become the rule. These "workarounds" are leading indicators of problems in a company's organization model. They are hastily invented substitutes for failed or inadequate processes and policies. For example, a salesperson might call her "friend" at headquarters to get an expedited pricing quote so she can get back to her customer in a day . . . rather than the week the process usually takes. That's one of the classic "workarounds." The good news is these "exceptions to the rule" are generally evidence of motivated employees trying to enhance the company and its service to customers.

The problem here is not the existence of the workarounds, but the inadequacies in the organization that prompted their creation. These one-off, informal exceptions are not only inefficient, they can be unfair; the rest of the sales organization does not benefit from this individual's invented advantage. Another concern is the message that management sends when it tacitly accepts these workarounds, particularly when it's a control process that has been bypassed. Finally, workarounds can weaken a company's leverage or scale advantage. For example, if business units develop their own workarounds in purchasing materials, they undermine the company's opportunities to consolidate spending and negotiate volume discounts.

At Commonwealth Bank of Australia, they even coined a term for the workarounds that surfaced throughout the branch system. They called them unauthorized productive processes, an apt name, since it covered both the "productive" benefit and the "unauthorized" detriment associated with these enterprising schemes. *Unauthorized productive processes* were the legacy of government ownership and a highly regulated market. When these artificial limits were lifted, workarounds proliferated to fill the void as ingenious employees looked "beyond the book" to find better and more profitable ways to run their part of the business. As CEO David Murray concedes, "Unless competitive decisions were triggered by experienced people in the field, they might not get made." Of course, these local calls violated protocol, and there were no formal processes and functions to disseminate these good ideas and best practices, so their productive benefit was limited. In fact, "unauthorized productive processes" arguably did more harm than good as they challenged existing policies and procedures, creating confusion, possibly even resentment in the ranks.

What does it feel like to have to "work around" the entrenched management of an Outgrown organization? Let's consider the case of Bob Krueger, a fifty-year-old general manager at *Danville Beverages*, a soft drink manufacturer and distributor based in Grand Rapids, Michigan. A family-owned and run company, Danville Beverages was founded by Don Danville in the 1940s and passed on to his children, Don Jr., Elizabeth, and Julie, who now oversee the business. Don Jr. is the CEO, and Elizabeth and Julie serve as co-chief operating officers, though Bob and others in the organization have no idea how they divvy up that responsibility. An eighteen-year veteran of Danville Beverages, Bob is now in charge of the Eastern Region, which encompasses Ohio, Pennsylvania, and New York, and fears he has reached the end of the line in terms of his career prospects. Out to dinner with his wife, Carole, he relays his latest frustration with the organization.

"It looks like we're going to lose the *Pit Stop* convenience stores as a customer," Bob laments. "They want those new flavored milks that are all the rage, but Don, Elizabeth, and Julie won't invest to build the production capability. It would cost a little over three hundred thousand, and I project payoff in less than three years, but I can't even get them to look at my figures. It's been six months I've been after them. Now we stand to lose a three-million-dollar client."

His wife, Carole, asks, "Isn't there some way you could come up with the money . . . divert some resources or something?"

"I'm only authorized to make purchases of up to fifty thousand, and it was like pulling teeth to get *that* level of approval. If your last name isn't Danville, it's hard to get any money out of those three. Last year, I was able to upgrade our packaging line by spreading the bill out over several purchase orders, but I can't finagle three hundred thousand out of Corporate. They just don't get the need for investment in the New York market. Maybe it's time for a new job."

The Emperor Has No Clothes

The increasing ineffectiveness of the Outgrown organization is an open secret in the organization, particularly to those on the front lines. They confront this lamentable truth every day in their inter-actions with customers, suppliers, even competitors. Yet—as with most of the information evident to those on the front lines—this knowledge makes its way to headquarters only with great diffi-culty. Griping remains backroom chatter. There aren't many people willing to take on "Rome." While it might be the right thing to do for the health of the organization, it's too risky personally.

After Bob tells Carole about the latest "veto" handed down by the siblings running Danville Beverages, she sympathizes, "I remem-ber when they hired you away from *P&A Grocery* with all those promises of career advancement and an equity stake. What hap-pened? They treat you like a hired hand . . . and then they tie it be-hind your back. How do the other general managers feel?"

Bob groans. "They're in the same boat, but they don't want to rock it. Gerry and Michelle had a great idea last year for a promo-tional campaign for the seltzer line, but they never even presented it. There are no incentives to stick your neck out like that. So, in-stead, we get together every couple of months and disparage the Danvilles. I'm the only one who even challenges Don Jr. The rest just swallow and smile. I don't know, maybe I should do the same. Who would hire me? It's not like I have any real experience manag-ing a business or running a P&L."

OUTGROWN: THE REMEDIES

So, what can Outgrown organizations do to stem the spread of these symptoms? First, they can harken back to what made them successful in their early days and reignite the torch of entre-preneurship among the next generation of leadership. They do that by democratizing decision-making, unblocking the flow of in-formation, and institutionalizing career development. The basic prescription is to refocus headquarters on the helm and allow busi-ness units greater autonomy.

Reignite the Torch of Entrepreneurship

Many Outgrown organizations started as a gleam in a young entrepreneur's eye and became classic success stories, epitomes of ingenuity and industry. The regrettable reality, however, is not all of these success stories have happy endings. As the business grows, the organization fails to evolve. Instead of adding fuel to the entrepreneurial fire by stimulating idea generation and decision-making throughout the organization, top management starves it of oxygen and dampens the flames that spring up from below. The original leaders hold on too tightly to decision-making authority, even when it's obvious they don't have the requisite market knowledge to make informed choices.

Most companies of any size—but particularly Outgrown organizations—need to accept that the executive suite is no longer capable of making every important decision across the company. These individuals, isolated from the market, cannot absorb and process all the information that should be brought to bear against the myriad choices that are made daily, particularly since the information underlying these decisions is often idiosyncratic and time sensitive. Senior management needs to stoke the embers of the company's entrepreneurial heritage by delegating decision-making to business unit executives—those closest to the customer and most likely to succeed to the executive office. Only then can the Outgrown organization increase the speed and effectiveness of decision-making and, ultimately, improve results.

When Cargill took a proactive, "blank slate" look at the way it was organized to do business around the world in 1998, it carefully evaluated its products, services, and customers. Based on this review, it identified ninety-five "natural," market-facing business units (BUs), where before there had been twenty-three mostly global divisions.

It then demonstrated the courage of its convictions and atomized the entire company according to this new model. Cargill nearly quadrupled the number of its business units, not to mention business unit leaders, each of whom was given a P&L and a performance contract with the CEO. These individuals became the principal strategists and implementers within the company. "This model was a radical departure from our more traditional, hierarchical structure. Instantly, the world of the business unit leader was rendered more transparent and more complex. There were more decisions to be made, more expectations to be fulfilled," notes Jim Haymaker, the head of strategy who helped guide this transformation program, dubbed Strategic Intent.

"With Strategic Intent, we reset business unit expectations. We said to business unit leaders, in effect, 'Come back to us and propose new business unit boundaries if you need to . . . or redefine your market . . . or even your strategic space. That's okay. But with respect to how you behave and how we do business, we're going to be very clear.' It took a burden off the business unit leader's shoulders to know precisely what his degrees of freedom were, and this clarity has unleashed great entrepreneurial energy."

In 1992, David Murray did not have the luxury of picking and choosing from among a field of high-potential management candidates at Commonwealth Bank. "We were just too thin on the ground. So, what I did was leverage my skill and the skill of bright people I had known in the bank for some time to unleash Commonwealth's latent entrepreneurial energy. At the same time, I pulled some outside people into influential roles, and then I threw them all into the deep end. For example, I put some outsiders with limited banking experience on the Credit Committee or the Asset Liability Committee, so that they could learn fast."

The results were impressive, in fact so impressive that the Australian government sold its majority interest and fully privatized the bank in 1996. Today, Commonwealth Bank is a publicly listed corporation, the fourth largest in Australia, with the largest financial services distribution network in the country and more customers than any other banking institution.

Refocus Headquarters on the Helm

It's difficult for hands-on executives—particularly those who've built the company from scratch—to let go of day-to-day decision-making. The urge to get their hands dirty is partly why they got into business in the first place. But let go they must—and pursue a higher vocation, to lead the company through the next wave of growth and value creation.

No executive, no matter how smart she is or how hard she works, can make every important decision at a company. To stay successful, Outgrown organizations need to redraw the line between corporate and business unit decision-making. Historically, that line has been drawn close to the top of the Outgrown organization's hierarchy, but that top-down approach no longer works. The organization has gotten too big and complex to be remote controlled. Corporate headquarters should relinquish day-to-day decision-making and redirect its attention to enterprise-wide concerns, creating value in the linkages between the businesses rather than in the businesses themselves (e.g., portfolio management, governance, strategy, risk management). This new focus will require organizations to develop individuals who create value by leading rather than doing.

If you were a Cargill executive in 1998, one thing was certain: you knew the economics of agricultural commodity supply chains like the back of your hand. As Jim Haymaker puts it, "The people that succeeded in this corporation were people who understood their costs on the back of an envelope—what it cost to raise the corn, to move the corn, to process the corn, to price the corn. Our managers everywhere in the system were constantly working the economics of the chain . . . both the underlying economics and the price volatility." In other words, they were deeply involved in the business.

In the old Cargill, you spent a career proving your mettle moving, processing, and hedging tons of grain or corn until you ascended to the top of a global division, where you became master of all you surveyed.

That is, until 1999, when the company overhauled its entire organization. Suddenly, that massive global division disappeared, and, in its place, several smaller, customer-focused business units appeared. Division heads became platform leaders with no direct control over business unit assets or strategy. Instead, they served in a new role as "coaches" to freshly designated and more junior business unit leaders.

"The platform is there to approve strategies but not author them, to approve business units' requests for funds, to approve their investment plans, to approve the hiring of key new players, and also assist the business unit leaders with customer relationship development. However, there was no more matrix," says chief strategist Jim Haymaker, meaning the requirement that managers work initiatives through multiple reporting lines had been eliminated. "The dominant form of execution in the corporation, and the formulators of those strategies being executed, are the business units. The platform leader's role is to shape platform-level strategy, to empower and motivate these business unit leaders, and to encourage collaboration among them.

"Imagine the impact that had on a company with a culture of lifetime employment that supported a certain sense of entitlement," continues Haymaker. "You climb to the top of a global division, working your entire career to one day be in charge of a global organization. Now you're being asked to move someplace else, to give up your key assets. It was very hard.

"Platform leaders' ability and willingness to adapt to their new roles after the transformation was our greatest concern. They had the most to lose. These were people who had spent their lives building a business only to have their business card changed from president to coach. Now, contracts were being drawn up between their previous subordinates—the business unit heads—and the CEO. And that contract had symbolic impact, because it really marked a break from the traditional hierarchical organization."

Jim Haymaker credits Cargill's culture with making the transformation possible. "Without these division heads saying, 'Look, I've worked my whole life here, and this looks really ugly and painful. But we've all come up through the organization together, and if you're all in this boat, I'm on board with you,' we could not have done this!

"Because of their strong loyalty to the company and their shared experience, senior management had a degree of trust in this grand experiment that allowed them to make this huge leap that most corporations would not have been able to make."

Push Out Decisions and Measure Results

Having redirected the focus of headquarters on the helm, the Outgrown organization needs to support newly empowered business unit and functional leaders in the middle of the organization with the tools they will need to succeed. The overall solution will encompass all elements of the Outgrown organization's DNA, from structural decentralization to two-way information flows to more inclusive decision rights and appropriately aligned incentives. The important thing is to establish congruence among these four building blocks, so that decision makers have the information and incentives they need to make the right decisions for the company.

Naturally, top management will initially be loath to give up control, and those taking up the reins may be equally hesitant as their experience in running a business is limited. The key is to distribute decision-making while establishing a clear line of sight between the corporate center and the business units. In addition, it's important that Outgrown organizations put in place decision-making frameworks and metrics to assess results. Headquarters needs reassurance that the next generation is up to the job!

Cargill's Strategic Intent journey began with a white sheet of paper. In 1998, CEO Ernie Micek appointed eight members to the Strategic Intent Team and charged them with preparing the organization for the future. Their job was to take Cargill's deep capabilities and rich assets and fundamentally reconfigure them to serve the needs of customers over the long term. Recalls Jim Haymaker, "The individuals that he chose were all senior group-head level leaders of the corporation, and the likely next generation of company leadership. They were far enough from the top to have ideas about how the company could be better run, yet they were close enough to the marketplace to see what was working and what was not working for the customer. And because they were a level or two down, they were maverick enough to be willing to really detach from wherever we were going as a company, without a great deal of compunction. They were not deeply vested in the status quo and could plot a new course."

The team pored over dozens of scenarios and organization models in a few short months, and ultimately recommended reorienting the entire company around customer solutions along the agriculture and food chain. Cargill moved away from its inefficient, matrixed organization structure and established a networked organization oriented along product lines.

The concept behind a "networked" structure is that it distributes decision-making accountability *throughout* the organization as opposed to focusing it at the top of the hierarchy. In a networked organization, there are "nodes" of decision-making authority at various levels, and responsible units work across the organization to get things done. In Cargill's new model, ninety-five business units were created around customer needs and solutions, and contracts were established between the business unit head and the CEO.

While business platforms existed as an intervening layer, the contract was between the business unit and the CEO. "One of the things that we were trying to get from this restructuring was a clear line of sight on units that were buried in the old vertical hierarchy," says Haymaker. "There were business units in the old structure that had potentially ten pieces under them, ten sub-BUs. At the top of the corporation, you had very little knowledge of what was going on in those ten sub-P&Ls. How much strategic attention was each getting? How much talent was it getting? How much of a drag was it on the overall profitability of the division? Now, all of a sudden, we had a degree of transparency, and, more importantly, accountability that we had never had before. We had clarity around strategy and the implementation of that strategy.

"The contracts that each business unit now signs with the CEO have proved catalytic in reinforcing our customer focus," says Haymaker. "These contracts articulate the key metrics of every one of our businesses and set forth the goals we are striving for. Over the past several years, the contracts have become, in effect, a perpetual performance guide. Even when they're not up for negotiation, they're always there. They're always operating. And if you're not clearing those hurdles, you're not creating value for the corporation . . . and you know it."

Cargill also started asking every business unit for a five-year forecast in support of their strategic plan. There was huge pushback from some of the trading operations, who claimed they couldn't forecast the next two months, let alone five years. And they were right.

"Yes, it's impossible to forecast commodity markets five years out," concedes Haymaker. "On the other hand, you can't do without a forecast. The very action of doing it is such an important discipline to stretch your thinking and especially your foresight. And that's what we wanted. Our new leadership wanted to exercise the minds and the judgment of these new decision-makers. They wanted business unit leaders to put a stake in the ground around their business model and what they thought it could do."

Legitimize the Productive Workarounds

When organizations are not running smoothly, the points of friction and dysfunction in the operating model can often be valuable sources of information. Rather than systematically sweep away problems and issues, you should "mine" them for useful intelligence. Workarounds are a treasure trove of valuable information on how to run the organization better, serve customers more effectively, and communicate more clearly. The secret is to legitimize those that work and leverage their productive benefit more broadly across the organization.

The traditional prescription for addressing workarounds has been to identify and eliminate these makeshift solutions, but this approach is flawed in our opinion. By weeding out workarounds in the business units, you do not actually address the root cause of the problem, only its symptoms. And you send the signal that what is not "official" is automatically bad. To improve your organization's operational efficiency over the long run, you need to understand the obstacles that these clever stratagems are meant to circumvent . . . and then remove those obstacles . . . not necessarily the workaround itself. In fact, workarounds can and often should become "legitimized" as best practices. This is the surest way to eliminate duplicative and wasted effort. It's wise to remember the adage "Necessity is the mother of invention." Workarounds exist for a reason. Your job is to discover why and use it to your advantage.

"Historically, people in the branch system had very good information about competitors' tactics," notes Commonwealth Bank CEO David Murray, "But by the time it went up the command-and-control chain and back down again, the whole market would have moved again." The enterprising few found ways to work around this bottleneck, devising those "unauthorized productive processes" to get work done or cross-sell products. Generally built around informal networks of colleagues and friends who would help each other out, these processes were ultimately legitimized at the branch level as the One-Team Referral System.

So successful was this small branch initiative that it was recently rolled out company-wide as an intelligence gathering and cross-selling tool. As Murray describes it, "We simply decided in one meeting—it took us two minutes—that we would scale up this system." Every person at Commonwealth Bank of Australia can now refer customers or other pressing business to the right party in the organization directly using the One Team Referral

System. Adds Murray, "We can now expedite market intelligence from the field by putting it on the system, where it can be transferred directly to a Line of Business manager, who can instantly decide what response to make to competitive moves."

Workarounds often surface when an Outgrown organization's centralized support services fail to deliver. At one global transportation company we've worked with, the IT department spawned a host of workarounds. Since it had to support large mainframes as well as a series of complex, homegrown legacy applications across various operations, the central IT department spent most of its time keeping systems running, as opposed to anticipating customer needs. Major application enhancements took up to two years to deliver, and smaller-scale applications received little, if any, support.

As a result, the IT department's customers—the various operating units—resorted to unsanctioned workarounds to get critical information technology projects completed and services performed. For instance, they would hire their own "shadow" IT staffs and pay them using non-IT job codes to escape detection. Ultimately, the company conducted a full assessment of its IT operations and determined there were opportunities to not only serve customers better, but also to cut the annual run-rate by $30 to $50 million. Rather than legitimize the workarounds, it established a more effective and transparent market for IT services within the company that allowed the IT department to prioritize its workload and the operating units to manage their demand. By imposing market forces (i.e., supply and demand) on internal IT, the company gave units the ability to "bid" for a higher place on the IT schedule for more critical, time-sensitive projects.

Professionalize the Management Model

Long gone are the "garage" days of ad hoc processes and informal controls. The Outgrown organization has already graduated from that stage in its lifecycle, and it needs an organization model that institutionalizes what works, while eliminating what doesn't. What doesn't work is clear, for example, "silo" thinking, second-guessing, inflated performance appraisals, and compensation without consequence. Turn these on their head and you see what does work and what characterizes a professional management model: an enterprise-wide perspective, appropriate delegation of decision rights, realistic performance appraisals, and pay that fairly and accurately reflects performance.

To build this sort of coherent and aligned organization, you need to temper the pursuit of growth with effective risk management controls and establish professional standards throughout your organization. People should know what is expected of them and have the tools, the information, and the authority to perform those responsibilities well. Professionalizing the organization model does not mean casting it in stone. It means taking a more disciplined, analytical and process-based approach to getting things done, one that better matches the scale and scope of a more mature enterprise.

In describing Cargill's dramatic and ongoing organizational transformation, Jim Haymaker says, "We were trying to achieve a huge amount, and we knew that the guide posts for this journey would be our strategy and principles . . . and the behaviors we sought to instill. In fact, we soon recognized that the key to overhauling the organization was not so much moving the lines and boxes around, but instilling new behaviors at every level.

"One of the six key behaviors we identified—and highlighted as it marked a departure from Cargill convention—was what we called discuss, decide, support. At Cargill, our operating paradigm had too often been 'discuss, decide, discuss.' Career managers felt they had the right to challenge a decision if they were just fundamentally uncomfortable with it. And that feeling ran deep in all of us.

"The new order couldn't move forward with that kind of dissent. Now, we get the best minds in the room—in terms of capabilities

FIGURE 5.1—CARGILL'S SIX KEY BEHAVIORS

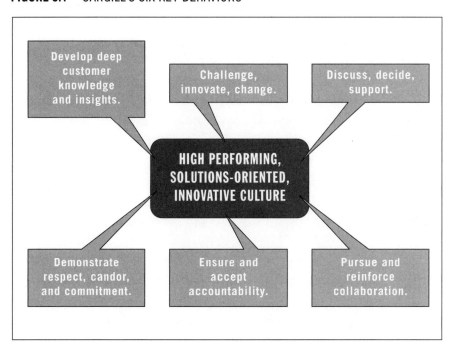

not hierarchy—to make the decision. We'll vet it, we'll make a call, and then we will expect everyone to get in line and really implement it. If it's not going well, we'll step back, we'll do a postmortem, and we may correct course. But, you can't get great execution unless you have compliance with the decisions that are made."

Business units at Cargill now have to operate within a set of parameters in terms of quality standards, performance hurdles, and corporate requirements. These are the constraints within which business unit leaders map a strategic direction in terms of market share, differentiation, and performance. "Sure, you find people trying to renegotiate their hurdle or renegotiate this or that, but there are fewer and fewer over time. The transparency between the business units and corporate is much greater than before. There is no place to hide and less room for excuses," notes Haymaker.

"The key is the clarity of the parameters. We have tried to be black and white, rather than fuzzy and gray. To the extent that we can be explicit about minimum requirements, decision rights, and behavior standards, we have clarified the world of the leader enormously.

"So, what are the tensions here? There's the fundamental tension between imposing on the organization a structure, a set of behaviors, a whole variety of new constructs on the one hand . . . while, on the other, letting them understand where they can exercise their own degrees of freedom, where they can be creative, where they can custom-fit the metric to their purpose. It's tight/loose.

"What was never loose were those things we deemed corporate requirements. In its simplest form, this was and is a very short list. We ended up with eleven of them. And they have become the beacon illuminating the minimal standard of systems and behaviors required in any Cargill business model."

The corporate requirements establish a floor that business units can use to estimate their cost of operating. It gives them a quantifiable sense of the minimum drag on their results imposed by corporate "must-have" services, so that they can compare themselves with their lowest-cost competitors. Moreover, it gives new managers and newly acquired operations a very clear sense of what is expected of them. The corporate requirements stipulate Cargill's threshold expectations in terms of behavior, system configuration, and when you must use company lawyers or insurance, for example. "You can always raise your hand and ask for an exception," says Haymaker, "but they're not often granted."

The first thing that David Murray did as CEO of Commonwealth Bank of Australia was overhaul the traditional Friday management meeting. "This weekly ritual could go from five minutes to three hours, and no one knew at the start. There was no agenda," recalls Murray. "It was a derivation of what the British banks used to call 'morning prayers,' where the management team just got together and had a chat." In a deregulated marketplace, this kind of collegial "coffee break" was not a particularly productive or professional management tool. "So, within one week, we pulled together all of the sales reports, competitive pricing reports, and interest-rate sensitivity reports, and literally stapled them together as the document by which we would manage the bank every Friday."

More recently, Murray and his team established key performance metrics around total shareholder return and rolled out a rigorous service and sales management system across the whole organization. Teams at every level meet or teleconference every week to discuss a lead topic and share best practices. Murray recalls, "Some weeks, we pick an area like Business Banking that we want to push along. The senior team will then follow up with phone calls or visits to front-line people. Thirty or more phone calls to Business Banking relationship managers in one week has a remarkable effect on the organization."

Cultivate Leadership at All Levels

Now that the organization has outgrown its old model, it's time to not only distribute decision rights, but also cultivate the next generation of senior management. One of the central challenges of the Outgrown organization is to extend the mantle of leadership beyond the "founding family" or tight management team. This is an organization driven from the top with few middle-management layers. The opportunities to exercise leadership skills have historically been scant, and there's little in the way of formal training.

As the management model is "professionalized," leadership needs to institute formal training and development programs to identify, promote, and reward exceptional potential. Promotions should include not only the vertical steps up the organizational ladder but also lateral transfers across the organization to enhance individuals' portfolios of skills. In designing career development programs, HR professionals should explicitly address the profound cultural shifts that employees are working through as they transition to a new, more accountable organization model.

In leading the transition from a government bank to a fully privatized commercial bank, David Murray ushered out an entrenched seniority-based culture and system of motivators, and inaugurated a new merit-based model. It was anything but easy. "People who come from a regulated and regimented environment like a government bank are steeped in the civil-service model where you spend a lifetime being steadily promoted until you retire. Your position is a matter of seniority, not ability. Many of those who came to the bank from the outside—and there's a lot by now—come from power-based private-sector models. They're used to doing what the person in charge wants done. And of course, neither is merit based. We're moving very assertively to a merit-based system now, where people are promoted and compensated based on their skills and contribution, not length of service or corporate politics."

To cultivate the upcoming generations of management, Commonwealth Bank introduced in the 1990s what it calls the Manager One Removed model, in which an employee's boss's boss takes responsibility for her coaching and development. As Murray describes it, "If you reported to Paul, and Paul reports to me, I am responsible for your development, not Paul. Paul is accountable for your team's performance." By encouraging a relationship between an employee and her "Manager One Removed," the organization effectively breaks through the impediments of a seniority-steeped culture and identifies up-and-coming leaders. It keeps promising employees on the radar screen and pushes them faster and further than might otherwise be the case.

In the "Manager One Removed" model, each manager has an "Effective Leadership Unit" consisting of his direct reports as well as his manager(s). These Effective Leadership Units convene three or four times a year to discuss business issues, collaborate on solutions, communicate change initiatives, review case studies, or play out competitive scenarios. These sessions are an excellent development forum for everyone involved. "They represent a fantastic cross-learning opportunity," observes Murray. "All three levels get to know each other much more directly." Managers can better assess team members' talents and help them develop. They can also build more effective succession coverage plans, since they now have a very good idea of where each team member could move, vertically or laterally, and in what time frame. This model also reduces unpleasant surprises by giving people the opportunity to raise issues in a collegial setting where they can address and gain input from not only their manager, but their manager's manager.

To motivate promising talent and to cement their commitment to the now decentralized organization model, Cargill's senior leadership team created five different compensation models. "I think the corporate leadership team may have spent more time in the first year of Strategic Intent on motivating alignment than on any other topic," says Jim Haymaker. "Fledgling units that were just getting off the ground, for example, might use a project-related scheme that deferred compensation for several years in anticipation of a breakthrough. The traders, as you might expect, had a separate system entirely."

The idea was that different compensation models fostered different behaviors and the right model for a business was dependent on a host of factors from the nature of the competition in its market to the time frame over which it would deliver results. So, if the business was being incubated and would not deliver results for a few years, a deferred compensation scheme might make sense.

Then, there were the entrepreneurial incentives. "We distanced ourselves from the word 'autonomy,'" says Haymaker, "because autonomy suggests you could go off on your own and do whatever you wanted. At the end of the day, this was a directed conglomerate, or as we preferred to call it, federation of businesses, bound together by a common strategic intent and a need to collaborate to succeed. Still, there was no mistaking the tremendous unleashing of entrepreneurial energy. Business unit leaders had more options in responding to changing market conditions, more freedom to run their businesses."

"In terms of career development, there were more places to go now, and being a business unit leader became a desirable job. Not all units are created equal; some are massive, and some are tiny.

But just being a member of that group; there is a great feeling associated with that."

Today, Cargill has a number of programs and educational modules designed to groom the next generation of leaders. The firm created the Leadership Forum to bring the top people in the company together every two years. The Cargill Leadership Academy also drives key ideas through the ranks by having leaders teach future leaders. The company has created a set of ten booklets on how to migrate the business unit to a customer solutions model. They now have a road map at the business unit level on how to do this. And they're being trained in the critical skills needed to succeed in solutions-selling from customer engagement to continuous product differentiation to the role of R&D.

The firm has an extensive talent management process through which it identifies the top two hundred leaders, the next five hundred, and so on. "No matter how big you get, you better know your leaders, and you better understand who fits best in what parts of the organization and what they're capable of. At the end of the day, these are the people that will fuel the growth of your business," concludes Haymaker.

CARGILL: POSTSCRIPT

It's ironic, but Jim Haymaker credits Cargill's historic culture with its ability to modernize. "I'm not sure any of us fully appreciated during the design phase what a powerful role our culture would play in motivating this new strategic direction. But it proved to be the vehicle that carried us through."

Six years into this twelve-year journey, Cargill is flourishing. Earnings increased significantly as soon as the changes took hold. In fact, since the launch of Strategic Intent in the fall of 1999 through early 2005, Cargill's shareholder value has steadily increased at a compound annual growth rate of 18 percent, ex-dividends. "Once performance took off, it took off rapidly and exceeded our forecasts. In addition to the accountability and performance payoff, we got a good collaboration dividend," notes Haymaker.

The power of Strategic Intent is the boldness of its ambition. It was a change program specifically designed to challenge the core beliefs of a venerated, family-run organization. The scope and the scale of the effort were so profound, that the company knew going in that it would be grappling with the consequences for a decade or more. Very few companies could afford such a long-term aspiration and fewer still could maintain the momentum required to bring it to fruition.

Cargill—still under the direction of CEO Warren Staley, who began his tenure as this program was getting underway—is a stronger, more focused company today with 105,000 employees and operations in 59 countries. Nearly a century and a half old, it has not only survived but thrived when so many other once powerful companies have struggled or faded away.

"What's wonderful about Strategic Intent is that it is an ambition that is so large that it can carry us for a long time and challenge the organization for a decade or more. From the beginning, it was inspiring to many people. It was not just about shareholder value. We felt that shareholder value would result, but it was about creating a very different kind of company and, if you will, weaving together the potential of the company's many capabilities and markets and people in a way that would really energize them to overcome a whole host of barriers . . . some structural, some system related, many cultural," says Haymaker.

"We're still only six years into this journey. And while we're smarter today than we were when we started this process, I can't even imagine how much smarter yet we have to get to succeed across the next six years of this. It's humbling."

The central challenge Cargill faced in undertaking this transformation was a common one for Outgrown organizations. How do you retain the benefits of sheer scale while embracing a more entrepreneurial model and mindset? There are many who view these two goals as antithetical. But Cargill has risen to the challenge. It has fashioned an oasis of entrepreneurialism in what was once a vast, family-run, hierarchical organization. And it has done so without sacrificing its hallowed status as a private company or the heart of its culture.

But what about Bob? How do we address his plight? He needs his employer, Danville Beverages, to invest $300,000 in a new product line for his region, and he can't get the attention of the senior decision makers. It is all too tempting for someone in Bob's situation to simply roll over and play dead in the face of such overwhelming apathy, and many Outgrown managers do. After all, if the owners don't care enough about the bottom line to see the value of his idea, why should he? In fact, many Outgrown organizations eventually wither and die because they are starved of the good ideas and entrepreneurial energy that people on the customer front lines could bring to the table if they weren't so discouraged.

For Bob, of course, it would be easier if Danville Beverages was healthy and able to recognize and invest in his good idea right away. But that's not the hand he's been dealt. Instead, Bob needs to focus on what positive moves he can make now with the $50,000 spending authorization he already has. He can't "fix" Danville Beverages single-handedly or overnight, but he can model the right behaviors in his own region and lead greater change by the power of his example. Moreover, he can develop his own management skills rather than waiting for his employer to "train" him.

Perhaps rather than building a full $300,000 production line, Bob could negotiate a trial agreement with a local bottler to produce the new product under Danville's label for distribution in Bob's region. Once the trial is underway and Bob can demonstrate some tangible success, he can make a more compelling case to the Danvilles. Or perhaps Bob's small-scale success in the East will attract attention from the other regional GMs, and together they can find ways to extend or expand the experiment. If all the regional GMs approach the Danvilles together asking for this breakthrough new product Bob has launched, the Danvilles would be hard-pressed to refuse.

The fact is that a little success goes a long way, even in Outgrown organizations. After reaping the fruits of a little entrepreneurial energy, the Danvilles may well begin to ask themselves, and their managers, how to get more of these results. At that point, the door would be open to talk about any and all of the remedies in this chapter. By trying something small in order to develop a proof point that can become a step toward a larger solution, Bob tests the old proverb "It is better to light a single candle than to curse the darkness."

While they confront the same execution challenges other "unhealthy" profiles face, Outgrown organizations often have a warm and close-knit culture that can—if properly recognized and motivated—enable the tremendous changes needed to stay competitive. While certain of these remedies are bitter medicine, many serve to inspire the organization's workforce with a glimpse of a more fulfilling and rewarding career. Outgrown organizations have the seeds of success within them; they just have to cultivate them.

SIX

THE OVERMANAGED ORGANIZATION
"We're from Corporate and We're Here to Help"

Burdened with multiple layers of management, the Overmanaged organization is a case study in "analysis paralysis." When it does move, it does so slowly and reactively, often pursuing opportunities later or less vigorously than its competitors. More consumed with the trees than the forest, managers spend their time checking subordinates' work rather than scanning the horizon for new opportunities or threats. Self-starters and results-oriented individuals are easily frustrated by this frequently bureaucratic and highly political organization.

Working outside of headquarters in an Overmanaged organization, you're almost certainly going to have your decisions reversed by someone in Corporate who knows less about customer needs than you. You've perhaps been approached by customers about a new program they saw advertised that you've never heard of. If you're staff, you spend an inordinate amount of time anticipating questions that never come up and running analyses that go straight to the shredder. There's a lot of wasted effort and stagnant information in the Overmanaged organization. Ritual promotions up the extended corporate ladder ensure that mediocrity prevails over merit.

Michael Munnell could barely contain his enthusiasm. For the first time in his ten-year career at *Tunka Steel*, he had been placed in charge of a high-priority special project and was hopeful that it would expedite his promotion to VP. For the past four months, he had been leading the task force that was developing a China strategy for Tunka, and he was ready to submit to the CEO the team's formal recommendation: a strategic alliance with *Chung-hua Steel*. In fact, Michael and his team had already negotiated the deal terms with Chung-hua, which had picked Tunka over three other competitive offers. Time was of the essence, and Michael was hopeful that he would get the go-ahead to seal the deal in the next day or so.

When his boss, Hal Cooper, gave him the assignment, he emphasized how important the fast-growing China market was for Tunka and told Michael that the CEO, Mel Papadakis, was fast-tracking the project and investing the team with full authority and accountability. When Michael later presented to Hal the team's findings and his strong recommendation, Hal reacted very well. "You've done an excellent job making your case, Michael."

Then he uttered those dreaded words, "Let me bring it up with Bob at the weekly staff meeting. If he likes it, we can get it on the docket for the Corporate Strategic Planning Committee." Bob Reiser was Hal's boss and a group senior vice president, but he was better known among Michael's fellow directors by his nickname, "Black Hole Bob." Great ideas went into Reiser's office, but they never came out. This was not the expedited review that Hal had promised Michael . . . and it was definitely not the swift decision that Michael had assured Chung-hua.

When Michael alerted his team to the next steps, Fergus, a grizzled twenty-year Tunka veteran, sighed, "And so it begins. This is how Corporate smothers most signs of life around here. I'll bet we won't have a decision for months. If the Strategic Planning Committee even sees this deal, they will question most of what we've done. They'll conduct their own independent analysis, rerun all the numbers, and come to the same conclusion. It won't matter, though. This deal will be long gone."

Fergus called it. The Chung-hua deal sat on Bob Reiser's desk for a week and then languished in the Corporate Strategic Planning Committee for the next two months. There was periodic contact as committee members asked clarifying questions, but no recommendation emerged. They reviewed all of the analysis, challenged some important assumptions, redid a lot of the projections, and kept Michael and his team out of the loop, for the most part. In the end, they tweaked some of the conclusions, but the fundamental recommendations were unchanged.

By that time, however, Chung-hua had already entered into talks with Tunka's main competitor, *Draggar Steel*. Still, there was a chance they could salvage the alliance. Michael spent days in the office and nights on the phone to China nursing the deal, hoping against hope that he would suddenly get the green light . . . but deep down he felt duped. The high-priority, mission-critical assignment he was supposedly responsible for had been hijacked by the higher-ups.

Michael was becoming increasingly demoralized as he realized just how many layers stood between him and final approval for the strategic alliance he had negotiated with Chung-hua Steel. His abiding hope that Tunka's top management would come through with a firm decision had proved misplaced. As soon as the Corporate Strategic Planning Committee finished its review of the Chung-hua partnership, it handed the proposed deal over to the finance department, which, once again, ran the numbers to see if they met the company's investment criteria. By the time Finance was through with its analysis, another week had passed, and Mel Papadakis, the company's CEO, finally got involved. Michael found this odd as Papadakis had earmarked this initiative as a personal priority and supposedly fast-tracked it. When Papadakis announced that he was bringing the deal in front of the Executive Committee to get a formal endorsement before bringing it to the Board of Directors for approval, Michael's forehead hit his desk. How many more rubber stamps could this deal take?

In Michael's mind—having studied the Chinese market, talked with regulators, trade officials, and steel executives, and run every possible scenario—this alliance was a no-brainer. China was fast becoming a critical market for Tunka, and it was clear the company could not succeed without an alliance partner who understood how the market in China worked. They had found such a partner in Chung-hua . . . and they were not alone. Tunka's competitors were knocking down Chung-hua's door with contracts in hand, but thanks to Michael's forceful arguments, Tunka had won. Four months later, however, Michael's personal charisma and commitment to this undertaking were wearing thin. Tunka needed to put its money where Michael's mouth was.

Michael felt the lump in his throat again. He had appealed to his boss, Hal, numerous times, but to no avail. It seemed no one had the clout or courage to accelerate this excruciating decision-making process. Hal kept telling Michael, "Don't worry. It's just a simple staff review." Meanwhile, both Hal and his boss, Bob, had been promoted in the last round of promotions, and Michael was still a director. He had hoped that his work putting together the alliance would merit an early promotion to VP, but no. He would be promoted along with the rest of his peers next year; merit played no part.

As Michael worked late preparing yet another summary of his findings and recommendation for the Executive Committee, he was interrupted by a phone call. With a sinking stomach, he picked up the receiver to hear the news he had been anticipating for weeks: Chung-hua was announcing a joint venture with Draggar Steel. Michael turned his computer off midsentence . . . and went home.

Overmanaged organizations illustrate the dark side of the command-and-control management model. Entrenched and isolated top-down decision-making fails to deliver results; it is an unfortunate legacy of a management structure that has not evolved with the times. Moreover, it debilitates those at lower levels with potential; they feel "nibbled to death by ducks."

Similar to the Outgrown organization, the Overmanaged organization operates from the top down, but Overmanaged organizations have more "fat" in their midsection. In fact, when you work for an Overmanaged organization, you wade through layers of management to get things done. You attend meetings in auditoriums, because no conference room is big enough to hold all the attendees. You prepare endless "back pocket" pages—just in case—that are never pulled out. You cringe when you read memos from executives who don't understand market trends. While decision-making is centralized, information still resides in the field, for the most part . . . leading to delayed and/or ineffective execution.

The self-reported profitability of Overmanaged firms is the worst according to our research; in fact, Overmanaged respondents' perception of their relative performance is more negative than any other profile.[1] In general, Overmanaged respondents paint the bleakest picture of their organization's ability to deliver results.[2] Step off the senior executive floor, and the average person at an Overmanaged organization is none too pleased and none too confident. Often, they're just biding their time until something better comes along.

OVERMANAGED: THE SYMPTOMS

The symptoms of an Overmanaged organization are easy to spot. Structurally, it has lots and lots of layers, so line employees are isolated from top managers, who nevertheless try to command and control them. By the time these directives are filtered through multiple layers of management, however, the plot is lost.

"Command and Control" Fails to Deliver

If there's one thing that every employee at an Overmanaged company can agree on, it's that they fail to quickly translate important strategic and operational decisions into action. The bureaucracy of the organization hobbles its ability to execute; it is so consumed with red tape and internal politics that it routinely misses key market opportunities.[3] Decisions are hopelessly delayed as line operations wait for a decision from headquarters. Meanwhile, headquarters does not get the information it needs from the field to make smart choices.[4] Senior managers have all the authority, but none of the market intelligence needed to make decisions on mission-critical issues such as new regulations, geopolitical developments, and breakthrough technologies. In short, the Overmanaged organization is paralyzed by a decision-making apparatus that shows signs of rigor mortis.

A rapidly growing consumer products company, blessed with a visionary founder and a groundbreaking product, was nonetheless losing steam. While young and brimming with creative talent and energy, the organization was almost arthritic in the marketplace. It was slow to capitalize on the category it had essentially created and was beginning to falter in fulfilling its commitments to retail customers. While the founder had done all the right things by bringing in professional management to run the business while he stepped back into a more creative role, he could not seem to let go of the reins. He and his handpicked crew still exercised virtual veto authority over key decisions about product development, brand position, marketing/pricing, even senior hires. As one manager put it, "We say we have moved from command-and-control mode, but the founder and some of the original team are not letting go."

The result was an organization chart that looked decentralized but an actual operating model rife with second-guessing, mixed signals, and missed opportunities. While decision rights were ostensibly assigned to line management, they were still being exercised by the founder and his cadre, who consistently overruled line managers' decisions about how to go to market. In this tug-of-war, both sides threw up their hands when it came time to accept responsibility for product shipment delays and inventory mismanagement. A "blame culture" took root and thrived.

At about this time, the company arranged an off-site, at which its top hundred people took the *Org DNA Profiler*[SM]. The predominant profile that emerged, not surprisingly, was Overmanaged. It was clear that execution was a real problem; less than a quarter of the managers polled felt that important strategic and operational decisions were quickly translated into action. A stunning 86 percent felt that decisions were second-guessed, and over 90 percent of the respondents said that information did not flow freely across organizational boundaries. These Overmanaged behaviors were costing the organization its goodwill in the marketplace. As one executive said, "We have inflicted more pain on ourselves than our competitors have."

We're from Corporate, and We're Here to Help . . .

The Overmanaged firm is a study in micromanagement at its most extreme; peering over shoulders is habitual.[5] The bloated midsection of the company, eager to justify their positions, "make work," manifesting an insatiable desire for detail and requesting tremendous volumes of information that have to be assimilated and reconciled at each level. Excessive time is spent requesting, tracking, and approving spending, personnel, and operating decisions.

While senior managers may be cut off from the information flow by layers of corporate hierarchy, they don't hesitate to second-guess the decisions of their subordinates.[6] Corporate headquarters's inability to delegate decision rights to those employees closest to the relevant information leads to organizational sclerosis. It's little wonder that talent attraction and retention is a challenge; the bureaucracy frustrates those with initiative and drive.

Layers, Layers Everywhere But Not a Chance to Think

The organizational chart of the Overmanaged firm is shaped like an hourglass with multiple layers and narrow spans of control, particularly in the middle. The result is often bureaucratic build-up, broken-down decision-making, and a general lack of innovation.

Employees laboring at the customer-facing end of this attenuated organization structure are hamstrung by the endless approvals needed to get anything done. Their career prospects are not enticing and their creativity is thwarted. The view at the top is equally uninspiring . . . and crowded.

The hourglass organization is the outcome of a paternalistic culture that rewards faithful, solid performers who "do their time" with an automatic promotion every three years. Moreover, it is understood that you will be promoted *up*, not *over*. A lateral promotion is an oxymoron in the Overmanaged organization.

The expectation of automatic vertical advancement places pressure on the organization to create additional—and largely artificial—levels of management. It's not unusual at an Overmanaged company for people to introduce themselves with their name *and* level, "I'm John Doe, Salary Grade Eleven." This deep hierarchy is a breeding ground for mediocrity, as unseasoned, unskilled managers are routinely elevated above their level of competence. Since there's little risk of autonomy and accountability, these flaws go largely unnoticed—the result being undistinguished careers at Overmanaged corporations that span decades, mostly on autopilot. Ineffective appraisal and career development processes perpetuate the talent vacuum.[7]

Bottlenecked Decision-making

Because information flows are so poor up and down the organization, line managers and senior managers are rarely "on the same page" regarding key business indicators. Senior management lacks important market information from the field, and line managers lack data on how their divisions contribute to overall company performance.[8] Unclear ownership and accountability perpetuate irresponsible or inconsistent decisions and behavior, which become apparent to the outside world.[9]

The ramifications of this breakdown in decision rights are enormous. Additional layers of management become institutionalized to "chaperone" employees as they make day-to-day decisions.

Meanwhile, employees feel they have no license to improve the organization and no incentive to deliver against critical objectives. Redundant levels and approvals enable everyone to "pass the buck" until no one is actually making the decision.

The problem is often too much information, rather than too little. Overmanaged organizations are expert navel gazers. Everything is measured, evaluated, second-guessed. A manager at one automotive company we've worked with put it succinctly when he said, "I have so many charts and so much data being fed to me that I feel like I'm drinking from a fire hose. I can't sort through it all." The useful pieces of information are like needles lost in a haystack of data dumps.

CHIQUITA BRANDS INTERNATIONAL: EMPOWERING AN OVERMANAGED ENTERPRISE

For decades, Chiquita Brands International had many of the telltale symptoms of an Overmanaged organization. It had a deeply embedded "command and control" culture, excessive layers of management, cut-off information flows, and a decision-making regimen that was described as autocratic. Paraphrasing Cyrus Freidheim, who served as chairman and CEO from 2002 to 2004, Chiquita had been run for at least thirty years as a dictatorship.[10]

Freidheim joined the board of Chiquita when it emerged from bankruptcy in 2002 and was appointed CEO by his fellow directors to lead the $2.5 billion global produce giant out of the woods. "During its hundred-year history, Chiquita has gone through ups and downs that would have killed most companies," Freidheim observes. Nicknamed "The Octopus" since its tentacles ran so deep into the infrastructure of the Central American countries where it owns banana plantations, Chiquita (formerly United Fruit) had been pilloried in the press for its poor environmental and labor relations record. Its financial fortunes were equally spotty. Prior to its bankruptcy, the company had lost money for ten consecutive years.

Chiquita's recent performance decline began in the early 1990s when its internal inefficiencies were exacerbated by a strategic bet on the growth promise of the new European Union. The company invested more than a billion dollars in new ships and banana farms in anticipation of the EU opening up the closed European produce market. In 1993, when the decision was made not to open the market to the extent anticipated, "Chiquita took it on the chin," says Freidheim.

The cash finally ran out eight years later, and the company declared Chapter 11. Freidheim stepped into a troubled and dispirited company, noting that it "had just gotten the hell kicked out of them. Anxiety was very high. People had no idea what was going to happen."

As Freidheim describes it, "Chiquita was highly centralized. The CEO basically made all the decisions of any size or note. If he took an interest in some part of the business, for whatever reason, he would have it report directly to him. When I got there, I had over fifteen direct reports. A lot of them were small businesses that really had nothing to do with the core."

Chiquita's was a "command and control" culture. Top management did not regularly seek counsel from others around or subordinate to them, and that philosophy trickled down the ranks. At Chiquita, division heads tended to run operations from a distance rather than engage in a more collaborative management style. As a result, middle managers did not get the experience and development they needed to assume executive responsibilities.

Managers would approach Freidheim with day-to-day operating issues. "They had a strategy that they had developed—which was really an operating plan—and they would come back item by item," notes Freidheim. Minor requests to sign off on personnel hires or individual compensation issues or advertising concepts would land in the CEO's inbox. Says Freidheim, "If I'm the one approving advertising, the company has some real challenges! But that was the way Chiquita operated. The CEO stamped everything."

As a result, critical decisions could languish in the chief executive's overburdened inbox. Regional operations either "left the reservation" and made their own decisions or idled as they waited for direction. Information, including best practices, moved slowly, and motivators did not always prompt the right behaviors. In fact, compensation was essentially an entitlement; even when the company was in bankruptcy, several hundred managers continued to receive significant bonuses, amounting to between 30 and 50 percent of their annual salaries.

Freidheim's first order of business was to set up teams composed of middle managers from across the organization to take a hard look at every business and every cost-reduction opportunity. The people who led those teams were second- and third-level managers. "They had never been asked to do anything like this," notes Freidheim. "They'd never been given what turned out to be fairly significant authority and responsibility to figure out what was wrong and what needed to be done to fix it. There had been little dialogue among operations. The organization was siloed as well as centralized."

Cyrus Freidheim was hardly an expert in the production and distribution of fruits and vegetables, but he had plenty of experience turning around the performance of struggling enterprises during his thirty-six years as a management consultant. Moreover, he had the blessing of the board and the respect of the organization. "My knowledge of the banana business was really limited—I knew what they tasted like—" says Freidheim with amusement, "but I did know this much: we had to put the firm back on solid financial footing, position it for new profitable growth, and put in place a strong leadership team for the future."

These were the three imperatives that guided the Chiquita organization over the next two years as it emerged from bankruptcy and swapped Overmanaged ill health for more robust results.

Structure: Peel Back the Layers

After Chiquita emerged from bankruptcy protection in 2002, it dramatically restructured its organization. The number of layers in its management hierarchy was halved in several areas as the company exited marginal businesses, shed noncore assets, and consolidated its production operations (i.e., banana plantations).

As Freidheim puts it, "Our aim was to simplify our whole system so that, in fact, linkages were limited and very direct. Now, there aren't as many cooks spoiling the broth as before. We had whole layers of people who were just span-breakers; all they did was coordinate other people's work. We got rid of the span-breakers."

Decision Rights: Breaking the Bottlenecks

Meanwhile, Chiquita elevated promising talent within the organization. "We had one guy who had grown up in the Columbian farms and done a great job there and moved to Costa Rica to head several divisions. He had an ability to motivate workers on the ground that was unbelievable; this guy's as good as any I've ever seen," says Freidheim, "so we made him head of all Chiquita farms."

Moreover, the company shifted responsibility for individual ports from the local farm manager and consolidated the entire "cold chain" (the distribution of perishable produce from packing house to supermarket) into one centrally managed process. Now one division has accountability for keeping a banana fresh and handled appropriately from the time it is put into a box until it is delivered to the customer. This cold chain represents about 25 percent of Chiquita's production costs, and about 15 percent of its bananas failed to make it to the store in saleable condition, so this was a high priority.

The result of several of these efforts was a large increase in productivity on Chiquita-owned banana farms, a major improvement in delivered quality, a reduction in unprofitable farms and noncore businesses, and a doubling of net operating income in 2003.

Information: Banana Best Practices

Cyrus Freidheim was struck in his early days at Chiquita by how closely and zealously information was hoarded. He recalls a tour of Chiquita's banana farms when he first arrived: "Some places they carried the stems, bananas down, others, bananas up. And I asked, 'Why?' Clearly there was a best practice, yet every farm was doing things a little differently."

Chiquita was very inventive in the way it broke down these barriers to information flow. It brought together in one place all the workers from its various plantations to compete in what has become known as the Banana Olympics. "How fast can you strip the tree? How fast can you box the bananas?" recalls Freidheim. "The object is to win the contest, but, in the process, you share knowledge. I was so impressed I brought the board down with me one time to see for themselves."

The Banana Olympics might seem trivial or frivolous, but, along with other measures, they improved the company's labor relations dramatically. "We had been having serious labor problems. Every time we would change anything, even if it was in the workers' interest, we'd have a strike. The managers created a new definition of success. Doing well was winning the quality game and winning the productivity game.

"Thereafter, every time I went down there, I would ask to see the new ideas and they would come out with all kinds of stuff . . . the double-row system that they've got . . . or a new irrigation approach . . . or that new bagging system. It was just constant innovation."

Motivators: Paying for Results

Part of paying for results is *not* paying when there is poor performance. That's the first thing Chiquita did postbankruptcy. "We set a floor in the first year," says Cyrus Freidheim. "It turned out to be the most unpopular thing a new CEO could have done, because we didn't make the floor. And therefore, there were no bonuses. And for most of these people, they couldn't remember when there were no bonuses."

The second thing the company did was freeze top managers' salaries for two years, while bumping up their bonus payout if they hit certain performance targets. "In the first year, there was no joy in Mudville when we didn't get anything. When we said there were going to be no bonuses, HR told me, 'Everybody's going to leave'; nobody left. As a matter of fact, during the entire time I was there over a two-year period, I don't know that we lost anybody in the top fifty voluntarily."

Postscript

Since 2002, Chiquita has made giant strides in reducing its debt, increasing its productivity, and improving the quality of not only its product but also its environmental and labor practices. While it still has some distance to travel, the company, now led by Procter & Gamble veteran Fernando Aguirre, is moving in the right direction.

By delegating more authority to middle managers and charging them with the responsibility for looking into every business and cost-reduction opportunity, Freidheim and his team were able to restore Chiquita to profitability. These up-and-coming middle managers were in a position to diagnose problems—not just in their silo but across the organization—assess alternative solutions and present recommendations to senior management. Even more striking, most of these recommendations were then implemented in the line operations. This participative process marked a sharp departure from past practice.

As the teams spread out over the organization to do their work, the opportunities for radical productivity improvements became manifest. Notes Freidheim, "If you take the number of actual bananas that grow in an area and look at how many of those bananas get into the supermarket and into a customer's shopping cart, it's less than three-quarters. That's a tremendous amount of waste."

Managers identified ways to motivate farmhands, disseminate best practices, and improve the quality and efficacy of the "cold chain." Farms and ports were decoupled organizationally to improve overall supply-chain management. Previously, farm managers had been responsible for their local port, which was a major diversion in an area they didn't understand. Finally, people with marketing skills were recruited and cultivated to help leverage the globally recognized but underutilized brand.

Perhaps Cyrus Freidheim puts it best when he frames Chiquita's ongoing challenge as follows: "Can you change the DNA of a company like Chiquita? Can we grow from a production-distribution company into a marketing company? That is a major change. I'd like to think Chiquita can."

OVERMANAGED: THE REMEDIES

The objective in renovating and rightsizing the Overmanaged organization is not just the obvious potential for stripping out excessive cost; it's the opportunity to elevate revenues by streamlining decision-making, enhancing customer responsiveness, and unleashing innovation. Achieving these benefits, however, requires a new approach to organizational restructuring, one predicated on true and lasting behavior change, rather than just slashing boxes on an organization chart. While we've been firm advocates of addressing decision rights, information, and motivators before changing structure, the Overmanaged organization is the one exception to that rule. Here the structure is so out of whack and such an impediment to progress that it should be tackled first.

Flatten the Organization

Massive layoffs are frequently the result of an Overmanaged organization trying to shortcut the road to recovery by summarily lopping off middle-management layers. This sort of indiscriminate approach rarely solves the problem. While proliferating lines and boxes on an org chart are an important indicator of an Overmanaged organization, they tend to be symptoms of a problem rather than the underlying cause. By the same logic, eliminating lines and boxes does not cure a dysfunctional organization; it merely forces the symptoms to appear elsewhere.

We're not arguing against select staff reductions, but organizations need to be judicious and foresighted in what they cut. Avoid the seduction of simplistic targets (e.g., "no more than 'x' management layers"). Sustained improvements hinge on developing the right size and number of layers based on the nature of work performed, the core business processes involved, and the interactions required to drive decisions. Companies need to step back and map out what an ideal organization would "look" like including not just the "lines and boxes" but also roles, responsibilities, controls, and accountability. The ultimate objectives are to "right-size" the organization so that it does not revert to old and inefficient habits and to reestablish a connection between the top of the organization and the bottom. Generally, that will involve some paring in the middle.

Remember Michael, the disheartened up-and-coming manager at Tunka Steel? When his special project came to an abrupt end thanks to upper management's inability to make a swift decision on his proposed China strategy, Michael returned to his regular job as sales director of the Flat Rolled Products division. This was the unit responsible for the production of flat rolled steel products and their sale to the auto industry and major appliance manufacturers.

Frustrated by the obvious delays and inefficiencies of the bureaucracy at the top of the company, Michael began to look at his own division and realized there were many of the same Overmanaged behaviors playing out in his own backyard. The difference was, here he could make positive changes stick. He could make Flat Rolled Product Sales a role model for the rest of the company.

Over the weekend, he took a look at the division's organization chart and noticed a profound spans-and-layers problem. In the sales department alone, there were eighty-five sales people reporting to fifteen district supervisors, who, in turn, reported to five zone sales managers, who reported to a national sales manager, who reported to Michael. Four layers of middle management, each with very narrow spans of control . . . and that didn't include the staff functions, including market analysis, financial reporting, IT, and human resources.

He recalled a benchmarking study that an internal staff group had done the previous year, which detailed the organization structure at competitive steel companies. At the time, Michael had barked at the staffers when they came to interview him, claiming that they didn't understand how things worked in his division. The study effort quickly faded away. Michael began to wonder if the district supervisors and regional sales managers reporting up to him had a nickname for him like the one he had given "Black Hole Bob."

Michael took a fresh look at the benchmarking group's findings and realized that it was not only possible to reduce the layers of management in his division, it was preferable. If he could streamline structure by eliminating two middle-management layers, he could also streamline information flows and decision-making and eliminate the bureaucratic delays that had killed his China partnership idea. He decided to work up a whole organizational model over the course of the next month that would fit with this new, leaner structure.

He sketched out a chart with eight direct reports, each charged with a sales "region." He eliminated "zones" and "districts" and assigned seven to ten sales people to each regional head, depending on the geographic coverage requirements. Then he put the chart back in his briefcase, because he knew that he couldn't implement structural change in the absence of other building block remedies. He thought that the lean structure would be a good forcing function, but it had to be implemented along with other key organizational changes.

Delegate Explicit Decision Rights

The only way to circumvent the second-guessing that runs rampant in the Overmanaged organization is to delegate decision rights . . . deliberately and explicitly. It is neither practical nor cost-effective for senior management to deliberate every decision in a large, complex organization. These tactical decision rights need to reside close to the market, while corporate should focus on enterprise-wide concerns: people, strategy, governance, controls, capital and resource allocation, and risk management. The result is an organization with a lean headquarters insulated from day-to-day operating issues and focused on supporting the business units.

Business units, of course, need to take up the decision rights gauntlet. To empower and equip them, Overmanaged organizations need to articulate clear decision-making principles, translate these principles into decision roles, and develop decision-making communication tools (e.g., frameworks, examples, FAQs) to transfer accountability smoothly. Decision rights should encompass who needs to be consulted before a decision is made, who has the authority to make a decision, who should be informed after the fact, and who is accountable for results. Then, the organization needs to institute a mechanism for enforcing these decision rights.

When he got back to the office on Monday, Michael of Tunka Steel pulled out the new organization chart he had drawn up for his division and thought about how to make it relevant to the way work got done in his unit. He started by diving into his inbox.

So crowded that it had overflowed onto his desk, the inbox was filled with countless forms and reports and authorizations. There was a form requesting excess vacation carryover from a salesman in Tennessee . . . with four signatures already on it from the district supervisor, zone manager, national manager, and human resources director; now it awaited Michael's signature. Michael thought to himself, "Why am I even on this distribution?"

There was an "FYI" summary analysis of actual and projected sales to six particular companies broken down by week. He remembered that this report had been commissioned five years ago to answer a particular question then regarding steel allocation; it had long since ceased to be relevant. Still, the report circulated every month to the entire sales management team; no one bothered to question why. Another report itemized discounts off of list by customer, salesperson, district supervisor, and regional manager. Michael began to recognize just how much unnecessary work was being generated by junior managers eager to please . . . at the request of senior managers eager to oversee. The result was clogged information arteries and stalled decision-making.

He opened his calendar and saw that it was filled with status briefings and update meetings on day-to-day operating issues. Every week, as an example, he had a discount review meeting, during which he signed off on every major discount with his regional managers, and at least five separate staff meetings with different departments in his division. Given the sheer number of attendees, most of these meetings took place in the large conference room.

By Friday, Michael had identified ample room for improvement. One by one, he started to lay out some changes, starting small and working his way up. First, he addressed the vacation approval process odyssey. If an employee's supervisor signed off on a vacation request, he ruled that was enough. An annual report on vacation accrual and usage would highlight any abnormalities. He also realized that if he held his managers accountable for their team's profit contribution, they could make their own decisions on discounting, within some broad parameters. The endless reports and sign-offs were consuming valuable management time and slowing down sales and service to customers. In the new regional structure, managers would not schedule "update" and "review" meetings; they would focus on action agendas and how to support the sales teams.

Bridge the Trust Gap With Information

Senior managers' double- and triple-checking of their subordinates' work suggests a lack of trust. They either don't trust that those below them are smart or talented enough to make the right decision, or that they share the same goals, or have the same information or perspective as senior management.

Information flows are unusually turgid in Overmanaged organizations. Both the bottom and the top of the corporate hierarchy are starved for accurate and relevant information. So, one of the most important remedies in rehabilitating an Overmanaged firm is to bridge the information chasms. That means establishing and institutionalizing robust communications vehicles to break through traditional roadblocks to the free flow of information. It also means implementing measures and incentives that sharpen the organization's focus on accountability and on the consequences for performance gains and losses.

At the consumer products company mentioned earlier, playing the "blame game" was a favorite pastime. As product commitments to retail customers went unfulfilled, the buck got passed. Marketing and Sales pointed their fingers at Operations, who, in turn, blamed Product Development, who, in turn, blamed IT.

When, during an off-site, the parties agreed to, yet again, document the problem with a memo, a senior executive threw a flag on the play, "Enough! Let's stop writing memos and start acting like a team to solve this problem together." This was a turning point. The senior executive turned to the product guy and asked, "What data do you need?" He replied, "I need to know what's ready for shipping, what's not ready, and what is being shipped each day to each major customer." The executive then turned to the CIO and asked, "How hard would it be to deliver this data daily?" He said, "Give me forty-eight hours, and I can get you that information on an ongoing basis." This helped the company overcome an important impediment to timely and accurate order fulfillment. This and the introduction of team-building decision rights and incentives helped the company banish the blame game.

Build Leaders at Every Level

You cannot ask unempowered middle managers to take the decision-making reins of the organization without training them in how to make decisions and developing their longer-term leadership potential. Otherwise, you risk going from "command and control" to "out of control." Leadership development is not something you can institute overnight, and it's not something you can undertake without truly decentralizing at least some degree of decision-making authority. It becomes nothing more than a classroom curriculum or a box-checking exercise if middle managers have no opportunity to exercise these new skills. Creating the next generations of organizational leaders is a multiyear, multistep exercise that needs to commence immediately.

First, you need to deprogram micromanagers in the upper levels of your organization. Senior managers need to be setting an example, rather than trying to do their subordinates' jobs. Train the next generation of middle management to delegate more decisions to the front lines, where relevant information resides. Management cannot be expected to know everything. In fact, "I don't know, but I'll find out" should be considered an acceptable answer to many queries.

Second, design more fulfilling career paths and staffing strategies to challenge and reward managers faced with fewer classic promotion opportunities. The notion of lateral promotions needs to be introduced at Overmanaged companies. Moving across the organization into new positions of responsibility cultivates a new breed of experienced managers who can break down internal barriers naturally based on the personal connections they have cultivated.

Finally, and perhaps most importantly, pay for results. Align compensation—both salary and variable—with clearly defined and tracked performance metrics that encourage the organization to mobilize and move forward. Retain "star" talent by compensating them accordingly. Showcase them as the new model of management.

The following Monday, Michael reviewed the concept and direction of the changes he was proposing with his boss, Hal, to secure his approval. During that meeting, Michael presented his case for streamlining the sales organization at Tunka Steel by removing the district and national levels. *District manager* was essentially a title that had been established to reward top salespeople with a heightened profile and some managerial responsibilities, but, frankly, many had complained about the administrative headaches, so Michael felt he could transition these individuals back to a full-time sales role with minimal disruption. The national sales director was another matter. The level had been created for a Tunka career employee, Lorraine Hasselmeyer, who had been the CEO's chief of staff for thirty-five years. She had petitioned for a line position, and this was how the company obliged her. As Lorraine was already sixty-seven, Michael proposed offering her a generous retirement package and using that opportunity to eliminate the largely redundant position. Hal said he would clear it with the CEO, Mel Papadakis, and try to get a sense of Lorraine's willingness to consider the package. Fortunately, Lorraine had long been considering a move to the South of France and saw this as a graceful exit.

Two weeks later, Michael met with his management team at Tunka Steel's headquarters and outlined his plans to remedy his division's Overmanaged symptoms. He announced Lorraine's decision to retire, using that as the prompt for the proposed leaner organization structure oriented around sales regions. He stressed the pushing down of accountability for day-to-day operations and described the expanded decision rights for both regional managers and sales people.

As the new sales organization had fewer layers of management, naturally some managers were initially disappointed with where they "fell" in the new org chart, but Michael was quick to outline a new system of motivators designed specifically to keep star talent. Bonuses would now be tied to an account's profit contribution rather than revenue, and added incentives were introduced for sales people who generated repeat business from key customers. Salaries were more clearly tiered to distinguish exceptional performers from average performers, and Michael made a point of introducing and explaining in detail the concept and value of lateral "promotions."

That said, Michael recognized there would be some attrition as managers reliant on "make work" lost their place in the hierarchy; this shedding of excess management weight was not only expected, it was welcomed.

Michael was candid in his assessment of this grand experiment. He acknowledged that Flat Rolled Products was stepping away from the Overmanaged pack at Tunka Steel and charting a new course. He shared with his managers the hope that they would stimulate a wave of change that might overtake the entire organization. Meanwhile, however, their day-to-day responsibilities would expand greatly, making their jobs both more challenging . . . and more difficult. Managers would take on expanded accountability.

While he planned to make himself available as a resource and to schedule intensive training for newly empowered managers, all Michael proffered in the way of decision-making "rules" was one page of guiding principles on how to make decisions: "single point accountability," "hold people accountable for results," and the like. He deliberately stopped short of telling decision-makers what to do. Instead, he appointed groups of three to deliberate and come back in two weeks with how the new organization would work. There was a Decision Making team, a Reporting and Meetings team, and a People Capabilities team, among others. Michael knew this far-reaching change would test his team, but he was committed to the result. The only way to fix what ailed Tunka was from the inside out.

The Overmanaged organization is a legacy of a command-and-control management style that might have worked well for a company in its earlier days, but has since become a liability. Overmanaged organizations cannot get out of their own way. They cannot react to market discontinuities or even seize opportunities. They forfeit what rightfully should be theirs to smaller, more agile competitors . . . a fatal mistake in a competitive environment where these fleet-footed rivals and finicky customers drive the pace of change ever faster.

The road to recovery is arguably longest and most tortuous for the Overmanaged organization, but it's not a death march. Many companies have persevered and emerged the more resilient for it.

SEVEN

THE JUST-IN-TIME ORGANIZATION
Succeeding by the Skin of Our Teeth

lthough not always proactive in preparing for change, this type of organization has demonstrated an ability to "turn on a dime" when necessary, without losing sight of the big picture. Just-in-Time organizations attract talented and motivated people. They're often fun and frenetic environments and great places to learn. There's an adventurous attitude that infuses the office and inspires creative outbursts, frequently real breakthroughs. But in the absence of consistent, disciplined structures and processes, the organization cannot fully capitalize on these opportunities nor replicate them. They often become "one-hit wonders," rather than a reliable source of competitive advantage.

Although it manages to hold on to good people and performs well financially, The Just-in-Time organization has not yet achieved peak performance. This type tends to miss opportunities by inches rather than miles, and to celebrate successes that are marginal rather than unequivocal. Despite its frustrations, however, it can be a stimulating and challenging place to work. It just needs to transition to a more stable and sustainable management model.

Bill Hsu, an associate at New York law firm *Taper, Parker & McDuff*, hung up the phone and tried to calm his racing heart. The partner he worked for, Jack McManus, had just called him from the offices of *Wi-Tel*, a large telecommunications company looking to launch a hostile takeover of one of its major competitors. They were interested in retaining Taper, Parker & McDuff, but wanted to be sure the firm had the experience and expertise to handle the assignment. Bill had just been given the job of putting together a credentials presentation on the firm and a briefing document outlining the merger process for Wi-Tel.

The presentation was scheduled for Monday noon. It was Friday. Clearly the ski weekend Bill had planned with his girlfriend, Elizabeth, was going to be a casualty, but he was excited. This was why he had joined the firm: the opportunity to work with Jack, whose copious energy and ambition had impressed him during recruiting, and the chance to work on a big M&A deal. For six months now, he'd been grinding out regulatory bulletins and FCC submissions. Finally, he was going to make his mark.

Thinking he could still salvage a Saturday-night dinner with Elizabeth, Bill called the firm's staffing manager to request immediate paralegal and secretarial help. He was told that no one was available; in-house resources were fully tapped for the next two weeks, and temps were not an option since this wasn't billable work. Bill was on his own.

Still, he was confident and enthusiastic. Taper, Parker & McDuff was well known for its work in M&A arena. True, that was mostly for oil and gas clients, but surely there were templates and qualifications documents he could leverage to build the credentials deck. He could then spend his time researching Wi-Tel and nailing the briefing document.

But when he checked the firm's intranet for a "leg up," he discovered that everything in Taper, Parker & McDuff's knowledge database was very dated. They had partner biographies in there that were years out of date. Many had left the firm; one had actually died. The few sample client documents available were irrelevant. When he asked around, the universal response he got was "Who has the time to populate the database? You have to 'sanitize' documents, write up case studies, and it's not billable. People are just too busy doing paying client work."

Bill found this hard to fathom. He was going to have to rely on the limited connections he'd developed over the six months he'd been with the firm to beg, borrow, or steal something he could use. He called Fiona, an associate in the oil and gas practice in London that he'd met briefly during recruiting, to ask if she had any firm credential information specific to merger support. She was racing against her own deadline, but said she would try to scout out something. They commiserated about how much easier this would be if the firm's knowledge database was kept current, and compared notes on how many vacation plans they had canceled. Bill felt a sinking feeling in the pit of his stomach. He then called Elizabeth to cancel their ski plans. In a sheepish voice, he asked her to walk the dog and drop by with some clothes for the weekend. He wasn't going anywhere.

As he hung up the phone with Elizabeth, he briefly registered the displeasure in her voice. It wasn't the first time he had canceled weekend plans with her on short notice. Nor was it the first time he had to scramble for information that should have been readily available. He had no problem putting in extra hours for the firm, but when the hours were unnecessary and spent reinventing wheels, it was aggravating.

By Monday morning, he had worked forty hours straight on a presentation that should have taken him at most a standard ten-hour work day. He never did find any usable M&A qualification material from the Oil & Gas work, but Fiona sent him a few pages from an old template Friday evening that he used to build a presentation. What he couldn't find in the firm's network, he pulled from his own memory of internal new-business memos and staff-meeting banter about other M&A work. He even referenced a paper he had written at Yale Law School. At 6 p.m. on Saturday, Bill e-mailed a draft to Jack, hoping that he could still manage dinner with Elizabeth and some sleep before dealing with the edits in the morning. As he was pulling on his coat, however, the phone rang and Jack's number in the Hamptons appeared on the caller ID screen. Bill picked up the receiver and immediately registered the upset in Jack's voice. The briefing document didn't cover as much of the firm's M&A experience as Jack had wanted. He started spewing client and partner names rapid-fire and told Bill to call the partners in charge of these deals and get the information needed to beef up the credentials . . . now. Jack told him he'd meet him at the office the following morning—Sunday—at seven.

Bill sank back into his chair and pulled out the firm directory. He'd been impressed when he first joined Taper, Parker & McDuff that even the partners' home phone numbers and faxes were listed. Now, he wasn't so sure. Clearly, being promoted to partner wasn't an invitation to leisure time on the weekends. As he interrupted partners' dinner hours, one after the other, he was surprised at how well they all took it. It seemed to be a familiar drill to them. They each said they would send some relevant materials as soon as they could log in to the network. He took advantage of the break to take a quick shower in the firm's men's room (the presence of which should have served as another warning sign). When he got back to his computer, he had eight e-mails in his inbox.

By the time Jack came in the next morning, Bill had a revised document ready. Jack scanned it and asked Bill to forward it to Leticia Morgan, a senior partner in the London Oil & Gas practice, Fiona's boss's boss. He then told Bill to meet him in the conference room. By the time Bill gathered his research and laptop and met Jack in the conference room, Jack already had Leticia on speaker phone. For the next two hours, she and Jack went through the briefing document line by line making changes, additions, and deletions. At two in the afternoon London time, Leticia made her excuses as she had to attend her niece's wedding reception; she'd already missed the ceremony itself. She said she would look at the revised document when she got to Heathrow later that night. She was taking a 6 p.m. flight to New York for the noon meeting the following day with the client.

Bill worked through the night as Leticia fed him changes from the plane and later from her hotel room. In the morning, he raced to the mail room to get copies made and jumped in a cab to join Leticia and Jack in the lobby of the client's building.

The presentation went off without a hitch. Leticia was spectacular, particularly given the two hours of sleep she had had the night before. Jack effectively established himself as the client contact and secured his booking credit. And Bill felt like a hero. He had delivered and impressed his boss and one of the firm's most senior partners with his ability to deliver under pressure. As they left Wi-Tel's offices with the assignment in hand, Jack encouraged Bill to take the rest of the day off.

Bill immediately called Elizabeth to see if she was free for an early dinner. She didn't answer. He then checked his home machine. Elizabeth had left a message two days before breaking up with him and taking custody of the dog.

Taper, Parker & McDuff is typical of the Just-in-Time organization. It delivers on its commitments, but it does so by the skin of its teeth. It's an exciting place to work that attracts talented individuals who perform well under pressure, but one wonders if the pressure is really necessary. If knowledge were routinely captured and shared, employees wouldn't have to reinvent the wheel on weekends or fly in last-minute saviors. Decisions could be made swiftly and efficiently with full information and commitments to clients could be met on a more timely and consistent basis. Moreover, the organization itself would be more robust as it could rely on institutionalized processes rather than heroic individuals. While it won this client and may well win the next one, there are signs of slippage. The next time, the best ideas may not make it to the briefing, and the client won't be impressed. Maybe Bill will decide that life is too short, quit, and take with him all the hard-earned lessons of the past weekend. The Just-in-Time organization needs to iron out the wrinkles in its organizational model and smooth work flows to ensure its continued good health and that of its people.

Many Just-in-Time companies are start-ups that have grown up but have yet to "professionalize" their organization. Still others are established, successful companies that are showing the first signs of losing their edge. Still, they manage to get the job done. To all external appearances, they are highly functioning organizations.

In fact, our research shows that people in Just-in-Time organizations overwhelmingly agree that "important strategic and operations decisions are quickly translated into action." Moreover, these companies are extremely agile and adept in dealing with discontinuous change in the marketplace. Just-in-Time organizations possess an almost youthful exuberance and energy; they run on pure adrenaline. They welcome an impossible challenge and—more often than not—succeed in overcoming it.

That said, Just-in-Time companies often seem to sprint when a more measured pace is warranted, even recommended. Over time this constant engine-revving stresses the organization. It's an unstable and unsustainable operating state.[1] Management needs to establish firm-wide processes and ensure accountability for performance to keep the organization from sliding down a slippery slope into chronic fatigue and disrepair.

THE JUST-IN-TIME ORGANIZATION: TRAITS

The Just-in-Time organization is nothing if not exciting. The energy and creative freedom it affords attract "out of the box" thinkers in droves. Fresh perspectives abound and, in turn, fuel ingenious solutions. But the organization's employees often have the candle lit at both ends, which can lead to burnout.

Culture of Controlled Chaos

Just-in-Time organizations are often fueled by a strong sense of mission. They want to chart new territory, inspire change, make a big difference. Not surprisingly, the people they attract to the enterprise are similarly minded. They're looking for the opportunity to get in on the ground floor and build something meaningful. The flip side of this almost evangelical zeal, however, is an often untamed corporate culture characterized by unclear and uncoordinated decision rights, "seat of the pants" market moves, and a general lack of discipline and coherence. In the mad scramble to meet deadlines and secure customers, the focus is overwhelmingly on the outcome, with little attention paid to the process used to get there. Lots of last-minute urgent requests interrupt steady workflows, creating a "hurry up and wait" pace as priorities compete for limited resources.

People don't spend a lot of time talking about the organization model, and when people from a "corporate" background come in and try to "administer" (e.g., set up regularly scheduled meetings, assign accountability, implement processes, make systems investments), their efforts are often greeted with disdain. Employees find it hard to focus on initiatives that may have high value but take months to work through. They assume it will get derailed along the way . . . and their career along with it. What works (and what gets rewarded) is what wins; the culture is very transaction focused, and almost superstitious in its overreliance on lucky talismans and proven rainmakers. For an organization that is largely "shooting from the hip," however, it scores an impressive number of bull's-eyes.

When Tim Shriver became CEO of Special Olympics in 1996, the movement was sprinting just to stay in place. While its people were still inspired by an almost missionary zeal for their work, the movement was losing momentum. What Shriver's mother, Eunice Kennedy Shriver, had started in Chicago's Soldier Field with a thousand athletes had, almost thirty years later, become a worldwide movement of one million athletes in almost 150 countries. The organization was stretched, resources were thin, and both staff and volunteers often felt overwhelmed. The head office in Washington, D.C., was not meeting the needs of local programs and information was not flowing freely between D.C. and programs around the world. There was a sense that the potential of the movement was being dissipated, not for lack of interest or enthusiasm, but rather because of organizational gaps and dysfunctions.

"While we had a lot to be proud of, we weren't growing," says Shriver. "We had taken the movement as far as the strength of our mission and the charisma of our founder could take us. We were stable, well accepted, but maybe a little too satisfied with our achievements. Growth was the key to our continued relevance and vitality."[2]

"Our mission was never our problem," notes Shriver. "In fact, it was this enormous asset. You could go to a rural village in Tanzania, and walk up to a volunteer wearing a Special Olympics T-shirt and ask, "Why do you do this?" and he'd recite the mission. He'd say he wanted to help people with intellectual disability develop physical fitness, demonstrate courage, and experience joy through year-round sports training and competition."

While a noble vision that has inspired thousands around the world to volunteer their time and energy over the past several decades, it was not enough to sustain and grow a global enterprise, as Shriver soon discovered. The Special Olympics organization had evolved around the strength of its mission and the charisma of its founder, but it had already gone as far as those qualities could take it.

"Our mission was not our problem," repeats Shriver. "Our problem was that we did not have the business processes or the organizational clarity to sustain a global enterprise. We had the mission to excite a global energy burst. We did not have the organizational strength at the head office to sustain it and help others at the regional levels expand on it.

"What I thought at the time was a relatively manageable problem, but which has proved to be an eight-year challenge, was the extent to which headquarters, as an element within the movement, was able to effectively create ownership, buy-in, and constituent participation in leadership decisions," says Shriver.

There weren't adequate channels for Special Olympics affiliates in the field to communicate their interests to headquarters, and for headquarters, in turn, to communicate the direction and goals of the organization to local programs. "The back-and-forth information flow was very much ad hoc, based on who knows whom and who calls whom to ask for what. It was very difficult, under those circumstances, to undergird any initiative we introduced with credibility in the field.

It was clear that Special Olympics had to morph its culture to accommodate organizationally sound, for-profit qualities. As Shriver notes, "That was the ticket to developing a more powerful entity that could sustain the life-changing benefits of our movement right down to the grassroots level."

Mavericks Meet Managers

There are two distinct groups in the Just-in-Time organization: the adventure-seeking mavericks . . . and the more cautious, professional managers. Mavericks regard the unstructured environment and strained resources of the firm with a certain fondness. They like the adrenaline rush; thrill-seeking is in their blood. Plus, they find the work fulfilling, because it's either highly remunerative financially or meaningful in its impact. Not surprisingly, the mavericks cast the culture of the place; they give it that sense of breathless anticipation and energy.

The managers, on the other hand, keep it running. What they lack in pure passion, they make up for in discipline and managerial skills. They are the more stable, reliable sorts, crossing the t's and dotting the i's of their maverick colleagues. The Just-in-Time organization's big "wins" are attributable to its mavericks; it owes its continued good health, however, to its managers. The fundamental challenge the organization faces is balancing the instincts of the maverick with the longer-term, more financially disciplined view of its managers. Needless to say, it's a hard balance to strike.

P.V. Kannan, the chairman and CEO of 24/7 Customer, knows how difficult it is to reconcile the maverick and managerial sides of a Just-in-Time organization. "I think people who sign on during the first phase of a company tend to have that start-up spirit instilled in them. I think it becomes part of their psyche. They feel, 'This is mine, and I need to take care of it," versus someone who says, 'My job is to manage this, and I'm going to do a really great job."[3]

Founded in April of 2000, 24/7 Customer is today one of the leading global providers of customer-service solutions to large corporations. Through a number of call centers and back-office operations centers in India, it processes claims for insurance carriers and conducts telemarketing for credit card and long-distance companies and it provides technical support on behalf of computer manufacturers, among other activities. With a client list that cuts a broad swath across the Global 500, 24/7 has grown from $0 to $50 million in revenues and from twenty to four thousand employees since Kannan and cofounder S. "Nags" Nagarajan started the firm five years ago.

The company has steadily collected both quality accolades and customer endorsements, but its runaway growth has extracted a heavy organizational toll. As new people come on board, it has become increasingly difficult to initiate them and equip them to take the necessary decisions to grow the business.

"I'm trying to solve this big problem in front of me as the CEO of a really fast-growing company, which is how do I get everyone aligned in the organization? How do I make sure, as we induct new members at the rate of one hundred, two hundred people a month, that they understand what they need to do and get it done?"[4]

The maverick, "on the fly" attitude that worked in wooing tentative customers in the early days is not going to satisfy the more robust demand of blue-chip companies looking for a committed, reliable service provider . . . and Kannan knows it. The rules of the game are changing and fortune will favor those with a predictable and, most importantly, scaleable business model.

"Growth creates its own set of what I call good problems," says Kannan. "And the main problem is essentially keeping the team focused on our goals. As we grow, we have to formalize the process of inducting new people and getting them to understand what 24/7 is all about, because with every new wave of hires, Nags and I are farther from the front lines. The next hundred we bring in will have less contact with the founders and the management team than the previous hundred. It's the necessary cost of growth.

"Every day, we're constantly solving issues and problems, but we've realized we have to become a bit more structured," notes Kannan. "We want to make sure that we have a solid framework in place to integrate acquisitions as well as manage change in a very standard and uniform manner across locations. Our internal processes need to be more robust. They need to be very consistent. And the cowboy mentality has to be dismantled slowly," says Kannan.

At the same time, the organization wants to preserve the energy and passion those "cowboys" brought to the enterprise. Kannan tells the story of a supervisor from 24/7's early days who approached him during a recent company off-site meeting and told him, "We've now got a whole bunch of professionals who have come in and really made operations run well and much more smoothly. We spend less of our time firefighting nowadays, so it's getting better. But they don't seem to have the passion."

Kannan remarks, "As the company has grown, there are fewer of those people who are driven only by passion. Now we have people who can run things, but may not necessarily have the same high degree of ownership."

Kannan tells another story of a second veteran front-line supervisor who picked up an analyst's report and e-mailed him about some factual errors. "I was amazed, first, that he got a copy of the report. It's not something that's distributed normally, so he must have picked it up in our library. Second, he read it, and third, he felt really badly that we missed an opportunity to get our message out. I didn't hear from many members of the management team on this, yet he felt compelled to reach out.

"That said, as 24/7 evolves and is perceived as a less risky venture, we're attracting impressive professional talent. The caliber of the résumés keeps improving, and we need high-level management skills to take us to the next level of growth."

* * *

Reinvented Wheels

While the firm may be out ahead of the market because of the entrepreneurial zeal of its individual employees, it finds it hard to duplicate its successes efficiently across the growing company. It doesn't effectively institutionalize best practices or codify knowledge, hence employees like our law associate Bill waste time reinventing wheels. Scalability—the ability to grow operations quickly without sacrificing quality—is a big concern, not only within the company, but for larger customers, who need the assurance that the company can adapt to changing requirements and deliver consistently. The cost implications of reinvented wheels and lost economies of scale are obvious. Not so obvious, but potentially fatal, are the revenue implications as skittish customers head to "known" quantities, who are less talented but more capable and consistent in their delivery. The Just-in-Time organization stands at the top of a slippery slope. The good news is it can regain its footing and the full confidence of customers with a more structured approach to transferring best practices and expanding operations.

Initially, 24/7 Customer won more new business than it lost, because it had a superior product and the technical competence to deliver better services at lower cost. As interest swelled in business-process outsourcing (i.e., the practice of transferring back-office operations such as customer service to firms who specialize in these functions), however, and blue chip companies came calling, 24/7's ad hoc execution style cost it new accounts. Potential customers were worried they could not repeat past successes reliably and predictably. There were too many reinvented wheels across the company.

"The first set of buyers were all risk takers. So they would come in and typically say, 'Look, I've got the interest of the CEO. We want to do a pilot, but we want to get started in two weeks.' They came in with wildly unrealistic expectations of start dates and learning curves. And our team fulfilled them." But, Kannan quickly recognized when that phase was over. "Fortune 500 customers don't want to hear, 'I'll get it done, I'm going to wing it.' Or, 'This deliverable normally takes two weeks, but I'm going to do it in three days.' They want predictability."

"A major computer manufacturer evaluated us about eighteen months back," recalls Kannan. "They said, 'Look, we want to see evidence that you could scale to a few thousand people in twenty-four months.'" The computer maker did not question 24/7's skills (e.g., answering phones in a timely fashion, technical support capabilities), but rather its ability to hire, equip, and train thousands of new call-center employees in a short time frame without falling off the rails. They wanted to see a delivery system that was reliant on institutional processes rather than individual actors. 24/7 has since signed the computer company on as a client and is expecting to scale the engagement to more than a thousand people in the next twelve months.

As Special Olympics grew from a summer day camp at Eunice Kennedy Shriver's home to a worldwide, year-round movement encompassing one million athletes in 150 countries, the need for organizational discipline and replicable, "turnkey" training and event programs became evident. Still, it took a long while for the organization to stop reinventing wheels. Take program appraisals, as an example.

Before headquarters took measures to improve it, the Special Olympics performance measurement system was informal to the point of unhelpful. Once every two years, a team of Special Olympics staffers would descend on a particular country and write up their anecdotal observations. "We'd find a sport director from Lithuania, and a PR director from Mexico, and an executive director from Kenya, and one staff person from headquarters," recalls Shriver. "And they'd all go to Poland for four days, and they'd observe games or board meetings, and interview folks. And they had a rough kind of instrument that they would follow: 'How's your volunteer training? How's your board development?' And so on."

Team members would send a report back to the board, or back to the executive director in Poland, and anecdotally describe their impressions of the program's efficacy, what they liked and didn't like. "When you look at it in retrospect, it's an incredibly primitive tool," says Shriver, "and no two were alike. So it was hard to look at Poland's report and then at Spain's and make any real comparisons. It was very subjective, and therefore had limited value. Second, it had no standardized measures that would allow for benchmarking or objective reporting. Third, there was no checklist recounting the twelve critical functional areas of an organization. And fourth, it was very difficult to share these reports. We'd do, say, thirty or forty of these a year and they would just pile up."

Firefighting Burnout

There is a great sense of urgency in the Just-in-Time organization. Everything is "life or death," and the immediate emergency inevitably takes higher priority over "road-building" for the future. Every day brings fresh fires that need to be put out, and that's where everyone directs their attention, even though yesterday's still-smoldering ashes are not yet extinguished. Sixteen-hour days and 2 a.m. e-mails are customary; some cars never leave the lot. Though Just-in-Time employees take a strange pride in such heroics, they are not built of steel and eventually burn out. The human body is not equipped to sprint a marathon.

In the early days, the heroes are lionized, as well they should be. They get it done, maybe not elegantly, but they deliver. As the firm matures, however, and transactions multiply, the "quick and dirty" fix is insufficient. Balls get dropped. Priorities blur. And, soon, it's not just employees who are burning out, but customers and suppliers, who become increasingly nervous about the company's ability to deliver a quality product on time . . . again and again.

Special Olympics is more than the Summer and Winter World Games that are held every two years. It is thousands of sports-training programs and athletic events that take place year-round, worldwide, encompassing twenty-six Olympic-type summer and winter sports and, by the end of 2004, more than 1.7 million athletes. Coordinating these myriad activities and their associated logistics is the full-time job of thousands of employees and the vocation of some one million volunteers around the world.

The last Special Olympics Summer World Games, held in Dublin, Ireland, ranked as the world's largest sporting event in 2003. More than 6,500 athletes from 150 countries participated in 18 competitive and 3 demonstration sports. The opening ceremonies filled a stadium with more than 70,000 people, and millions more watched on television.

Over the years, as the Special Olympics World Games have grown and attracted more publicity, they quietly usurped the movement's more mundane, year-round programs in terms of headquarters' attention. Months before the Games, all eyes were focused on this marquee event . . . and pulled from the movement's other activities and programs. Consequently, key people were overtaxed and core headquarters' role in developing community programs in towns from Atlanta to Ankara was neglected. While the movement continued to pull off terrific events, it was only through the Herculean efforts of its dedicated staff. Employees and volunteers alike were burning out by the late 1990s, and the movement was at risk of faltering.

SPECIAL OLYMPICS: THE BUSINESS OF PHILANTHROPY

All organizations wrestle with their organizational DNA. Not-for-profits are no exception. Decision rights, information, motivators, and structure are all as relevant to the effective execution of a charitable endeavor as they are to that of a business enterprise. Special Olympics was essentially a healthy organization; Just-in-Time organizations fall on the "healthy" side of the organizational DNA spectrum, but only just. There is still considerable room for improvement in each of the four building blocks.

In Special Olympics' case, the gaps were apparent:

- **Decision rights.** Unclear, both in terms of accountability and processes. People often did not understand what they were accountable for and how they were being measured.
- **Information.** The lack of IT infrastructure or any formal knowledge transfer capabilities made it exceedingly difficult to communicate consistently within the organization, leading to increasingly strained relationships between country programs, regional offices (e.g., Europe), and the Washington, D.C., headquarters. Programs were deluged with paper memos, but true knowledge-sharing was scant.
- **Motivators.** Given its not-for-profit status, the organization struggled to coordinate and motivate the efforts of a relatively small paid staff and legions of volunteers in an environment of limited funds. While a peer performance-review process allowed for some interaction among various country programs, opportunities to cooperate and collaborate were few. In the regions, resources were insufficient to deliver adequate training in key program-development areas (e.g., sports, fund-raising, organizational development, public relations).
- **Structure.** The head office in Washington, D.C., was disconnected from the programs in the field and viewed, by many in the field, as too large, too U.S. focused, and too expensive.

Special Olympics was a Just-in-Time organization. By all external accounts, it served its existing constituents well; it had a talented and dedicated staff. However, all too often, it scrambled to essentially reinvent a wheel that had already been crafted several times in various locations around the world. "Crises tended to overwhelm the day-to-day and strategic elements of our efforts," noted one insider.

The regions looked to the Special Olympics headquarters in Washington not only for inspiration, but also for practical leadership. "We couldn't respond well when these countries had challenges," Shriver recalls. "We just didn't have the capability. We'd get faxes from places, and they'd go into black holes. We understood that Special Olympics was life transforming and yet we didn't have the institutionalized capabilities to scale that message."

Shriver knew that Special Olympics' mission and values were clearly motivating and well understood by its staff, but the organization was frustrated in realizing its ambitions by its lack of infrastructure and alignment. The major challenge slowly became clear: Special Olympics needed to run more effectively and efficiently as a "business," without losing the strength and focus of its public-service mission.

As Shriver recalls, "The currency of that time in business circles was growth. And the power of that message resonated with me. At the same time, I felt frustrated by the widely held perception that growth was not a relevant challenge for organizations like ours . . . that we were the kind of people that did nice things, but we couldn't grow and double our revenues every two years like those smart business guys could. We needed to create a sense of urgency and develop a more entrepreneurial spirit."

Shriver draws the distinction between the business and the philanthropic communities with a quote from Warren Buffet: "I'm more interested in the artist than the painting." Says Shriver, "The perception is that not-for-profits focus all their time on the project, on the painting: How many people are we feeding at the soup kitchen? How many beds are there at the women's shelter? How much closer are we to the cure for cancer?

"They don't spend any time on the artist of this work . . . on the organization itself and its health. They don't spend time on board development or training capabilities or planning. They just focus all their energy on getting those five more services at the shelter . . . which is admirable, but shortsighted."

Shriver speaks from his own experience as an educator and career public servant. "My normal time horizon is somewhere between three hours and a week. I really was quite impatient. Still am," admits Shriver. "But I knew in my gut that our situation called for strong medicine. We needed to clarify who does what under what circumstances and in what location, and how to break down bridges . . . and oh, by the way, get better at doing plans."

The leadership of Special Olympics needed to transform the way the organization was structured, managed, and engaged to release its latent and significant potential. As Shriver describes it, "We were on mission. The leadership we were providing programmatically was good and well received. Our training capabilities were limited, but developing to the extent our budget allowed. I just thought we had to tinker with this 'little' problem we had, which is how do we most efficiently marshal our resources and get everybody on the same page?"

JUST-IN-TIME: THE TREATMENTS

The Just-in-Time organization is healthy; it gets things done and it provides its people with a lot of excitement and intellectual stimulation. But, it runs the risk of running itself ragged and lapsing into a state of ill health. Its focus should be on preventive treatments rather than drastic remedies. This type of organization should make refinements, not wholesale changes to its DNA to create a more coherent, layered, self-correcting organization where employees understand what's expected of them. While the firm will always rely on the skill and ingenuity of its talented employees, it needs to establish clear decision rights and processes that guide the actions of these stars, while cultivating more of them. Rather than running full tilt in an open field, the Just-in-Time organization needs to pull onto a paved surface with guardrails, where it will suffer less wear and tear and make more sure progress toward its goals.

Institutionalize Accountability and Process Discipline

Ad hoc decision-making doesn't deliver consistent results; the organization needs to introduce more structure and discipline to sustain its success. Management needs to make crystal clear who does what and how. That means clarifying decision rights and supporting decision-makers with the right systems and information. Not only should business processes be well defined, the organization should ensure that they are adhered to in a disciplined manner. The Just-in-Time organization has proven that it can deliver . . . it now needs to prove it can deliver consistently and efficiently. No more conflicting marching orders and wasted labor. Reliability, predictability, and stability are the new "watch words." There will naturally be exemptions from company policies and processes, but they will be exceptions to the rule, not standard operating procedure. In short, the Just-in-Time organization needs to embark on a balanced and regimented fitness program.

Luckily, 24/7 Customer's management saw some of the warning signs in its Just-in-Time behavior and anticipated the appropriate adjustments to its decision rights and motivators. "Rather than attacking problems on an ad hoc basis, we have introduced a decision-making framework, which is process driven. Problems are identified. They're handed off to different function heads. There's a date, and there's a tracking mechanism. And weekly, we look at outstanding issues as a team and ask, 'What are the things that we need to collectively work on?'" notes founder and CEO P.V. Kannan.

The firm has methodically identified and defined the 150 separate business processes it regularly performs and has assigned clear accountability for each. P.V. Kannan has instituted Monday management meetings with a disciplined agenda, one that covers all aspects of performance but really focuses on red flags. As Kannan describes it, "If someone is running a client program, he will produce a 'dashboard' for the rest of the team indicating—at a glance—program revenue, profitability, various SLA [service level agreement] measures, and, always, outstanding issues. A typical issue might be the inability to hire enough people with the right qualifications. The 'owners' of that issue are clearly identified and listed, and there's a date attached to resolution. And that resolution is driven by a defined process now, rather than being assigned as an ad hoc task to someone.

"If the process fails to resolve the problem or falls behind schedule, then let's talk about it. But if problems are identified, plugged into a process, and it's running, let's not waste time talking about it." The results have been astounding. "If you look back four months, we used to have sixty issues per program each week. Today there are no more than two or three," says Kannan.

In addition to installing clear decision rights for the 150 company processes it has defined, 24/7 has restructured operations around practices rather than programs to focus the company on areas of particular expertise (e.g., claims processing, inbound customer service) where it has a competitive edge. It has also eased information flows, arming front-line supervisors with detailed data on the metrics that drive the business as well as the financial performance of the company as a whole. New IT systems put in place not only streamline workflows but foster collaboration and the transfer of best practices.

P.V. Kannan and cofounder S. Nagarajan have been firm in their transfer of authority to the next generation at 24/7 Customer. In fact, it's an area where they give themselves grudging credit. "We've shown marked improvement in placing that sense of ownership for the success or failure of a client in the hands of the people who run it and the entire team surrounding them," says Kannan. "If they fail, Nags and I will spend time coaching, rather than trying to take on the problem. We now have close to ten people who manage all our clients . . . most, very well." Getting involved in day-to-day decision-making according to Kannan "is the number one time-waster."

"I tell people, 'Look, it's bad news if you're spending a lot of time with me.' And I repeat that often. If someone says, 'Hey, it's great. I get to talk to you more often.' I say, 'You don't understand; it's really bad news. If I don't talk to you for six months, *that's* great news. That means there are no issues to firefight.'"

Recognizing the worldwide movement could not be led from the top by sheer force of charisma anymore, Tim Shriver and the Special Olympics Board established a more formal and accountable organization model. After assessing a variety of organizational models against a range of criteria (e.g., fit with mission and strategy, ability to implement, flexibility, risk, access to resources), Shriver and the Special Olympics Board ultimately adopted a blended model with decentralized operations and centralized accountability and control. Seven regions were created and virtually all day-to-day decision-making was delegated to them and the local programs. Meanwhile, headquarters shifted its focus to more strategic concerns: identity and mission, metrics and accountability, fundraising, and overall capability-building and knowledge transfer. In short, the head office resolved to lead more and do less. It would equip the regional and local programs with the tools and resources to make operational decisions within an envelope of specific authorities.

The new model focuses on quality growth through autonomous and entrepreneurial regional teams focused on training, competition planning, games, and other sports events. These empowered operations—closer to coaches, community organizers, and athletes worldwide—are better able to serve their needs and expand the movement's footprint.

Regional managing directors appoint regional growth teams to help enlist athletes, build year-round programs, and raise funds. While the head office in D.C. specifies requirements at different stages of regional and office development, ultimately, the regional managing director determines how Special Olympics will meet these targets, based on the capabilities and potential of the movement in his or her corner of the world.

Program development, on the other hand, is centralized in the D.C. office along with a separate shared administrative-services unit to leverage the movement's scale and optimize efficiencies. As a percentage of total staff, the D.C. head office is now smaller, while the regions have grown more robust. Functional staff now located in the regions have a matrixed reporting relationship with central functional groups in the head office.

Shriver describes the reorganization with pride: "Moving that blend of skills and capabilities away from headquarters and into the regions—leaving headquarters to focus more fully on mission, strategy, and knowledge management—was, and continues to be, a big insight and a big change for us. The regional offices created as a result of this reorganization—with their specific focus on supporting the accredited programs in their regions—disseminate this knowledge and provide leadership in the region. Now, we have strong, indigenous leaders who have stature within the region and can help us with board development and door-opening and so on. We're still evolving, but I see this as one area where we've gotten a lot better."

Noting that there were other ways centralization could help the organization become more efficient, the D.C. team created the Special Olympics University as a resource for programs around the world. They also established processes for sharing knowledge, measuring and managing performance, and developing leadership skills. The redesigned strategic-planning process explicitly links regional plans to the movement's global agenda.

Don't Take Yes for an Answer . . . Reinforce Individual Promises

Based on their early success in delivering on unrealistic expectations, Just-in-Time companies can fall into the trap of overpromising. "Yes" comes too easily to people's lips when the responsible answer might well be, "I don't know, I'll get back to you." As the Just-in-Time firm matures, so must its organization model and planning processes. In making commitments, the organization needs to consider what it can consistently and repetitively deliver as an institution, not as a tired crew of miracle workers. Relying on the stamina of select individuals is risky business; the organization needs to reinforce their efforts. For example, Bill at Taper, Parker & McDuff could have saved hours of time if the firm had a more robust knowledge management network. The enterprise needs to set priorities for the week, month, and year and run the business accordingly. People at all levels need to clearly understand what is expected of them; in fact, those expectations should be documented for future reference. Feedback loops and follow-through reminders should be established, so projects do not slip off the radar screen, and managers need to rigorously follow up on the tasks and decisions assigned to their direct reports. Incentives should clearly reflect performance against specified expectations . . . not the number of fires fought. The organization needs to recondition itself from running sprints to running marathons to ensure the long-term health of the company.

Getting past the automatic "yes" and "on the fly" execution remains a challenge at 24/7 Customer, but Kannan is pressing his management team to commit upfront to planned results, and the culture is slowly changing as a result. Says Kannan, "I asked the operations leader of one of our largest accounts when we were ramping up the program whether we would be able to maintain the performance and service levels given that the program was expected to triple in volume over a relatively short four-month time frame. He said, 'Yes, provided certain assumptions work out.' That wasn't good enough. We cannot be making conditional commitments. You either get it done . . . or you don't.

"So, I forced him to take a stand. This was in front of the whole management team. I said, 'Look, there's no way we're going to accept that statement. You're hedging. Either you identify the impediments to achieving the goal, or you say, 'Look, I've gotten everything I need, I know what decisions I can take. I will take one hundred percent ownership for this.'

"And I think that made this person take that ownership stake. And it sent a clear message to the other folks in the room. Since that episode, I have never been personally involved in a single decision on this program. I know it's on track and that's it."

Tap the Organization's Brainpower

In the spirit of institutionalizing capabilities and commitments, the Just-in-Time organization needs to organize its information.

Mavericks can reinvent the wheel only so many times before their frustration crescendos. All-nighters can be invigorating when you're twenty-three, but not when you're thirty-five or forty-five . . . and when the effort is unnecessary. To truly tap the organization's substantial brainpower, don't waste it on boilerplate documents and weekend fire drills. Once a valuable model or template or design concept or client insight or best practice is developed, make it a public good—free and available to all in the organization. The time spent to arm employees with information will be more than recouped in the time they save . . . that can now be spent serving customers better.

"We had in the head office of Special Olympics two information-related roles that we, theoretically, understood were distinct, but did not separate in practice," says Tim Shriver. "One was the gathering of information . . . the creation of content experts and expertise . . . the pooling of best practices, what I'd call the knowledge center. This whole function—gathering, packaging, sorting, and repackaging information for distribution—was something we knew we were supposed to be doing.

"The second information role was that of knowledge transfer—more formal training and education—and that was also very clearly our responsibility. We have to run training in volleyball or board development or PR. So, we not only had to understand and manage the knowledge, we had to train other people in how to use it. And we were trying to do some or all of these things with using the same people in the same functional departments—Sports, Public Relations, and Fund-raising being the primary ones.

"I'll never forget people in the field complaining: 'We called the sports department to try to get some information about such-and-such a sports guide, and the guy was off in Europe. He wasn't even there to take our call.' And I thought to myself, 'Of course he's off in Europe. He's running a training program. What do you expect?'

"I underestimated the conflict and complexity of asking someone to be, say, the content expert on athlete leadership programs, while also asking him to take on training people from Singapore to San Francisco."

Special Olympics addressed that information challenge by distinguishing between curriculum development and training and focusing the former under the head office, while delegating the latter to the regions. The organization built up its functional expertise in Washington, D.C., and these "experts" then developed customized training modules (e.g., program planning, fund-raising, physical education) for programs in the field. Sports experts, as an example, developed CD-ROMs centrally, which were then translated into local languages and sent to places like China and Africa and Russia to help local trainers teach Special Olympics athletes how to kick a soccer ball, do floor exercises in gymnastics, or hit a golf ball.

Not only did Special Olympics fix its human information resources, but it established an impressive information technology infrastructure. Indeed, its knowledge-sharing systems are now the envy of the not-for-profit sector. "Ours is now a really very, very sophisticated IT system, particularly for the not-for-profit sector," notes Shriver. "When I show it to friends of mine at other not-for-profits, their eyes jump out of their heads. It's an 'Aha!' It's an enormously educational experience to see concretely what it means to build a sustainable organization.

"There's a lot of good successes here," he continues. "Our organizational assessment tool—what we call the Program Development System—is a fantastic tool. Its hub here in D.C. is constantly updated, and it's used very effectively by the programs in the regions. It's a great asset."

Special Olympics' new Web-enabled knowledge management site is being increasingly populated and is available in more and more languages. People around the globe can go there and find everything from best practices to old editions of their *Spirit* magazine.

"Our data may not be as quantitative as in the for-profit world, but it's as robust and informative. I could, as we're talking, go on to the knowledge management system, pull up the organizational profile for Poland, and tell you more about that country's program than you'd ever want to know."

Not only does this tool lend transparency to how programs perform around the world, but also, importantly, it vests these programs in the process of reporting the data and setting their own plans for growth.

"It almost intuitively creates a consistent structure for plans, because it says to a program: You're at Stage Two in the development of your board. To get to Stage Three, these are the three things you have to be able to check off. Not surprisingly, you'll see those three items appear on that program's plan for the next year," says Shriver.

To support its goal of quality growth, Special Olympics needed a firm sense of the number of athletes already participating in its events and programs around the world, so it conducted its first global census of Special Olympics athletes and captured valuable demographic data on athletes by region, country, sport, age, and gender. It was when the census indicated that nearly one million athletes participated in 2000 that the board adopted the ambitious goal of doubling that number by the end of 2005. (In East Asia, as an example, the goal is to increase participation from 83,000 athletes in 2000 to over half a million in 2005.) In so doing, they committed to becoming a worldwide movement led by athletes, and to changing the attitudes of the world's population.

To assess progress in achieving these strategic objectives, the organization developed a sophisticated performance measurement system around metrics (e.g., athlete coverage, fund-raising, knowledge sharing) focused on three key criteria—growth, quality, and innovation. Staff and program evaluations now hinge on performance against these metrics. Programs are rated in each of these functional areas on a scale of 1 to 4, from "emerging" to "very mature."

Shriver explains, "We enable programs to assess themselves and report progress using an electronic tool. The idea is to make the program self-monitoring but, at the same time, available to all, to the entire field. The outcome is a program profile that tells you where this program is both quantitatively (e.g., number of competitions, athletes, family members enrolled) and in each of these functional areas." More recently, it is refining its performance management systems even further to create a "balanced score-card" that captures—at a glance—the key metrics of success.

Don't Throw Out the Baby with the Bathwater

In introducing more professional processes and structures, Just-in-Time organizations also need to preserve the spark of innovation and initiative that fueled their previous success. While instituting a more reliable and stable business model, they need to continue to incubate creativity and cultivate entrepreneurialism. It's a deli-cate balance, and the potential for culture clash is palpable as you try to blend an appetite for adventure with early warning systems, but companies have successfully made the transition. The proper mix of motivators can play a key role. In a perfect world, the Just-in-Time organization retains the market focus, agility, and respon-siveness of its pioneering spirit with the discipline, acumen, and durability of its professional processes.

P.V. Kannan speaks of the need to keep the entrepreneurial "cow-boys" engaged in starting up new operations, while instilling management discipline and best practices across more mature operations. "We still need the cowboy mentality as we chart new territories. If 24/7 Customer goes and sets something up in an-other offshore market, I want to go in guns blazing." To be suc-cessful in establishing "greenfield" operations, the company needs the ingenuity and initiative of its mavericks, those who set up 24/7's operations in India so successfully. As Kannan points out, "Sometimes defining processes and getting too rigid early on in-hibits flexibility."

Kannan recalls a situation where the company had to launch a new center for one of its top clients with a very aggressive target of forty-five days. "Our normal time frame for starting up a new cen-ter in a new location is seventy-five days. To respond to this chal-lenge, we set up a crack team of 'cowboys' to develop and deliver the target. The team was given complete operational freedom to 'bend processes' to execute the plan. The team worked closely with our vendors to implement some innovative ideas, and we were able to deliver the center within forty-five days."

24/7 Customer could not have met this challenge using its traditional processes, but what's interesting is that it was able to leverage lessons learned on this project to reengineer some of those very processes. Now it regularly starts up new centers in sixty days, as opposed to seventy-five.

The heroes of the early days who pulled all-nighters to put out fires or respond to customers' requests-for-proposal (RFPs) put 24/7 on the map . . . and will continue to put it on the map in new locations. As operations mature, however, the organization needs to focus and discipline the company's sales and service approach so that it can fulfill its mission "to consistently outperform our customer's best center by ten percent or more."

What does that mean exactly? Well, if you're an entry-level worker in a call center in Bangalore, your ability to become a supervisor is directly tied to your ability to meet or exceed this 10 percent improvement goal. Says Kannan, "We talk about being ten percent better than any center that our clients currently use—whether it's in-house or outsourced. In short, we'll be the number one provider for them, based on the metrics they care about. That's how we differentiate ourselves . . . and so, that became an important component in how we reward people . . . that and profitability. In 2002, we started tracking how many people in each client program were exceeding that ten percent goal."

Here's a concrete example. Let's say it takes five minutes, on average, to process an insurance claim, with an error rate of .05 percent. That's the best performance the client's existing centers can produce. 24/7 is pledging to shave 10 percent off that time. In other words, its agents will process the claim in four and a half minutes, with the same or fewer errors. Those that meet this test advance more quickly to supervisor and qualify for cash incentives.

Ultimately, you become head of the process, running an operation with perhaps two hundred claims agents. "Again, your bonuses and everything are tied to your being the top center for the client," remarks Kannan. "Now our performance measurement systems track not only service-level agreement measures, but also the quality of a manager's people: What percentage of her team excels. What is the attrition rate? Because if she has too much attrition, knowledge and experience levels will decline and so will results."

Variable compensation remains a large component of the total pay package at 24/7 but is tied even more closely now to the financial performance of the company. In addition, more care is being paid to career development. As Kannan admits, "What we recognized—probably a little late—was you can promote someone and give them responsibilities, but at the same time, you have to put formal mechanisms in place to develop them. Initially we were in the situation where someone who does extremely well at one level moves to another level, does extremely well, then moves to the next level and fails completely. We've since introduced a career-planning mechanism, so that everyone's ambitions are realized but not necessarily exceeded."

The results of these process changes are clearly visible at 24/7. Eighteen months back, the company was the best performing center in the world for only 18 percent of its clients. This number has now swelled to over 70 percent. "The time taken to stabilize operations and exceed SLA's for any new program we add to our centers has dropped from a hundred and eighty days to under one hundred and twenty days," says Kannan.

Clearly, in a mission-focused organization such as Special Olympics, it's vital that you preserve the charisma and energy of its founder. In adding structure and process discipline to the organization, Tim Shriver has been careful not to subvert his mother's original vision; instead the board has put in place governance measures to sustain it. The board must include two of Eunice Kennedy Shriver's descendants, must agree unanimously to any changes in the movement's mission, and must explicitly review mission compliance at least every two years. Maintaining the balance between mission and process discipline is a critical job for SOI's leadership team.

The primary motivator at Special Olympics has always been, and will always be, its mission. As one insider exclaimed, "It is so inherently good!" Pride in the mission and the "product" is so strong, that other motivators common in the commercial sector (e.g., compensation, promotions, benefits) take a backseat. But the strength of the organization's mission can take people—even volunteers—only so far.

"In the reorganization, we set up high expectations for the kinds of managers we wanted on board. They had to be good at managing expectations, good at goal setting, good at aligning personal goals with the organization's goals. They had to manage and communicate knowledge well and clearly define roles and responsibilities.

"But, you have to keep in mind, that we, for the most part, hire people who come out of the not-for-profit sector, for whom those skills are secondary. This is not something they learned in their twenties and thirties. And so most of our staff are relearning, and we're helping them with training, but it takes time.

"We have not yet become good enough as individuals—and I include myself in this, not to be humble but to be honest—at how we shift our focus from the 'painting' to the 'artist.' We have to ensure that our focus on the project or the program is balanced by our focus on our own organizational health."

With that in mind, Special Olympics has developed a new staff professional-development strategy and introduced, as mentioned, a rigorous performance measurement system that reinforces accountability and control at all levels. Headquarters provides training on how to start a local program that covers key organizational issues (e.g., planning events) and outlines needed capabilities. In addition, the movement is developing turnkey modules on fundraising, sports, people management, and general skills.

"All of us are the kind of people who want to move beyond the issue of decision rights, and get back to the issue of how we get more athletes in the program in Calcutta," says Shriver. "Nobody here really cares deeply about decision rights or spends sleepless nights wondering how they're allocated. That's not why we're here. We're trying to learn how to exercise decision rights well, but we're here because we care about something else.

"And that's the key to motivating extraordinary effort. People who work for not-for-profit organizations are motivated largely through social return and the personal gratification of helping people. Our job in managing the Special Olympics organization is to make their efforts as effective as possible."

SPECIAL OLYMPICS: POSTSCRIPT

The efforts of both Special Olympics' headquarters staff and regional management around the world have placed the movement on the Road to Resilience. Its decision rights, information, motivators, and structure are more aligned, and these building blocks are working in concert to further the organization's mission and objectives.

"There is a lot of good news," concedes Shriver. "We have World Games that will take place over eight years in three countries outside the United States.[5] That's a direct outcome of this reorganization. Moreover, we've truly globalized the movement. Very few people in Lithuania would call Special Olympics a U.S. export; it's a European movement to the Lithuanians. It's a Middle Eastern movement to the Egyptians. That's a huge and positive change. Being able to stage the World Games in other markets contributes to the sustainability of the whole movement and allows us to develop other affirmative programs such as the Schools Outreach Project and Healthy Athletes, which today boasts cooperating centers everywhere from Massachusetts to China.[6]

They've enjoyed great support and buy-in from the regions as they implemented major changes. In the past four years, they have grown by more than 70 percent, adding over 700,000 athletes. The fact that the head office said "We want to reach two million athletes" did nothing to add a single athlete to the field. Every athlete that has joined did so because a local volunteer or employee found them, introduced them to a program, a volunteer, a coach, a competition . . . then gathered their data and sent it in.

"We have a team now," says Shriver. "We didn't have a team before. We have goals now. We didn't have goals before. We have buy-in now. We didn't have buy-in before. As a result, we're gathering momentum worldwide. Russia has grown, China has grown, Turkey is growing sporadically, but still is growing. Mexico is growing. They're growing because we have local management teams paying consistent, strong attention to the organizational development of each program. And headquarters now has good tools to assess these programs. We've focused on a lot of things and gotten a lot of things right, but our journey continues."

The Just-in-Time organization can act like a precocious child, dazzling its peers with its effortless wins, and then behaving in an immature or even foolish fashion. Oftentimes, this organization has grown so fast, it loses its footing, which places it in a precarious position as it is poised near the top of a slippery slope. Without the right tools and some traction, it can slide into dysfunction. But with the right processes and structures in place, it can reach a plateau of sustainable success.

EIGHT

THE MILITARY PRECISION ORGANIZATION
Flying in Formation

Often driven by a small, hands-on senior management team, the Military Precision organization hums like a well-oiled machine. Everyone knows his role and implements it diligently, creating the overall effect of fluid and consistent execution. This organization is hierarchical and operates under a highly controlled management model. It can conceive and execute brilliant strategies—often repeatedly—because it has drilled the organization and run it through every scenario in the manual. It's highly efficient and leverages its scale masterfully in executing large volumes of transactions.

While it provides for a certain level of autonomy in the field, the Military Precision organization's biggest ongoing challenge is preparing for growth beyond the tenure of its current leadership. Talented people need to be groomed, not just drilled, to release their full potential and to provide for smooth succession within the organization's management ranks. Moreover, feedback loops need to be institutionalized to ensure that top commanders understand—in real time—what's happening on the front lines. Military Precision organizations can be vulnerable to sudden shifts in the external market environment, as they do not typically deal well with significant and unexpected change.

Bright and early each Monday morning, the eight members of 7-Eleven's executive committee and invited guests convene to discuss strategic issues and survey the week that was and the week that will be. Armed with the "book" issued the Friday before, they know—for each of the 2,500 products in the 7-Eleven inventory—what is moving and what is not in their 5,800 stores across the United States and Canada. They have exhaustive intelligence on new products and promotions. They are ready to solve high-level issues and plot the tactical course for the week ahead.

By 11 a.m., the senior executive team has determined the week's priorities and is ready to relay them to the leadership of the company . . . all vice presidents and above. During the first half of this two-hour national videoconference, division VPs go over the updated forecast for the month and the quarter and discuss strategic topics. While the give and take is spirited, participants always reach agreement, in keeping with one of 7-Eleven's core operating principles, "Together when we leave." At noon, department heads, product directors, category managers, and sales and marketing managers join in for what is called the Obstacles Meeting to discuss issues at the store level that need to be escalated for corporate resolution. Topics cover the gamut from replenishing the stock of Gatorade during a heat wave in San Diego to fixing systems bugs in a new program rollout. Issues are identified and accountability clearly assigned. In fact, issue "owners" can expect to see their name on the following week's agenda for a resolution/progress report.

First, however, the financials. As president and CEO Jim Keyes notes, "Normally, this sort of detailed financial review would be done with a relatively small group. But I found that the management of this company was totally disconnected from the financials, so this is an education process. We call it the Leadership Meeting because, in effect, it's a leadership-development opportunity for people at department-head level or field level to understand the direct link between what they do and the earnings per share of the company."

Equipped with a similar "book" to the one issued to the executive committee the Friday before, these up-and-coming leaders can see sales, profits, and how they are stacking up against expectations. Managers who had previously considered only their department or unit now understand the performance of the whole and can flex tactics to help the company make its numbers.

The communications cascade does not end there. In truth, it is just beginning. As people emerge from the 11 a.m. meeting, many head to staff meetings and divisional communications meetings.

Then, on Tuesdays at 11:15 a.m., 7-Eleven's nearly eight hundred field consultants—who each oversee a group of stores and ensure compliance with corporate standards—are debriefed. The hour-long video teleconference starts with a message of the week from the company's chief operating officer, Gary Rose. Then, the call quickly covers case studies, new merchandising issues, featured products, learnings from test markets, everything the field consultants need to know to educate store owners and associates about that week's priorities. Finally, Jim Keyes wraps up with a closing message. Often he'll reference a visit he made to a 7-Eleven store that week or an upcoming special promotion or tie-in. When these field consultants head out into the field Wednesday through Friday, they know exactly what news to deliver to the stores, because they've heard it directly from the top. While time-consuming and repetitive, this weekly drill has been integral to 7-Eleven's resurgence and sustained success over the past eight years. In fact, as of March 2005, the company has reported thirty-four quarters of same-store sales growth, an unprecedented feat in the grocery/convenience store sector.

It's hard to believe that less than fifteen years ago, 7-Eleven, then known as Southland Corporation, filed for bankruptcy. A classic Fits-and-Starts company, it had lost focus as entrepreneurial store owners and unfocused corporate executives took the brand in inconsistent directions. The company diversified into unrelated businesses such as oil refining, auto parts, and real estate development. Meanwhile, the core business—convenience stores—was suboptimizing its purchasing leverage as each owner stocked his or her own shop. The highly decentralized structure that had worked in the early years of high growth started to sputter as gas stations and twenty-four-hour drugstores cottoned onto 7-Eleven's competitive formula. Indeed, they quickly commoditized many of 7-Eleven's core products—beer, soft drinks, cigarettes, even bread and milk—charging loss-leading prices for these items to get customers into their stores.

Jim Keyes has very personal memories of that chapter in the company's history, as he was the architect of the restructuring plan that ushered the renamed 7-Eleven out of bankruptcy. "I've had a unique career path," he observes wryly, "I was sort of the architect of the plan and then later on in my career, as chief financial officer, I got to fund the plan. And then I became chief operating officer, so I got to execute the plan. And now as CEO, I get to go sell the plan."[1]

He describes the old Southland as a boa constrictor who had swallowed a pig. "The irony was that we were not only decentralized, but we had built up a tremendous amount of corporate staff . . . which was inconsistent with the idea of being decentralized. So I depicted us as a boa constrictor, in which all of the authority was bunched somewhere in the middle at the division level. The decision-making authority was centralized, but it was centralized somewhere in middle management, which made us neither nimble at the street level, nor effective in leveraging our corporate purchasing power.

"And what I was trying to build was more of a rattlesnake. One end is pretty important with the rattle. And the other end is pretty important, too, with the fangs. And that's how we've restructured in this new environment. We've pushed more authority and decision-making into the store, because, with information technology, we now have decision-making tools that allow us to truly empower that store operator.

"We're also pushing more authority than ever before to corporate decision-makers so that we can truly leverage our buying power because we're a bigger customer of many products than Wal-Mart. And it was time we enjoyed the kind of buying power and leverage that Wal-Mart does. So, today we're trying to accomplish just that."

Central to that mission is communication, and that's why 7-Eleven has collapsed its management layers from eleven to seven, including the CEO and store manager (see Figure 8.1, page 192). And that's why it communicates, then communicates again, and then communicates again every week. "I refer to our business model," says Jim Keyes "as 'corporate entrepreneurship.' We encourage our store operators to be entrepreneurs, but not wild, rugged frontiersmen . . . who might, for example, stock bait because they are located near a lake. We've literally had 7-Eleven stores where the worms were right next to the cold sandwiches. A corporate entrepreneur is free thinking, risk taking, and will make decisions that are in the best interest of serving his customer. But he'll make those decisions within the parameters of a recommended product set. He's not just out there retailing worms."

7-Eleven exemplifies the Military Precision organization because it is top-down with a twist. It takes its direction from above, but its intelligence lies in the field . . . and it recognizes that. It's an organization bent on providing a consistent, quality customer experience to the thousands, often millions, that pass through its doors every day.

As its name implies, the Military Precision organization is disciplined and highly coordinated. It hews to its strategy unswervingly, and the strategy is generally very straightforward. This is an organization that gets things done very efficiently, because everyone is "in formation" and on the same page of the playbook. Senior management sets the strategy, and managers align to it quickly. Its decision rights and information flows are centralized. Information flows to where it is needed, which is up; directives, on the other hand, flow down.

Military Precision organizations perform like any well-trained sports team. There's a playbook, and the team drills these plays over and over, until they are instinctual. Consequently, when one of these playbook scenarios arises, the organization knows how to execute expeditiously. Everyone understands what's expected of them. That said, there is a certain latitude allowed the player on the field. As circumstances shift, for example, a shop or plant manager may have to call her own plays, and that's okay . . . as long as they are covered in the playbook.

The challenge comes when the game itself changes . . . when the market in which a Military Precision organization operates shifts suddenly and unexpectedly.[2] A competitor opens a store across the street. A disruptive technology usurps its value to the customer. The market trend it was riding abruptly fizzles. These are scenarios the standard playbook does not address. In these situations, management needs to come up with new plays and roll them out quickly. In order to do that, they must be able to scan the horizon and anticipate these disruptive competitive events, a skill that can be in short supply in the Military Precision organization. It doesn't like surprises.

By the same token, rarely does something good happen by accident or happy circumstance in the Military Precision organization (as can be the case in Just-in-Time firms). Once made, decisions aren't second-guessed (as in Overmanaged organizations); orders are orders and those who give them take responsibility.[3] This organization presents one, uniform face to the marketplace, and people understand their duties very clearly.[4] It's a do-or-die atmosphere, where employees well understand that their ability to deliver on performance commitments strongly influences career advancement and compensation.[5] Not surprisingly, there's an emphasis on training in these companies.

In short, Military Precision organizations are both efficient and effective, but they're not flawless.

THE MILITARY PRECISION ORGANIZATION: TRAITS

Military Precision organizations manifest certain distinguishing traits: disciplined, consistent, and lean operations and a well-defined chain of command.

Clear Chain of Command

There is no mistaking who's in charge in a Military Precision organization. Headquarters sets the direction and runs a tight ship, making sure field operations—those prosecuting the competitive offensive—have the tools they need to be most effective. Decision-making is crisp, clear, and controlled. Roles and responsibilities are unambiguous, and direction from the upper echelons is straightforward and unequivocal. This is a ship-shape, well-defined operating model that is attentive to the most minute detail and caters unswervingly to customers. While there's certain latitude granted to midlevel managers to do what's right in their local market, it is always clear where the boundaries are. Not much is subject to interpretation; everyone is on the same page.

7-Eleven makes major decisions at the top, and that is well understood and accepted at the store level, since these decisions are made on the basis of real-time data on what sells and what doesn't. Jim Keyes characterizes 7-Eleven's decision-making model as "controlled autonomy." For example, 7-Eleven strongly urges store managers to take full responsibility for all ordering decisions . . . as long as they stay within the strategic scope of a recommended overall product mix. Store managers exercise full sourcing discretion over as much as 25 percent of their inventory; the other three-quarters is subject to strict guidelines and is sourced from company-approved vendors. Plan-o-grams are centrally designed and controlled. There is a centralized price book that its 5,800 stores follow closely. Store-closure decisions are made on a quarterly basis using an eight-category Performance Framework; some two hundred stores are reviewed each quarter. Corporate hires have to be approved by no fewer than three executive committee members. This is a highly structured and disciplined organization. It has to be, given all its moving parts. Planning at 7-Eleven is as exalted as Merchandising.

Before 7:00 a.m. every morning, every executive in the company gets an e-mail summarizing sales from the prior day and month to date . . . by division and by category . . . so they know—before they've even finished their first cup of coffee—who to call and why.

In keeping with this highly disciplined approach to decision-making, 7-Eleven has a trim management structure. Today it operates with about two thirds the number of management layers it supported in its prebankruptcy days (see Figure 8.1). This stream-lined structure facilitates quicker information flows and more efficient execution.

CEO Jim Keyes describes his management style as similar to that of the coach of a football team: "I'm trying to establish a winning strategy, one that allows the organization to clear competitive obstacles. What plays will our competitors throw at us? We've got to have a game plan, and it's my job, ultimately, to come up

FIGURE 8.1—7-ELEVEN'S EFFICIENT ORGANIZATION STRUCTURE

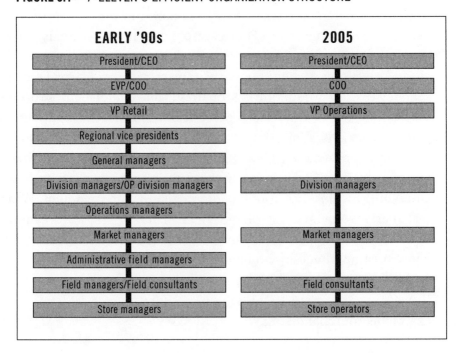

with one, but the coach can't throw the ball. He can't execute the plan. The coach has to be able to teach the players to do that.

"We've certainly had our growing pains as a team, but now we have a clear strategy and our people are well trained. They understand the playbook. They understand the nature of the game, that it's about winning. Before they didn't even know why the score was important; they were just out playing.

"Now that the coach's authority and credibility have been established, we can start to open up decision-making a bit . . . and encourage input when players come back for the huddle. It's okay to say, 'Hey, you dropped your coverage last time' to the guy next to you . . . or 'I'm open, so pass me the ball.' As long as the feedback is constructive and informed, we can use it. In fact, we've come to expect it, as we modify our plans."

Lean Mean Machine

The fundamental advantage of the Military Precision model is that it's less expensive to operate than more decentralized models. These are typically businesses that execute large volumes of similar transactions on a daily basis. The opportunities to leverage fixed costs and consolidate purchasing power are substantial. Successful Military Precision organizations wield scale as a weapon. They are no stranger to automation, which helps them not only ensure consistency, but lower execution costs dramatically. Not surprisingly, front-line employee costs in a Military Precision organization are quite low. The risks commensurate with greater rewards are being taken at higher levels. Many of these organizations are high-touch retail businesses that pass these savings on to the consumer. While it can't turn on a dime, the Military Precision organization can mobilize on one. The call to arms is heard instantly and clearly, and these organizations scale up and down very efficiently.

Gabriella Santiago, the newly promoted vice president of U.S. Operations for *No-Frills Rental Car*, was looking to make a big splash. Now that she was in line to be CEO some day, she wanted to elevate her profile in the organization, but how? She'd taken to reading management journals in search of a big idea or a road map to the top, but all the articles and CEO profiles seemed to be written about a different company. The guy in the corner office had either taken a huge bet on a new product, executed a major turnaround, or broken a union. No-Frills offered no such opportunity for "glory."

What it did offer was steady, if unspectacular, revenue gains of 3 percent a year and continuing earnings improvements of close to 6 percent year-on-year. These reliable numbers had translated into a 40 percent increase in shareholder value over the past five years, making No-Frills the darling of the industry on Wall Street. Gabriella liked to think that she had contributed to that reputation for results.

As director of the Midwest region for the past seven years, Gabriella had championed efforts to squeeze time and costs out of the business. She had piloted some new checkout and cleaning procedures in Indianapolis, for example, that had shaved seven minutes from the turnaround time for an economy-sized car. Within three months, she had rolled out these improvements across her region. The efficiency gains that resulted allowed her to reduce car inventory substantially, which had a very healthy effect on her region's bottom line.

While she explored ways to automate the more routine and repetitive tasks involved in renting, receiving, and prepping cars, she engaged her team in fun contests to identify ways to differentiate the experience they offered customers. Moreover, she devised a more flexible staff scheduling process that enabled her to meet diverse employee needs, while actually lowering labor costs. Her firm but fair management style won her the fierce loyalty of her employees, and she was able to slow employee turnover and motivate incremental effort from hourly workers, who before had spent their eight hours watching the clock and working the bare minimum.

As Gabriella reflected on the business, she realized that this steady, no-nonsense, execution-oriented philosophy was the "magic" she was looking for. When all was said and done, a good rental-car operation was basically a series of simple processes. You rent cars, receive them, clean them, and refuel them. You staff the locations to meet demand, and you manage the inventory. And each of these activities is performed hundreds of thousands of times a year.

When she looked at who had made it to the top at No-Frills, she realized that the formula for success was the one she had been practicing all along: stick to the basics, keep your eye on the customer, look for every opportunity to take time and costs out of the process. The company's former CEO, Dan Jakuboski, who had been hired away by the competition last year, had drilled the "3 by 3" rule into her head. He used to say, "Next year's target should be a three percent reduction in cost and a three percent increase in productivity (i.e., rental revenue per labor hour)."

No-Frills was not just the name of the company, it was Dan's operating philosophy. Five years ago, when the corporate headquarters' lease had come up for renewal, he seized the option to move to a lower cost location, even though it was a record earnings year for the company. Not only that, but he "downsized" the layout of the new offices by introducing a concept called hoteling. Managers who traveled a lot now had to bid for empty office space.

Gabriella concluded that she should take a page from Dan's book if she wanted to maintain her career trajectory. Keep looking for ways to do more with less; that was the secret to keeping both customers and shareholders happy.

Consistency Is Not a Hobgoblin

The "secret sauce" in the Military Precision organization's lean and mean formula is consistency. These companies have built their brand around the consistency of product, service, and experience they deliver to the customer. They've built their business model around the consistency of their processes and procedures. As mentioned, these companies execute similar transactions with astonishing frequency . . . tens or hundreds of thousands of transactions per day. Consistency is achieved and sustained through rules, tools, and automation. It should be noted, however, that consistency does not equal standardization. Military Precision organizations acknowledge the need to incorporate local input and preferences.

7-Eleven has moved from its prebankruptcy, decentralized model in which company-wide programs were executed haphazardly . . . to a highly focused and disciplined model in which stores implement consistently and "by the book." The book in this case is, actually, a booklet known as the "Five Fundamentals of Convenience," which is making the rounds as 7-Eleven introduces fresh foods to its product lineup across the country. The five fundamentals—each covered in a page—are Quality, Value, Assortment, Cleanliness, and Service, and the organization's performance measurement system is closely aligned with these five objectives.

Store cleanliness, for example, has become a high priority. Windows, floors, bathrooms, even the parking lot are expected to be pristine at all times, and the store's interior should be in a high state of order.[6] This is not just a topic for corporate bulletins and field consultant visits; it's fodder for Executive Committee sessions.

In keeping with this new strategy, 7-Eleven has reexercised control over the store inventory, creating a fresh-food supply network to ensure that the approximately 350 perishable SKUs it now stocks are delivered daily, sometimes twice daily.[7] The store manager retains the ability to tailor about 15 to 25 percent of her inventory to the specific tastes of her customers. She can source these from the company's overall merchandising inventory . . . or from local vendors.

Then there is another layer of products in the store that are regional or even market based. Finally, the bulk of the store's inventory are products that are foundational. Every store must have these—Coke, cigarettes, beer, beef jerky—the staples of any convenience store."

* * *

Consistency is at the heart of the Four Seasons hotel experience. It is that expectation of a familiar, luxurious, and uneventful experience that keeps guests coming back. They pay extra for no surprises. San Francisco Regional Vice President Stan Bromley, a thirty-five-year veteran in the trenches of hotel management, likes to say, "We're not nuclear physicists. We're butlers, welcoming our guests home. We need to be aware of our customers and their satisfaction all the time—listening to what they say and reading their body language—as if our livelihood depended upon it . . . because it does." Try having breakfast with Bromley in his San Francisco hotel. If you arrive first, you're likely to hear the types of questions he recently asked of his breakfast companion, "How long did you wait before you were greeted by someone? Did they act like they knew who you were? Did they seat you at a table promptly? How was the table set? Did they remove the extra place settings quickly? How long did you wait before they asked if you wanted coffee, tea, or juice? How hot was the coffee?"[8] It's this attention to detail and the discipline with which it's reinforced that keeps Four Seasons at the top of the hotel heap.

No complaint is too trivial at Four Seasons. When a guest recently commented that the bathroom towels weren't "thirsty enough," the hotel conducted an in-depth investigation and found that the dryers in the laundry room were set 15 degrees too high. Still, while the luxury hotel chain has built its business model around delivering a consistent and familiar level of premium service, it gives employees a lot of leeway in defining how to execute that mission. Bromley tells his employees to show that they care about their guests, but to do so in a genuine and comfortable way. Unlike other hotel chains where every service person uses a scripted response after a customer thanks them, Four Seasons encourages its staff to use their own words when interacting with customers.

THE MILITARY PRECISION ORGANIZATION: TREATMENTS

While the Military Precision organization is fundamentally healthy, it does have its blind spots. Given its highly disciplined management structure, it can be rigid and unyielding in the face of sudden competitive threats. Moreover, it can suffer from high turnover as employees come to view themselves as interchangeable cogs in the corporate wheel. To avoid these pitfalls, the Military Precision organization should apply the following preventive treatments.

Cascade Communications, Elevate Intelligence

You cannot overcommunicate in the Military Precision organization. As our opening story on 7-Eleven illustrates, the senior command in these organizations can communicate the same message five times in a twenty-four-hour window. To deliver the consistent, efficient service that is its trademark, the Military Precision organization needs to be firm, clear, and, yes, redundant in the directives it passes down. The more that frontline individuals hear "news" directly from the top, the better, which argues for a flatter management structure with fewer layers of intervening directors and VPs to garble messages. Since Military Precision organizations are generally dispersed, communications technology (e.g., video teleconferencing, e-mails, IT alert systems) is an invaluable asset that can enhance tremendously the efficiency of information flows, both down the organization and up. As priorities and solutions hatched in Corporate are cascaded down via video conferences and e-mails, so real-time data and employee/customer suggestions are fed up the organization via internal IT systems. Information flows both ways in this organization as in most healthy organizations; the distinction is the liquidity of the information. Military Precision organizations tend not to get bogged down in lengthy discussions, debates, or management retreats. Instead, direction, current priorities, and customer data are communicated in rapid-fire fashion. The aim is to create a seamless exchange of relevant and real-time information that gets to the right people on time.

"We're not any smarter today than we were twenty years ago," observes 7-Eleven's chief executive Jim Keyes, "but we have communications technology in place to enlighten us instantly and empower our franchisees and store managers."

An example of this communications technology at work is 7-Eleven's foray into music retailing with Jessica Simpson's holiday album in 2004. Sony Music was taking a risk, giving a nontraditional retailer a sixty-day exclusive on its top recording star. Her previous two albums went platinum. Corporate needed to get the word out that this was a high priority.

"Traditionally, we would have just put it out there and hoped that our eight hundred field consultants would be able to communicate this very important message to their store managers during their weekly visits," says Keyes. "'This product needs to be in a certain place on the sales counter. It needs to have the appropriate signage, and you should be playing the music in the background so people can hear it.'"

Instead of relying on that word of mouth, however, 7-Eleven can now underline the urgency of this promotion by playing a few cuts from the album at the Tuesday video teleconference. "I can introduce the president of Sony music, so that the field consultants can hear from his mouth how relevant and important this product is to them and to us," says Keyes. "I can share with them the opportunity that if we are successful with this, we will get the next Jennifer Lopez release or the next Harry Potter book."

Finally, there's another tool at Keyes' fingertips, the company's new retail information system. "With this system I can place a 'gateway' icon on every store's computer screen that they have to click to open up their system. And the icon is my smiling face telling them how important it is for them to merchandise and sell this product," says Keyes. Now, *that's* communicating.

Of course, the other side of this technology is headquarters' ability to gather enormous amounts of data from the stores to help manage the enterprise better and anticipate inventory needs. "The magic of our retail information systems is the ability to take vast amounts of data and convert it into easy-to-use graphs and charts that convey useful information on how our twenty-five hundred products are selling every hour of every day," notes Keyes. This information is not only useful to corporate headquarters, it's available on the handheld computer of the sales associate stocking tuna fish sandwiches. He can hit a button and see sales for that item over the past eight days. He can check the weather and see the correlation between tuna fish sandwich sales and rainy days.

"We've captured the drivers—the probable drivers—of sales on that product, so the stores can make informed choices. As Lent approaches, for example, they'll be reminded by a flashing icon that says, 'Don't forget! It's Lent!' If they're located next to a Catholic church, that's relevant information." Interestingly, 7-Eleven stops short of automatically replenishing store inventories. In fact, it doesn't even offer recommendations on how many items to order. "That's true retailing, and that's the domain of that eight-dollar-an-hour sales associate who's charged with managing that section. They know the external environmental factors that influence tuna fish sales better than we do."

Reward the Messenger

While the Military Precision organization communicates a lot . . . more than most . . . the format for these "exchanges" tends to be very structured and scheduled. These are not free-form debates. Moreover, the top-down tone of the organization can discourage many people from speaking up. There is a natural tendency in a centrally controlled environment to tell senior management what you think they want to hear. To overcome this tendency, management needs to encourage some constructive insubordination. Institutionalize and make explicit feedback loops through which employees and customers can surface concerns or complaints. This sort of dialogue is a sign of good health. Curiosity and creativity need to be cultivated, within reason, so that employees at all levels stake ownership in the company's success.

At a weekly field consultant meeting in January of 2005, Don Thomas, VP of 7-Eleven's Central Division, presented a case study on sandwich wraps. With more than 1,200 people either in the conference room in Dallas or participating via video teleconferencing from around the country, you would have expected a pretty stiff presentation concluding with a sales pitch on the wraps. Instead, Don talked through the case study like he was sharing his findings with a colleague across a desk. He showed pictures of the wraps. He reported test-market results and the drivers of success. (Interestingly, stores near offices or shopping malls enjoyed better results.) He sized the financial potential of this new product category (up to $70 per store per day). But he also acknowledged the gaps in his information. "We could have sampled the product better than we did. We need to know what customers are buying *with* the wraps, and we haven't tested that yet." He didn't admit this in response to a pointed question from senior management. He volunteered this error as part of the "conversation" he was leading.

7-Eleven has institutionalized this sort of "confessional" management style. In fact, Jim Keyes, the company's president and CEO vigorously encourages the dissemination of bad news. At a recent national conference of 7-Eleven employees, he outlined a bad shopping experience he had had at a store. "I prefaced it by saying, 'This is countercultural to the old Southland habit of never embarrassing anyone, but I had a bad experience in my store. And I want to tell you about it.'

"And I named the store. I know right now there's buzz all over this company about that. And I know there's buzz in that specific area. 'What are we going to do about that store?' And that's precisely the kind of culture I'm trying to create. I want people to feel that ownership stake in the problem. It's our collective responsibility to make sure that no one has that experience in *any* of our stores."

Keyes raises the analogy of a neighborhood association. "If one of your neighbors was letting his grass grow three feet tall, you're not going to just drive by and say, 'Not my job.' You're going to send a letter to the neighborhood association, and they're going to—even at the risk of embarrassing your neighbor—point out that he really needs to mow his lawn.

"In a corporate environment, there's a tendency for people to shake their heads about the guy in the next department or about the store that's not clean, but that's it. There's a reluctance to get involved, because they either want to avoid embarrassing a colleague or they fear that their own heads will roll as the messenger of bad tidings. I tried to model a different sort of behavior at our national conference. I said, 'I'm not suggesting that someone needs to be fired. I'm not trying to humiliate anybody by pointing out an area of weakness. But it's my job as a customer of 7-Eleven and a stakeholder in 7-Eleven to point out if something's not acceptable.'"

A single purpose dictates the priorities of every employee who works at the Four Seasons hotels around the world: to operate the finest hotel in that city. "We set out to redefine luxury as service, and to provide a support system at our hotels to replace the one left behind at home or the office," says Regional Vice President Stan Bromley. Toward that end, he cultivates an environment in which hotel housekeepers and concierges feel free to speak up. "Our employees know more about our guests than anyone else," says Bromley. "And they trust the system. They know that they can tell management when something is wrong, and that we will do something about it. They will speak up and give you two or three chances to show that you will act. After that, they hit the Delete key. They have little patience for managers who listen but don't do anything about a problem. How do you find out what is on an employee's mind? Ask them and then actually wait for their answer before moving along."

Hotel staff know what issues to raise, because they have been well trained in the Four Seasons way. "We advise all staff to make sure that every decision they make squares with our goals, beliefs, and values . . . and they honor that obligation, because they feel respected. If we were seen as only caring about profits and prestige, rather than our customers and employees, they would not believe in our values, and we would be communicating across a trust gap."

Build Leaders, Not Robots

High turnover can be a problem on the front lines of the Military Precision organization. The industry with the greatest proportion of Military Precision organizations—retail—averages 140 percent turnover a year. Retail jobs, as a rule, pay a fair but modest wage, and the opportunities for advancement are not obvious. Military Precision organizations make them obvious. They devote time and money to developing state-of-the-art training programs and building the skills of high-potential talent. While striving to build a consistent, high-functioning machine, senior management also tries not to take all the thinking out of the job. The challenge for the Military Precision organization is to achieve the benefits of centralized direction and decision-making without turning employees into robots. They delegate authority and decision rights to frontline managers and associates, as appropriate and deserved. This also means giving people the opportunity to learn by doing . . . and failing . . . and communicating that that's how people learn and develop. Making an extra effort to emphasize lateral, not just upward, moves is another good way to broaden the horizons and skill sets of future leaders.

"Our vulnerability," admits 7-Eleven CEO Jim Keyes, "is it's too easy for frontline employees to say, 'Just tell me what to do.' Everybody's going to default to that 'bare minimum' kind of solution." Employees who are punching clocks don't necessarily bring initiative to the job. From management's perspective it's often easier to give store managers or associates the answers rather than teach them how to come up with it for themselves.

"It requires constant communication," says Keyes. "And it requires those of us at the top to keep changing. I have changed my leadership style probably ten times in the last five years to try and find that right approach to cascading leadership throughout the organization. I don't want managers in this company. I want decision-makers. I want that concept of leadership to be embraced by everyone down to the hourly employee. That's easy to say, but it's very, very difficult to do."

Still, for four years, 7-Eleven has been doing it through a strategy called Retailer Initiative. The program does just what its name implies; it arms local store managers and their employees with the information and the authority to take the initiative in running their store. In what may be the convenience industry's most intense and thorough training program, candidates are certified to take on increasing levels of responsibility, starting with writing an order.

During a two-day training program, store clerks learn how to use 7-Eleven's proprietary data management system to ascertain what customers are buying from their store each day. With thirty to forty new items added per week, it's a remarkably robust system, and employees need to be schooled on how to leverage its full potential. Managers and hourly associates learn how to analyze trends, develop hypotheses, and make considered choices. They are taught the two key metrics that drive the business: store sales per day and inventory turns. When they emerge, they have a much greater sense of ownership in running the business . . . and they get a pay raise. Not surprisingly, employee turnover has dropped since Retailer Initiative was introduced.

Keyes's view is that the knowledge of what sells on a day-to-day basis lives in each store, and the deeper you go, the richer that knowledge. "So, we ask the store manager or franchisee to delegate decision-making to that hourly sales associate. Ask her to manage a section of the store and develop a point of view."

"So, say you're a college student working part-time to help cover expenses. Five years ago you would have been handed a mop and shown how to ring up sales. Today we give you a computer—a handheld computer—and the opportunity to exercise significant decision-making responsibility. We'll train you and then turn you loose on a section of the store. We want to hear what you have to say; we want your inexperience. Because what we want you to do is look at that section from the customer's perspective and develop a hypothesis about what would make those products more appealing."

"In a lot of ways it's retailing at its purest. We've talked about it for twenty years, but we've never been able to really do it . . . truly empower that person at the point of sale to make decisions. They've never had the proper tools. Now they do."

While he jokes that he never dreamed as a child of being a retailer, Keyes now considers retailing to be the best possible window on the basics of business . . . because of the immediacy of the feedback. "If I'm developing a new product for Boeing, I may not see the results within the span of my career. If I'm testing a new product at 7-Eleven, I'm going to know how it did tomorrow morning. In fact, we were more accurate than the exit polls in predicting the results of the last presidential election based on our sale of Bush and Kerry coffee cups."

Stan Bromley of Four Seasons Hotels and Resorts lists the three key drivers of the hotel chain's success—"people, products, and profits"—and the order is very deliberate. Just as Jim Keyes recognizes the importance of the hourly sales associate at 7-Eleven's convenience stores, so Four Seasons executives acknowledge that their business is in the hands of the hotel receptionists and door attendants who greet their guests. While they impose rigorous standards as a "floor" for employee conduct (e.g., the phone should not ring more than three times before the caller hears a live human voice), they let the individual employee define the "ceiling" . . . within reasonable limits.

By now, the story of the door attendant in Washington, D.C., is folklore at Four Seasons. He helped a guest into an airport taxi and bid her good-bye before realizing he was still holding her briefcase. He took it upon himself to call the guest, an attorney in New York, and discovered that she needed the documents in the briefcase for an early-morning meeting. He then approached hotel management to ask if he could take the shuttle to New York to return the briefcase that evening. His request was not only approved, it was applauded. The names and locations in the story sometimes get jumbled in the telling and retelling. Sometimes it is a female desk clerk. Sometimes the guest is leaving New York, but the message remains the same: Do what is necessary to keep our guests happy.

Prepare for the Next War

Stop, look, and listen. While the relentless consistency of the Military Precision model is its strength, it can also be a rut if management automatically defaults to doing tomorrow what worked today. The top brass needs to be constantly scanning the horizon for the next opportunity or competitive threat that could make or break the company. Typically, a centralized staff group is tasked with this responsibility of applying a fresh eye to the future. That might mean staging the occasional coup or turning the business model on its ear. The key is to hone the organization's peripheral vision and not be caught off-guard.

Jim Keyes remembers a piece of counsel he got from John Thompson, former president and CEO of 7-Eleven's predecessor company, Southland Corporation. Thompson related a story his father, the original founder of the business, had told him: "He had said that the convenience industry would never mature, and, in fact, if anything, it would only grow as society became busier and busier. He added, however, that the products we define as convenience certainly could mature and that if we didn't constantly change and innovate, we would not survive as a company or industry."

And, in fact, 7-Eleven did stumble and fall in the early 1990s because it failed to innovate its product set, among other things. As convenience needs changed, the company failed to make the necessary adjustments. "We fell into the trap of defining market share in terms of number of stores, and we stopped creating value in each new store," concedes Keyes.

While the company has made significant progress in gathering and responding to customer intelligence, executives can still cite examples where the company missed an opportunity. "We offered video rental before Blockbuster," recalls Keyes. "But we fired before we said ready, aim—and we didn't have any of the computer infrastructure or inventory management tools in place to manage returns."

Another more recent example involves Lance Armstrong and his Live Strong initiative. 7-Eleven had been working with Lance Armstrong, his trainer, and his team in developing a line of high-performance foods. "Think of it as the Gatorade of fast food," says Keyes. "What do you eat before you go play ball?"

While they were in the midst of those discussions, Armstrong introduced the Live Strong yellow armband to support his cancer foundation. "We're seeing these armbands on his people," says Keyes. "This is a trend that we had the opportunity to catch before it took off in the stores. We missed it. By the time I asked the question, 'Can we sell those?' they were sold out."

Of course, for every example of an opportunity missed, there's an example of one 7-Eleven is capitalizing on, even creating. An example is the aluminum bottle.

"We sell a lot of Budweiser beer," notes Keyes. "In fact, we're their largest customer. But it's become a commoditized product in a lot of places because mass retailers are selling a twelve-pack of beer for cost to get traffic into their stores. So we're always trying to find ways to differentiate."

So, 7-Eleven imported a hot trend from Japan, where all manner of carbonated beverages are being sold in aluminum bottles. "We took the idea to Budweiser and said we'd like to work with you to develop an aluminum bottle." This represented a major investment and Budweiser was initially resistant. Working through a collaborative process, however, 7-Eleven convinced them that their stores would be the ideal test market for this packaging concept. "The intent of this whole program is to come up with a way to sell beer and capture premium. First, it's a cooler-looking package, but it actually has some differentiating product attributes as well. It keeps the beer fresher and colder longer than traditional glass bottles or cans.

"Will this product work? I don't know, but so far it's actually been quite a successful product in our tests," says Keyes. And it furthers a cultural shift that 7-Eleven needs to make to stay competitive.

"Ultimately that's my goal—27,000 stores, 350,000 people that are engaged . . . that are saying, 'Hey, check this new package out' or 'I just saw this new idea in some mom-and-pop store in Thailand. Let's get this back to the merchandising people.' That's what I want. It's a cultural shift that starts with my instilling a sense of intellectual curiosity and healthy competition in the management ranks.

"My CIO never wants to get an e-mail from me saying, 'Did you see this new technology that could be relevant in our stores?' He should always be on the cusp of the emerging trends and be telling *me* about these new things.

"It's not a 'gotcha' culture I'm describing, and I'm not trying to bring back old turf battles. It's more a spirited competition to see who's going to come up with the newest, latest, and greatest way to satisfy the customer."

Gabriella Santiago had not been VP of U.S. Operations for No-Frills Rental Car long before the "perfect storm" hit. Four months into her new job, she noticed a significant reduction in rental volume for reasons that defied easy explanation. Typically, rentals slowed when the economy slowed, and business travel dropped off, but all the economic indicators were positive. Business travelers were still renting cars; they just weren't renting them from No-Frills.

Moving down her mental checklist, she next assessed turnaround times and labor cost measures. Never better. She was perplexed. She had never run up against this sort of situation before. Typically, when there was a problem, she tweaked a few dials, adjusted a few levers, and resolved the issue. She couldn't tweak her way out of this hole, however.

So, she picked up the monthly volume report one more time and scrutinized the breakdowns in the appendix for further in-

sight. This is where she discovered her answer. No-Frills was losing a disproportionate amount of business at the busiest U.S. air-
ports, where a big-name competitor, *Glide-n-Ride,* was piloting a
Terminal Drop initiative. Frequent renters could call ahead and
arrange to drop off their rental cars directly at the terminal. A
Glide-n-Ride employee would meet them, hand them their re-
ceipt, and return the car to the lot for an extra $20. The manage-
ment team at No-Frills had actually discussed this idea three
months before, when Glide-n-Ride announced their initiative
with great fanfare, but they had quickly dismissed it. They assumed the initiative would fail as had so many of Glide-n-Ride's
nutty schemes. Who would pay $20 to save ten minutes? It turns
out . . . a lot of busy business people.

No-Frills had always prided itself on the economical, consistent quality experience it offered its customers; her fellow managers were loath to go out on a limb. But Gabriella realized that
Terminal Drop was a game-changing move, and they had to react
swiftly. They had already seen a good number of their most valued
repeat customers switch to Glide-n-Ride. She marshaled the facts,
conducted quick research with preferred renters, and presented a
strong case for following Glide-n-Ride into the market . . . and up-
ping the ante. Not only would No-Frills allow preferred renters to
return vehicles at the terminal, they could pick them up there,
too . . . with sufficient notice. She called the program Rent & Roll.

Within six months, No-Frills had recovered the ground it had
lost and had started to eat into Glide-n-Ride's share of the business
traveler segment. Looking back on the experience, Gabriella recognized where No-Frills had stumbled—because of the blinders it
was wearing—but she took pride in how the organization had finally acknowledged the problem and embraced the solution.

Any other organization type can improve by striving to become resilient, but not the Military Precision organization. It offers an alternative destination. The Resilient model is characterized by a
high degree of autonomy and flexibility at all levels; as a result it's

an expensive organization to run. The genius of the Military Precision model is that it gets the execution at minimal cost, and that is critical for organizations with a heavy transactional focus. The Military Precision organization draws from a broader labor pool and has systematized many day-to-day decisions, so it is more inexpensive to run. Pursuing certain resilient behaviors would generate unnecessary expenses and only undermine this model's efficiency. Indeed, in applying the preventive treatments suggested in this chapter, you should ensure that you don't go overboard and subvert what makes the model work (e.g., by overpaying for bells and whistles you don't need). Military Precision is tried and true; it works.

NINE

THE RESILIENT ORGANIZATION
As Good as It Gets

Flexible enough to adapt quickly to external market shifts, the Resilient organization remains steadfastly focused on and aligned behind a coherent business strategy. This forward-looking and self-correcting type of organization anticipates changes routinely and addresses them proactively. When it does hit a bump in the road—as all companies do—the Resilient organization distinguishes itself in its response, which is immediate, thorough, and constructive. It attracts motivated team players and offers them not only a stimulating work environment, but also the resources and authority necessary to solve complex problems.

Resilient is the healthiest of all the organizational types. The firm is in good working order, but that's no invitation to complacency. Consistently resilient companies know better than to believe their own press. They're always scanning the horizon for the next competitive battle or market innovation.

Resilient organizations—as the name implies—adapt and recover lost ground quickly, because they have a coherent, focused organizational model. Organizationally speaking, they're in excellent shape—as close to "zero defects" as it gets. Not surprisingly, our research confirms that people in Resilient companies report "better than average" profitability more often than do respondents from any other organizational type.

Nothing exists "just because" in the Resilient organization;

every position, process, and policy has a purpose . . . and that purpose is aligned with the strategic objectives of the enterprise. Does that mean that Resilient companies are problem-free or that they're on autopilot? No. Resilience is not an end state. It's a never-ending journey. Once achieved, it is not maintained without continuing effort. The companies we feature in this chapter and the next have demonstrated the hallmarks of resilient behavior, but they, too, deal with ongoing organizational challenges. In fact, Caterpillar—the company we devote the next chapter to—is a case study in Resilience, precisely because it has rebounded so successfully from the adversity it encountered in the 1980s.

The Road to Resilience is littered with bumps and potholes that can derail a company's progress. No organization can anticipate or prevent all of these unexpected detours, but the Resilient organization handles them better than most . . . and when it is diverted or delayed, it bounces back more readily. Why? Because it has clear and compelling guiding principles and faith in its people and their collective conviction. Management isn't pulling up the organization by its roots every three months to see if it's growing; neither does it leave people to their own devices without an ethical compass to guide them. The Resilient organization fosters a culture grounded in core values that are understood, endorsed, lived, and reinforced by everyone.

TOP TEN ORGANIZATIONAL TRAITS

So, what does it feel like to work in a Resilient organization? In a word, fulfilling. All of the organization's building blocks perform as they should, both individually and collectively. In fact, the hallmark of the Resilient organization is the seamless manner in which all four building blocks—decision rights, information, motivators, and structure—integrate with one another to drive the organization and its performance forward. This seamless alignment is what enables these organizations to demonstrate the following ten winning behaviors . . . which, together, drive results.

1. Entertain the Inconceivable

Resilient companies benchmark themselves—not against others in their industry, but against the theoretical limits of the human imagination. They take the view that anything that can be conceived can be done. These organizations reach beyond best-in-class in looking for role models. They look past their market, the next five years, the status quo in preparing their organizations to compete. They imagine bogeymen around every corner. Resilient organizations are the first to recognize a burning platform; in fact, they often light the match. They see the handwriting on the wall and anticipate and adapt their organizations to change, always with a focused and productive sense of urgency. They break the mold, so they can be the first to cast the next one.

Fred Smith created the overnight shipping business. Before he founded FedEx, the industry did not exist. He had an idea in college that as business and society became more automated, the need for quick replacement computer parts would grow. Organizations would come to rely on keeping their computers up and running. That meant a faster, more dependable and more far-reaching delivery system for vital components. "It was that simple an observation," notes Smith.

What was simple in theory, however, was anything but simple to execute. To realize his ambition, Smith had to finance and build a nationwide, hub-and-spoke network (before, incidentally, the major airlines did); anything less would have been inadequate. "The problem with FedEx," says Smith, "was that you couldn't start small and expand, as you could with most businesses." So, the twenty-nine-year-old Smith put up his own cash, that of his family, and $90 million in venture capital to set up a twenty-five-city network. "We leased some planes and then started to test the system. For two weeks, we flew empty boxes back and forth throughout the country. Then, on April 17, 1973, we went live."[1]

The rest is history . . . a history of entertaining the inconceivable.

FedEx's days of pushing the envelope—literally—continue to this day. After approximately two years, the company broke even and quickly dominated the industry it had created: domestic express shipping. "We were the high-flyer, number one in the express business and growing like crazy every year," notes corporate vice president and twenty-five-year FedEx veteran Bill Cahill.[2]

In 1989, the company broke the mold again and made a dramatic bid to extend its presence internationally. It acquired a struggling outfit called Flying Tigers. As Cahill describes it, "It was a big, primarily Asia-driven, freight company with big, old planes." The company had been steadily losing money, and its operations were shrinking. FedEx employees were mystified. They could not comprehend what their fast-growing successful company would want with Flying Tigers. Thanks to a concerted and massive communications effort, however, they soon came to understand the appeal: international landing rights. As Cahill observes, "You can't replicate those international landing rights today. You couldn't buy them no matter how much money you had."

In what has become typical FedEx style, the company acquired Flying Tigers and absorbed all five thousand or so of its employees. The communications effort was just as thorough with these new employees as it was with FedEx veterans. "There was no stone unturned, it was an A to Z effort, and it took a few years," says Cahill. "As we integrated Flying Tigers, we said to their employees, 'You're now part of our company. You're part of FedEx, and these are our plans for our collective future. Here's how we're going to treat you. This is how we're going to convert existing programs you have.' It was a dedicated and collaborative effort."

Now the world's largest full-service, all-cargo airline, FedEx focused on global express shipping until the mid-1990s, when it lit yet another match under its comfortable and profitable platform. FedEx scanned its horizons and saw the likely impact of e-mail on the document side of its express shipping stronghold. Rather than throw up walls and hunker down, FedEx embraced the Internet as a transactional access point for customers. With the launch of fedex.com in 1994, FedEx was exploiting the Web to provide customers with instant information about their packages. Meanwhile, it acknowledged the maturing market for express document delivery and moved into the ground-based small package business with its acquisition of The Caliber System in 1998. Caliber's crown jewel, RPS, provided FedEx with a foothold in the traditional ground shipping business and anticipated the marketplace's needs for a more comprehensive air/ground solution.

Another of Caliber's subsidiaries, Viking Freight, was merged with a subsequent acquisition, American Freightways, in 2001 to create FedEx Freight. Now, FedEx could offer customers an unmatched portfolio of shipping services.

Enough? No, FedEx has never limited its aspirations to the industry it created and now competes in. Once again anticipating the needs of the market—in this case consumers and small- to medium-sized businesses—FedEx expanded upon its long-term partnership with Kinko's by acquiring it in 2004 and rebranding it FedEx Kinko's. With this acquisition, FedEx instantly established a worldwide retail storefront for pickups and drop-offs and positioned itself on the passing lane of the digital information superhighway. As Bill Cahill puts it, "Kinko's was known as your friendly, local copy center, but we saw it as an access point for all kinds of professional services and digital economy transactions."

Today, FedEx is a $27 billion enterprise consisting of four core operating companies—Express, Ground, Freight, and Kinko's—and employing a quarter of a million people worldwide. It has consistently recognized and realized the inconceivable, from the very concept of overnight package delivery, to combining air and ground transportation into one integrated offering, to leading the fights on Capitol Hill to deregulate the airline and trucking industries. It has demonstrated consistent resilience for thirty-plus years.

2. Build a Culture of Commitment and Accountability

Every organization makes commitments. It's how they define these commitments, translate them into decision rights, and measure performance against them that distinguishes Resilient organizations. Commitments and the decision rights that result are not soft or subject to interpretation; they are etched in stone and obvious to all, particularly to the individuals held accountable. In fact, a Resilient organization's commitments are hard currency backed by the "gold standard" of full and clear accountability. Just as people accept paper money in a gold-backed monetary system, the market invests on the mere promises of a Resilient company . . . because they know that promises made by this firm are as good as results. They are backed by appropriate and unambiguous decision rights that are transparent, both internally and externally. There's nothing to hide and nowhere to hide it. Therefore, shifting blame is a futile exercise. Welcome to a true meritocracy; this is an organization that extracts the best from its people, because it expects and rewards no less.

Nissan Motor Co. Ltd. distributes a *Values Reference Manual* to all new managers in which thirty-two key words are explicitly defined. *Commitment* is defined as "taking responsibility for accomplishing the objective. The objective to be accomplished is expressed by numerical values, and pledged. Once individuals have committed, they must achieve the objective except under extraordinary circumstances. When they do not accomplish the objective, individuals must be prepared to accept the consequences." In October of 1999, now Chairman and CEO Carlos Ghosn defined "consequences" in vivid terms when he put his own job on the line if the company failed to accomplish the three objectives of Nissan's Revival Plan within three years. "I said that if any one of the three main commitments—any *one* of them—was missed, I would resign, and with me all the members of the Executive Committee," recalls Ghosn.[3] "And this helped a lot in communicating the sense and meaning of 'commitment' within the organization."

At that time, Nissan was mired in nearly $20 billion of debt and burdened with overcapacity and an aging product line; in fact, the ailing automaker had failed to turn a profit for eight years. It was an organization caught up in the internal blame game, so focused on finger-pointing, it was squandering its prodigious engineering talents and falling further behind in the marketplace. Indeed, while its rival Toyota thrived, Nissan was on the brink of bankruptcy and searching for salvation. The Nissan Revival Plan, developed by nine cross-functional teams (CFTs) of Nissan high-potential managers, promised that salvation, and the organization delivered . . . well ahead of schedule.

The transformation of Nissan is one of the great business turn-around stories of recent times and—while a tribute to the leadership abilities of Carlos Ghosn—it is also a paean to the people of Nissan who shouldered the bulk of the bottom-line responsibility and got the job done. Today, Nissan is on the verge of embarking on its third three-year plan, each one as ambitious as the last, and is further refining decision rights through what they call DOA—delegations of authority. These are simple statements posted on the company's intranet clearly defining who does what and who is accountable.

Ghosn hastens to add: "Everything is quantified. What you cannot measure, you should not do. And measurement is not only about how much you should do and how far you should go, but also about *when* you should do it. Timing is extremely important to the organization. Any objective that is set without regard to timing is irrelevant. It exists in a vacuum. So, we are deliberate and precise in placing milestones on the organizational calendar."

3. Move the Goal Posts . . . Every Three Years

Most Resilient companies, like Nissan, are known for their rolling and continuous transformations. To motivate employees and move the organization forward, management moves out the goal posts, typically every few years . . . whether or not they feel the hot breath of competition on their necks. These transformation agendas are grounded in the foundational values and principles of the organization and have clearly defined end states; everyone understands the destination, and the guideposts they must pass along the way. But the route is not mapped. Each unit, team, and individual must define the journey and chart a course. The organizational building blocks are designed and aligned to facilitate their progress, so everyone has the right information, incentives, and authority to be effective. The objectives to be achieved are ambitious; they are designed to stretch the organization and the people who populate it, but not until they break. Senior management needs to exercise its best judgment and intuition in setting goals that are challenging but manageable.

As company head Carlos Ghosn observes, "We constantly go from three years to three years." When he took over the reins in 1999, the organization embarked on the ambitious Nissan Revival Plan, which not only restored the company to profitability within three years, it catapulted it to the top of the large automotive heap in terms of operating margin. No sooner had the organization achieved its NRP objectives, but it was off and running toward Nissan 180 (one million additional cars sold, 8 percent operating margin, 0 debt). Commencing in 2005, it embarks on Nissan Value Up, a new three-year transformation program aimed at improving process quality in areas outside of manufacturing (e.g., Logistics, Finance, Human Resources).

Carlos Ghosn describes Nissan's approach to "moving the goalposts": "First we outline a vision, which is usually a little vague, a little tentative. It's meant to put the organization in the right mindset and condition behavior, but it won't tell you what to do tomorrow or one year from now. From the vision, we develop—over several months—a three-year plan. This is the way we work.

"Everybody knows the plan, helps prepare the plan, executes the plan. The plan, in turn, drives the budget, which is a yearly objective. So you move from a long-term mindset to three-year goals to annual budget commitments."

Beyond defining outcomes and key milestones, Nissan's senior management does not dictate a path for achieving the organization's objectives. For example, in product development, product directors control every aspect of the process of designing and building a car. As one VP observes, "We have six or seven program directors, and no two of them work in a similar way . . . so the process of what you do between milestones can be very different from one vehicle program to another. The idea is not to document the process but to be very clear on what is required at each milestone . . . who participates in decision-making and who is accountable for which outputs."

"In general, ours is a very pragmatic approach," notes Ghosn. "We agree on the right set of breakthrough objectives for the next three years. Then we determine how the organization needs to adapt through what we call 'accelerated *kaizen*,' a fast-track, continuous improvement process, something the Japanese do very well. Then we assess the tools at our disposal, and we say, 'Okay, what should we introduce? What should we modify? What should we change about the way we do business to deliver the results?' And we fine-tune all the time and make small step changes."

4. Show the Courage of Your Convictions

Resilient companies do not follow fashion. They do not succumb to the latest business fads, nor do they court the fancy of Wall Street. By the same token, Resilient companies do not accept the status quo as an article of faith simply because "that's the way it's always been done." They chart a strategic course based on their best instincts and information, and they stay the course as long as their own market intelligence validates it. The same holds true for organizational changes. They shake up things as necessary—that's part of being resilient—but they don't change for change's sake or to curry favor with the board, analysts, or shareholders. Resilient organizations have faith in their people and their capacity to make effective decisions and execute them even as strategic objectives change. Therefore, they are more sure-footed in pursuing these objectives . . . and in dealing with temporary setbacks. They don't collect "flavor of the month" organization improvements that others are implementing and try to "shoehorn" them into their model, but they also don't look the other way when the need for improvement is apparent. They have a solid foundation built around core values that not only guide decision-making but also inspire and motivate employees at all levels.

Since its inception, FedEx has taken an inordinate interest in its people and their satisfaction, and has stood by its "people-first" principles through good times and bad. In fact, FedEx Express, the original and largest operating company, has long distilled its operating philosophy as PSP—People, Service, Profit. Bill Cahill explains: "This enterprise is a three-legged stool. It was founded on the ability to satisfy employees (people), customers (service), and shareholders (profit), and absent our ability to satisfy any *one* of those constituencies, the enterprise doesn't work. Fred Smith has always said, 'If you take care of the employees, they will take care of the customers, who will, in turn, provide profit to the shareholders.' But he takes it a step further and completes the loop. Profits not only accrue to the benefit of shareholders; they also cycle back to employees in the form of better benefits, incentive bonuses, improved pay, and brighter career prospects. And we also take the profits and reinvest them in the business to make our service better to customers."

Founder and CEO Fred Smith draws on his military service in Vietnam in defining leadership: "In the military, you have to trust that people will put in extra effort to achieve organizational goals. If not, people could be killed or maimed. So to me, the short definition of leadership is getting discretionary effort out of people. I don't want my employees thinking about the minimum amount of effort they have to put in to keep from getting fired. I want them thinking about the best possible job they could do if everybody was giving one hundred percent of their effort."[4]

With that in mind, FedEx long ago adopted a "no layoff" philosophy, and it has stood by that philosophy for thirty-plus years . . . even when it became clear that it was hurting the bottom line. "Shortly after 9/11, the economy went into a tailspin, and we hit a period where growth in our air express business was stagnant," recalls Cahill. "The market was maturing. We had done everything we possibly could to reconfigure our domestic express network so that it was in line with our business growth potential. But we still had too much overhead in the form of professional and managerial staff."

So, the company launched an initiative designed to improve profitability and staff efficiency at FedEx Express. While the initiative centered on process redesign, it also included a voluntary separation and early-retirement program, which proved so generous that 3,600 people ended up taking advantage of it, more than the company had anticipated. Bill Cahill remembers attending one of the many good-bye parties held across the company, and was surprised at the positive reaction. "There were a lot of tears in the audience, but after the ceremony I went around and talked to a lot of people, and, quite frankly, people were saying, 'Boy, FedEx sure treated me well.' And these are people that are on their way out the door, and they're saying, 'This is too good a deal to turn down.' It was sad from the standpoint of old friends parting in large numbers, but at the same time people were saying, 'Well, it's on to the next thing in my life because FedEx took care of me.' Overall, it went over exceptionally well. Now, did it cost us money? It sure did, more than maybe it could have. But in the long run, it was the investment in the positive employee relations that will serve us well, and people will remember that FedEx treated people right.

"PSP is the underpinning of the people focus around here. When I first got here and the company was still in start-up mode— running fast to keep up with customer demand—we didn't have a policy manual. We made up the rules as we went along. So you did things that made sense and did right by people. That's a judgment call, and as you get bigger, those calls become codified and policies are created. But our fundamental culture hasn't changed. We've had to make some hard business decisions, but those who have left, those who have stayed, and those who have recently come on board know that we stand by our people.

"I used to tell managers that came to work for me, 'You can screw up every now and then, but if you lose sight of managing your people, if you screw up on the people part of the business, you won't last here very long.' People are forgiving of mistakes from an operational standpoint, but you don't mess with your people. You treat them right. You treat them with respect and dignity, do the right thing by them within the confines of the rules and regulations you have, and you'll be fine as a manager. It is still a roller coaster, mind you. There's something new every day. The organization continues to shift and change, but it's still FedEx—it's just a bigger, broader FedEx."

While demonstrating respect for Nissan and its employees, Ghosn did not let the "sacred cows" of Japanese business like lifetime employment, *keiretsu* cross-holdings, and seniority-based promotions get in the organization's way.[5] A non-Nissan gaijin (foreigner), he leveraged his "outsider status" and the courage of his convictions to chart a new course. He promptly shut down plants, laid off employees, and tore asunder cozy supply networks and equity cross-investments with traditional business partners. He broke with Japanese business practice again when he built a new assembly plant in Canton, Mississippi, and is shaking up the market with groundbreaking new vehicle designs and exploratory outsourcing relationships with India and China.

"We've transformed a culture of analysis and what I would call 'passive consensus' into a culture of action and stretch," says Ghosn. "Nothing is discussed without leading to a decision, and that decision leads to an action, and that action is always a stretch. With every single action, we are trying to go a little bit beyond the perceived limits of the organization, step by step. That's how you increase the potential of the whole company."

Another cultural innovation is transparency. Says Ghosn, "Transparency is obviously a little bit new to an organization based in Japan, a society known for its inscrutability. But we were crystal clear from the beginning, outlining three years in advance exactly what we were going to do and how we were going to do it— not only internally, but also externally."

Finally, Nissan has embraced diversity in a way that is unique to Japanese businesses, which tend to view foreign incursions as a threat or a distraction. As Ghosn points out, "We've totally up-ended this notion by saying diversity is a wealth. We have American people, Japanese people, French people working together. We've made sure that the Japanese youngsters in our organization can access jobs of responsibility; they don't have to wait until they hit fifty-five to be considered for a corporate officer-level position. We're promoting more women into decision-making roles in Design, in Engineering, in Marketing, in the sales process. They're our consumers, too."

In short, Nissan has demonstrated the courage of its convictions in a different way than has FedEx. It has broken with tradition and charted a new course, but, still, it has drawn on the underlying will and conviction of its people to fulfill its bold ambitions.

5. Bounce Back from Adversity

Even the most Resilient organizations encounter setbacks. Healthy DNA does not protect a system from all external risk factors; it does, however, facilitate a quick internal reaction. When Resilient organizations suffer a discontinuity in their marketplace—be it technological innovation, economic downturn, or competitive challenge—they detect it early and mobilize a response quickly. They don't waste time and resources assigning blame and applying makeup. They confront the enemy head on. They cauterize wounds and defend core market positions. More important, they seize offensive opportunities to pursue growth aggressively. *Resilience* is defined as "the ability to recover strength, spirits, etc., quickly." These organizations live up to that name.

With more than $50 billion in revenues, Procter & Gamble is America's largest household- and consumer-products company and a master brand builder, but even masters "hit the wall," to use CFO Clayton Daley's expression. In the two quarters before

A.G. Lafley took the helm as CEO, P&G issued four profit warnings and saw its stock price plummet 43 percent. For the first time, the company failed to double its sales in the 1990s, a goal it had achieved every decade since 1940. Losing share ascendancy to competitors Kimberly-Clark and Colgate-Palmolive in some of its core product lines, Procter & Gamble was also losing leverage with customers like Wal-Mart who were growing more and more powerful. Lafley, a twenty-three-year P&G veteran took a long, hard look at the organization. He replaced nearly half of the organization's top 30 executives and lopped 9,600 jobs from the company payroll. He outsourced IT and some manufacturing, and refocused the company around its core strengths and product lines.

At the same time, however, he has opened up new horizons by suggesting that half of all new products should come from outside the company and reinforcing cross-functional collaboration. The result is restored market leadership, strong profitability, and solid shareholder returns during Lafley's tenure, not to mention new innovations like Iams-branded pet health insurance, Swiffer Dusters, and Mr. Clean AutoDry. Says Clayton Daley, "In 2000, we were recovering from a time when a number of our new brands and launches had failed. We were occupied with turning the business around: restructuring, downsizing, and rebuilding our big brands. Now, we're growing again, and we're focused on sustaining that growth, and setting ourselves up so we don't get in trouble again. Three years ago the guy in the corner office said, 'We're going to use total shareholder return (TSR) as our measure of value.[6] We're going to evaluate management performance on it, base bonus payments on it, and use it as a strategic tool.' And by now, it's institutionalized; it provides us with a standardized measure to evaluate performance and investment choices at every level of management. We put all strategic projections through the TSR screen, so that we have some confidence that every strategy can build shareholder value. You could walk into any general manager's office in this company and ask somebody about TSR and they could tell you what it is and how they use it to evaluate their business decisions, large and small."[7]

★   ★   ★

While FedEx's failures are few, there is one that springs readily to the lips of old-timers: Zapmail. Zapmail was the company's attempt in the early 1980s to create a high-speed digital facsimile system. It made perfect sense; a large portion of FedEx's revenues at the time came from moving documents . . . and fax machines were not as cheap and ubiquitous as they are today. The idea of transmitting documents electronically was a natural evolution of FedEx's core business. "Unfortunately, the Zapmail technology was built around a very large satellite that could only be launched by the space shuttle," notes founder and Chairman Fred Smith. "And the space shuttle blew up."[8]

Soon fax machines and printers were on desks everywhere, and Zapmail's window of opportunity had closed. As Bill Cahill, head of HR, says, "It was one of those things that didn't work, so we shut it down, absorbed all the employees that were assigned to it, and moved on. It's not like everything has always worked around here. But I think that success is when you learn from your failures. We learned a valuable lesson and turned our attention to developing a worldwide express market with the acquisition of Flying Tigers. Everybody got over it and said, 'Okay, let's move on, let's go get more boxes and documents.'"

Smith sums up the experience and FedEx's ability to bounce back from adversity with this observation: "The point is, at that juncture, we knew we had to change. We couldn't just sit there. Companies that don't recognize that their business is going to be commoditized and don't take some risks—some of which are going to work and some of which aren't—are going to end up getting punched up by the marketplace."[9]

6. Think Horizontal

When you think of most organizations, you think of a hierarchy, a structure that operates from top to bottom. In business, we are conditioned to think in vertical terms. The chain of command runs up and down; you are generally promoted up a level. Resilient organizations, however, manage to introduce a second dimension to their world view. They capture full value by flattening their organizations and working across vertical boundaries, breaking down silos, transferring best practices, collaborating cross-functionally, and promoting laterally. They think horizontal . . . and reap the benefits of a more coordinated, efficient, and broadly competent organization.

The flow of information up and down and across organizational boundaries is critical to maintaining a Resilient organization. If someone in another business unit or function can serve a customer better with information you have, you give it to her. You do so because you recognize that a greater good is served and because you are motivated through shared objectives, common metrics, or outright bonuses for working collaboratively. Silo walls and NIH ("not invented here") thinking fade into oblivion in the Resilient organization. Instead, it's how do we get ahead . . . so I get ahead?

Much of the success of Nissan's turnaround can be attributed to the nine Cross-Functional Teams (CFTs) that engineered and executed it. Composed of promising middle managers, these CFTs were the horizontal agent of change at Nissan. Having used CFTs in previous turnaround situations, Carlos Ghosn was a strong advocate and spent his first days at Nissan identifying the high-potential men and women he would recruit for these teams. Their mission—and no one failed to accept it—was to take on one of the key drivers of performance at Nissan (e.g., product complexity, organizational structure, business development) and come up with a plan to fix it . . . within three months, while doing their regular jobs.[10] The ultimate goal of the CFTs was to resurrect the flagging company; along the way, they broke the "black box" of Nissan's functional silos. Today, CFTs still exist across the organization, challenging the status quo and illuminating opportunities.

"In my experience," notes Ghosn, "executives in a company rarely reach across boundaries. Typically, engineers prefer solving problems with other engineers; salespeople like to work with fellow salespeople, and Americans feel more comfortable with other Americans. The trouble is that people working in the functional or regional teams tend not to ask themselves as many hard questions as they should."[11] The genius of the CFT is quite simple. "It's people from different geographies and different functions and different generations working together—not to address a specific functional problem or a specific regional problem—but to address a company opportunity from the only two perspectives that matter: that of customer satisfaction and company profit."

FedEx stays horizontal in a variety of ways. First, it has never had in more than thirty years of operation more than five layers of management. Notes Bill Cahill, "It's been that way since the beginning, and the reason is simple: it's to keep information flowing up and down without having to go through fifteen to twenty layers of complex organization."

The company has also woven a horizontal dimension into its new credo: "Operate independently, compete collectively, manage collaboratively." Given its steady expansion over the years into new sectors of the global economy, FedEx Corporate is now an umbrella organization encompassing four main operating companies and a host of other businesses and functional services. Senior management feels strongly that these companies should operate independently as they each offer distinct "products." Cahill elaborates, "We've got FedEx Express and FedEx Ground, two companies which provide shipping services, but to unique customer segments, which require very different networks. These companies have fundamentally different service characteristics, so they need to 'operate independently.' You're not going to mix up a package that's due at eight-thirty the next morning with a parcel that's not due for four days. But at the same time, they both carry the FedEx brand, therefore they're 'competing collectively.' These businesses are linked to one another, share with one another, are accountable to one another. And they share some of the same support services (e.g., IT and marketing) provided by the central FedEx Services company."

It's the "manage collaboratively" part of the triad, however, that brings home the horizontality of FedEx. All of the operating companies have a long history of cross-functional task forces, but now the enterprise is taking this approach to a whole new level by, among other things, creating the Senior Management Committee (SMC). Made up of the CEOs of Express, Ground, Freight, and Kinko's and the heads of Finance, Legal, Marketing, Communications, Sales, and IT, the SMC collectively manages the enterprise, while its members also manage their individual units within the enterprise.

As Bill Cahill points out, "There's an awful lot of collaboration that goes on and has always gone on. Now we are saying, 'We will manage between companies, and we need to collaborate,' which quite frankly—from a staff-guy standpoint—is the most difficult of the three operating imperatives, because you can't do things with authority, you have to use the power of persuasion. You either build a good case or people do not buy in. It's a very subtle balance you have to strike. You don't impose change. You don't order things. You try and build consensus, good business cases, and once you do that, it becomes obvious to everyone, 'Oh yeah, that's a pretty good deal,' and then you can move forward collectively."

7. Self-Correct

Resilient organizations have developed and institutionalized internal mechanisms for finding and correcting problems before they reach task-force or profit-warning proportions. Information is timely, robust, and accessible to those who need it, and systems and processes have feedback loops that are automatic; they don't have to be triggered from the outside. In short, Resilient companies are self-correcting organisms that learn as they grow. As the DNA building blocks are refined over time, the overall organization becomes more intelligent and agile. It moves up step-by-step until it reaches a whole new level of performance. The organizational characteristic we're describing here is more than an early-warning light; it's a self-generating remedial system that fixes problems before they even reach the radar screen.

Procter & Gamble's chief financial officer, Clayton Daley, wears many hats. He is responsible not only for traditional accounting issues but he also serves in a more strategic role as the arbiter of quality growth. "We focus on sustainable top-line growth: getting our initiative success rate up and making sure that we have a disciplined qualification process for launching new products—whether they're completely new products, geographic expansions, or updates to an existing brand. How do we meet or beat our sales targets? How do we deliver quality growth, without taking excessive risks?

"The old game around here was: 'If I'm a brand manager, my job is to sell my project to management, and hope I've moved on to my next job before the results come in.' If you've got a rigorous system, which we do now, of going back and evaluating your batting average on these projects, and holding management accountable, then you've got a system that is very self-correcting. When I see gamesmanship today, it's people promising a little less, because they know they will be held accountable. That's not all bad. If that means they have a little more difficulty making the sale on their project, then that's exactly the discipline I'd like to have in the system."

The nine Cross-Functional Teams originally charged with developing the Nissan Revival Plan in 1999 proved so effective that they continue their work to this day. In fact, three more global teams have been deployed, and still other CFTs will be part of Nissan's new three-year quality initiative, Value-Up, as well as the integration work associated with Nissan's alliance with Renault. Initially tasked with extracting efficiencies from individual functional areas (e.g., Purchasing, R&D, Sales, and Marketing) the CFTs have gone beyond their initial mandate and now regularly tackle cross-functional issues and opportunities (e.g., how to sell cars to women). If they spot a problem, they go ahead and fix it, knowing that if they don't, another CFT will be formed to do it. In short, they have become the vehicle through which a now resilient Nissan self-corrects.

"We always tell the CFTs, 'You are the wake-up call for this organization,'" comments CEO Carlos Ghosn. "You are the people who are responsible for systematically looking outside, benchmarking, seeing the dysfunctions, and coming up with better ideas for higher levels of performance."

8. Listen to the Complainers

Resilient organizations do not ignore squeaky wheels; they listen and learn. Complaints are, by their very nature, unpleasant. No one likes to hear what they are doing wrong, but Resilient companies understand that complaints are also opportunities . . . invitations to improve what isn't working smoothly. Therefore, Resilient companies institutionalize mechanisms for surfacing and addressing dissatisfaction not only among customers but also among employees. These are the individuals "at the coal face" who really understand how the business operates . . . or doesn't. To enhance performance, you must find ways to solicit their input—town hall meetings, ethics hotlines, interviews with customers and customers' customers. Employees, in particular, need to feel free to air substantive grievances without fear of retribution. All of this is so much posturing, however, if the organization does not do anything to acknowledge and address the behavior being questioned. Resilient organizations act on complaints and end up making positive changes to the organization that accrue to the benefit of everyone, not just the original complainer.

"We have formal complaint systems at all of our companies," says FedEx HR head Bill Cahill. "Express, for example, calls theirs the GFTP (Guaranteed Fair Treatment Program). Moreover, there are also well-understood informal ways for employees to register dissatisfaction. Everybody's got an 'open door' policy here.

"If I have a grievance, I get to take it to my boss and say, 'Look, I disagree with that decision,' or 'I feel I should have gotten that job,'" says Cahill. An employee has to put his complaint in writing, and his boss has to give an answer within a specified time frame. If the complainant doesn't like the decision, he can take it up to the next level. Some cases progress to the very top of the organization, where a committee composed of rotating senior officers and executive officers issues a final decision.

"The point is, whether you win or lose, your voice is heard," notes Cahill. "And management gains valuable intelligence about the organization. Over time, if you keep hearing the same complaint out of the same area, you say, 'Where there's smoke, there's fire. Somebody go look into that.' Again and again, I've seen positive changes made as a result of these complaints, beyond the satisfaction of the individual."

In addition to formal complaint reviews, FedEx circulates employee surveys every year . . . in every business. Says Cahill, "We basically say to employees, 'Tell us what you think, anonymously.' Over a two-week period, we can poll a couple of hundred thousand people." Questions run the gamut. They cover employees' impressions of their manager, the company, pay and benefits, and, importantly, the service that FedEx provides its customers. The surveys even poll employees on their intentions to stay with or leave the company.

The reports that are generated as a result of this feedback do not languish in a binder; they are incorporated in management development plans and monitored on an ongoing basis. The data are cut down to the individual manager level, so each manager gets a clear read on what percentage of her employees reacted favorably, neutrally, or unfavorably to each question regarding her performance. All these individual scores are rolled up into a "leadership index." As Cahill points out, "Managers understand that if they don't treat their people right, it will come back to haunt them."

"Now we try not to make this feedback a final report card per se, since there is always a temptation for people to play with the numbers to get rid of the boss. It may be a bad work group that we've just sent that manager into to clean up. And so you have to look behind the numbers, but over time, a meaningful trend develops. You're getting a score every single year. You're building a track record on how well you manage people. And your director sees that, and the VP gets a roll-up, the senior VP gets a roll-up, then the operating head, and, ultimately, Smith gets to look at the whole company."

FedEx doesn't listen to just its employees, it assesses how it's doing with customers through a process called SQI (Service Quality Index). Similar to the employee surveys, SQI measures certain key customer satisfaction metrics: "How many packages were delivered right day late? How many packages were delivered wrong day late? How many phone calls didn't we answer within a specified timeframe?" Notes Cahill, "The more egregious our error, the more weight it carries in the scoring formula."

FedEx does not stop there. It also holds customer summits. "It's 'Go talk to the customer,' and we take this to the nth degree," says Cahill. "There are constantly customer summits going on, with marketing people doing research and sales people organizing speakers. Once a year, the Senior Management Committee holds a meeting for all senior vice presidents and above from all the companies, and it's called *The* Customer Summit. And we bring customers in, and we break up into small groups, and sit down and talk to a customer and listen to what they have to say about their experience with FedEx. I did this last summer, and I can assure you they don't bring in just the happy customers. We get to hear about the areas where we can improve as well. Now they're very polite about it, but they make no bones about telling you that your courier isn't polite enough, or you'd better get a new plane because it's not arriving on time.

"You get an instant sense of appreciation—even if you're not in operations or sales—what this business is all about and why we're here."

9. Put Your Motivators Where Your Mouth Is

The Resilient organization does not pay you for one behavior and promote you for another. All oars—both financial (e.g., raises, bonuses, benefits) and nonfinancial (e.g., promotions, transfers, exposure)—pull in the same direction and clearly point toward what is valued. It's not "Yes, I know we should do the right thing for the company . . . but that's not the signal I'm getting from my boss." Another trademark of the Resilient organization is a performance appraisal system that clearly differentiates between above-average and subpar performers. Delivering a negative review is a difficult, often uncomfortable experience, but the alternative is an organization overrun by mediocrity—not just because poor performers stay and fail to improve, but also because strong performers witness this lack of consequence and become disillusioned. A Resilient organization avoids this dilemma by being straight with employees and by linking motivators to what matters.

Everyone at FedEx knows what the corporate objectives are. Every year, CEO Fred Smith solicits the input of the organization and then writes them out . . . for all to see. He reviews recent results, strengths and weaknesses, and priority initiatives and then exhorts the organization to join forces to accomplish the company's goals. He sums up his approach to people management as follows:

"Workers want to know what's expected of them and how they're doing. They have to have report cards. They also want to know what's in it for them, so we put in a lot of award programs, a lot of profit sharing, and a lot of internal promotions. Simple stuff. Just telling people they did a good job. You also have to communicate with your people and make sure they understand that what they're doing means something. We still tell our employees what we always told them: You're delivering the most important commerce in the history of the world. You're not delivering sand and gravel. You're delivering someone's pacemaker, chemotherapy drugs, the part that keeps the F-18s flying, or the legal brief that decides the case."[12]

Bill Cahill elaborates: "We have one simple objective that links everyone, and that is corporate-wide profitability. It may not be in Ground's best interest to take a particular piece of business, but that lower margin may be worth it, if it benefits the corporation—if we get more Express business or Freight business as a result. So, while you operate independently and your pay is, in large part, determined by how you perform as individual companies, there is a fairly significant piece of your annual bonus as an officer that's linked to corporate-wide profitability. And of course, all of your long-term compensation—and we have both cash and stock programs—are based on enterprise performance."

FedEx has made a concerted effort in recent years to raise the performance bar in employee appraisals. "Initially, people had more of an 'everybody-gets-the-same-treatment' mindset," notes Cahill, "and that was probably okay for the Eighties and maybe the early Nineties when we were growing rapidly. The bell curve skewed right. But when we got into the late Nineties and the Two thousands, we realized that we had to take a harder look at what constituted 'good' performance; otherwise we ran the risk of running off our best people. The view was 'Why should I break my back if the guy next to me is delivering half the effort and getting paid the same?' Now, we tell managers, 'There's a pool. Take your very best performers and give them *more* than their share; the worst performers should get less than average. We've watched the bar get raised every year, and the bell curve is more balanced now."

"Now, instead of a hundred percent of your bonus, you can get up to a hundred and fifty percent of your bonus. But if you're at the bottom end, you might get zero percent. But we don't subscribe to the notion of a forced ranking. We may give guidelines, but there's no forcing . . . just steady reinforcement of pay for performance."

Another motivating commitment that FedEx has made is its promotion-from-within policy. "An overwhelming number of employees—up to eighty-five percent of the organization—grew up in the FedEx organization," says twenty-five-year veteran Cahill. "I'm an example of that, but we've got others: the CEO of FedEx Express started as a courier; the executive vice president of International at Express started as a handler. We trained them well. They were successful at what they did, and they got promoted for it. And they've been very successful."

10. Refuse to Rest on Your Laurels

Resilient organizations are not complacent; in fact, they take the view that a little paranoia is good for you. Despite irrefutable success, Resilient companies never gloat or take satisfaction in their victories. They reward their people for a job well done and then move the finish line. To maintain their market leadership, they need to spend more time fine-tuning their organization and less time publicizing their successes. In fact, quite a few Resilient companies have an active aversion to media exposure, however fawning. It demotivates employees and takes the organization's focus off the ball. What matters is what's measured: results.

Procter & Gamble resists compliments and shuns the limelight with the best of them. Chairman, President, and CEO A.G. Lafley is the opposite of flashy. "Though he is arguably one of the most successful CEOs in corporate America today, A.G.'s more or less the same guy he was when I met him twenty-four years ago," says CFO Clayton Daley. And that style carries over to the company, which is presently focused on its core product line and trademark strengths. "Our challenge," notes Daley "is to focus on what P&G does well. We have to always think of ourselves as the underdog. We have put a number of competitors on the defensive. And they are not going to want to stay there."

Carlos Ghosn, architect of one of the most stunning turnarounds in recent business history, opens our interview with the words, "Saying that we are a Resilient company is a generous statement. We're not a Resilient organization, we're *trying* to be a Resilient organization."

He adds, "If you ask the question, 'Would you have done any-thing differently?' I would tell you, 'Everything.' But that's nor-mal. We're in the business of systematically looking for bad news, for the dysfunctions, for what we could have done better. Because these are the seeds for future growth and enhanced performance. For example, before launching our next transformation program 'Nissan Value-Up' we're going to spend a lot of time going over what went wrong with 'Nissan 180.' We delivered on all three commitments; the results are great. It was a successful plan . . . but there is always room to change the process so the next plan will be even more successful and easier to deliver than the last one. You can't just declare a plan successful and agree to do more of the same thing. That's preparing yourself for the fall."

Resilience is not perfection. It is the committed and passionate pursuit of perfection, and the acknowledgment that the journey is the reward, not the destination. Any objective, once achieved, ceases to be worthy; it becomes yet another milestone in a contin-uing quest for even higher levels of performance. The healthiest companies and those with the healthiest potential recognize this reality and focus their attention and energy on driving progress rather than declaring victory. One such company—Caterpillar—is featured in the next chapter.

TEN

CATERPILLAR'S JOURNEY TO RESILIENCE
The Cat That Came Back

Caterpillar Inc. is a $30 billion global company known principally as a manufacturer of large construction and earthmoving equipment. While it operates in many cyclical industries that have been hard-hit by recession over the last several years, Cat has delivered twelve straight years of profit, nearly tripling both its top and bottom lines since 1993. Its global markets reach from Peoria to Pretoria, from New York to New Delhi, with innovative products that routinely win quality awards, and a dealer network that delivers some of the best customer service in the world. In 2003, shareholder returns were the second highest among companies in the Dow Jones Industrial Index, and the *Financial Times* named Cat twenty-seventh in its list of most respected companies in the world. In 2005, *Forbes* magazine listed Cat as the best-managed industrial corporation in America.

Cat is a highly tuned, well-aligned organization where the building blocks of decision rights, information, motivators, and structure are tightly coordinated into a coherent whole. Employees know what the objective is, know what needs to be done to reach it, are motivated to get there, and have the authority to make things happen. As a result, Cat can repeatedly move decisively and quickly in its markets, and has established leadership positions in most of them.

These traits are undergirded by Cat's organization, which has remained fundamentally unchanged for the last fifteen years, compelling proof of precisely how resilient Cat's organization is.

But Cat hasn't always been a Resilient organization. In the 1980s, after enjoying a fifty-year period of uninterrupted profits, Cat's DNA had become so badly misaligned that its very existence was threatened. Today's successful Caterpillar was made possible only through an extreme makeover of all four building blocks.

Cat's market-leading position was built and sustained by superior product technology. Cat has always had world-class engineering capabilities developing innovative products that up until the 1980s customers could not seem to live without, despite Cat's premium pricing. The products also came with superior customer service delivered through a world-class network of independent dealers. As George Schaefer, CEO of Caterpillar from 1985 to 1990, put it, "We decided what the customers needed, built it, and said, 'Here it is.' And things were just fine."[1]

Driven by the strength of its product, Cat used (and still uses) a relatively straightforward "make-ship-sell" business model: machines were manufactured in Cat plants, sold by Cat's marketing divisions around the globe, and then shipped to Cat's independent dealers worldwide. The dealers would then sell the machines to end-users in the construction, transportation, mining, forestry, energy, and other industries.

THE OVERMANAGED ORGANIZATION

But in the 1980s, Cat's market-leading position masked a classically Overmanaged organization. Its highly centralized decision-making process, manifested in a hierarchical central bureaucracy, resulted in a slow, inward-focused organization increasingly out of touch with the market. But because the company had been reliably (and sometimes spectacularly) profitable, any organizational issues went largely ignored if not unnoticed. Glen Barton, who was chairman and CEO of Caterpillar from 1999 to 2004, says that "we had been so successful through the years that no one could envision that we were perhaps not doing as well as we could have been doing."[2]

Caterpillar has always been highly integrated, manufacturing many of the components used in its final products rather than buying them from other companies. In the 1980s it was organized in strong functional divisions—Engineering, Manufacturing, Pricing, Marketing, etc.—each responsible for a piece of Cat's overall business process. They were all organized in functional "General Offices" or "G.O.s," each with its own executive vice president reporting to the company president. Over time, the G.O.s became extremely powerful and made all the important decisions in the company. "Everything revolved around the General Offices. They were the kingpin of decisions," recalls George Schaefer.

But the General Offices were not tied together through metrics or motivators to keep them pulling in the same direction. While full of extraordinarily talented managers, the functional organizations rarely communicated with one another. Each G.O. served its narrow functional purpose well, but any sense of an overall company purpose was missing.

The pricing G.O. was especially powerful. If a sales rep in Botswana wanted to give a discount on a tractor, the decision had to be made by the pricing G.O. at company headquarters in Peoria, Illinois, frequently by relatively low-level staffers. Market share wasn't their concern—that was the marketing G.O.'s problem. Pricing G.O. made little connection between price and value to the customer. Without accountability for share or volume, Pricing "could make pretty much unilateral decisions, and the only thing that stopped them from going further was the volume of complaints that would occur every time a major change was made."[3]

In theory, such centralized pricing could work if those in the pricing G.O. had all the information they needed to make good pricing decisions, but they didn't. At the time, Cat had no visibility into its profitability by product or country—it could see only the profitability of the company as a whole. Without product or regional profitability measures, pricing G.O. set worldwide prices almost exclusively on the basis of cost: if the projections for the coming year were too low, pricing G.O. would simply raise prices to make up the difference. Don Fites, Cat chairman and CEO from 1990 to 1999, explains that "in those days, prices weren't market driven. Those of us who were actually in the marketplace, who were trying to sell against Komatsu when Cat's prices were already at a twenty percent premium—we knew we weren't going to sell much. Pricing was always a great frustration."[4]

When George Schaefer was the controller of Cat's manufacturing facility in Grenoble, France, there were plans to open a cafeteria in the plant so that workers could stay on-site for a half-hour lunch break rather than going home for the two-hour lunch that was customary in France at the time. It was a huge change in the culture, and while workers agreed to the shortened lunch break on-site, they insisted upon having beer and wine served in the cafeteria. "A hot shot from General Office came through and told us that we could not serve beer and wine in the cafeteria," recalls Schaefer. "G.O. said 'everything's going to go to pot in the afternoon: performance will be down, the scrap will go up, the frequency of accidents will go up.' Well, General Office didn't know what the real Frenchman was like! We finally overruled General Office, but we very quickly put the systems in place to check all these afternoon things, and performance improved! So that shows you how much General Office knew."

This fundamental disconnect between centralized decision rights with relevant information residing only in the field is a hallmark of an overmanaged organization. With incomplete and often wrong information, G.O.s would often reverse decisions made by the executives in the field who had better information and a clearer picture of the competitive reality. "It just took a long time to get decisions going up and down the functional silos, and they really weren't good business decisions; they were more functional decisions."[5]

The G.O.s were set up as cost centers, measured on and held accountable for whether their expenditures were within their budgets. However, the manager responsible didn't know whether the expenditures generated enough revenue to justify them. Even the revenue-generating divisions did not have profitability information. "You didn't even get an operating statement. Regional management might be given a gross sales figure and a calculated share of market, but they didn't have a clue about how much it was costing them to get those sales."[6]

In the late 1980s, the only person in the organization who was responsible for any kind of bottom line was George Schaefer, the chairman and CEO.

Bottlenecked Decision-making

Like all Overmanaged organizations, Cat had become inwardly focused. Lack of information about the external market caused executives to focus instead on the internal workings of the organization, analyzing issues to death and second-guessing decisions made at lower levels. Jim Owens, Cat's current CEO and a managing director in Indonesia at the time, recalls that "we had everything being decided on the seventh floor [of the headquarters building in Peoria] for much of the Eighties. Everything for the whole company came to the top. We were not nimble in response to entrepreneurial opportunities. By the time decisions got there, they had certainly been whitewashed and varnished several times over along the way, and there was a strong consensus that had emerged, because nobody wanted to bring dissenting opinions to the executive office. It was a lot easier in those days. We didn't have to decide anything!"[7]

Don Fites recalls that in the sales organizations, "you spent most of your time trying to get special pricing. There were forms you had to fill out and justify, and sometimes these things took weeks to turn around. And on a big deal, rather than being out there trying to sell the quality of your product, all the marketing and sales people spent a great deal of time trying to get exceptions to list prices. And finally, a majority of the product in many of these areas was being sold under special pricing, not regular pricing, so it came to a point where [the centrally controlled pricing] was almost self-defeating."

As it became increasingly inwardly focused, Cat slowly grew out of touch with the realities of the market. Managers had very deep but very narrow functional expertise. "Most of the people who were senior leaders in the company never had broad experience in the company. They had come up within a function. The head of Pricing had been in Pricing his whole life. The head of Marketing had been in Marketing his whole life. They had no view to anything outside of their functional responsibilities, and so they only knew the process."[8]

Ironically, many organizations with very strong market positions by virtue of innovative products or other protections do not realize that their DNA is gradually becoming misaligned until their competitive position comes under attack. Cat was no exception. Its organizational flaws and frustrations never got much attention, because Cat's product and dealer strength could effectively overwhelm any competitive threat. And, frankly, most people in the organization were pretty comfortable. "It was a lot [easier] for a lot of people, because accountability was just doing what Peoria was telling them. In one way, you had less risk of a heart attack. You just had to do what you were told to do. No initiative, no risk."[9]

And Then, the Iceberg

In the early Eighties, the invisible hand finally wiped away this comfortable existence. In 1982, Caterpillar posted the first annual loss of its fifty-year history—and couldn't seem to pull out of it: In the three years from 1982 to 1984, Caterpillar lost a billion dollars. In 1983 and 1984, it lost a million dollars per day, seven days a week.

The global recession, combined with runaway inflation in the early Eighties, had turned Cat's formerly cozy markets into attractive new opportunities for several competitors, key among them Japan's Komatsu. As George Schaefer recalls, "Japan reared up, and Komatsu in particular decided to take us on. And I mean they took us on full bore. They went into the Middle East markets and just devastated us. They were coming in with prices forty percent below ours on comparable equipment. Then they started to attack us in North America, and we had to just rear up and say, 'That's enough, we have to preserve this market!' And of course you know what happens to prices when you maintain market share?"

Facing significant competitive challenge for the first time in its history, Caterpillar was shocked out of its complacency. It was "almost like hitting a wall. Everything we had done and practices we had put in place and policies we were executing were irrelevant because new entrants had come into our competitive space and had changed the rules of engagement. The bad news is, it happened. The good news is, it was a wakeup call."[10]

The Lifeboats

Schaefer and his first lieutenant, Pete Donis, recognized that one of Caterpillar's most important competitive assets was its distribution system, and that whatever happened, that distribution system had to be protected. So they decided to continue selling to dealers at a price that allowed the dealers to make a small profit. While that policy led Cat to lose a million dollars a day, they did not lose a single dealer.

Cat managed to protect its distribution network, but the crisis brought front and center the fact that its costs were too high. So Cat launched a massive, $1.8 billion manufacturing modernization program called Plant With A Future (PWAF), which would dramatically reduce its manufacturing costs.

In 1985, the rising tide of a recovering global economy lifted a lot of boats, including Caterpillar's, and the company returned to profitability. By 1988, Cat had surpassed its then-record 1981 profit levels, and much of the organization was feeling relieved and perhaps a bit smug at having survived the most threatening period in its history. But some in senior management still had nagging concerns: the PWAF cost-reduction initiative had done little to solve the problems that made Cat internally focused, slow, and unresponsive at the customer face. George Schaefer worried that the company was slipping too easily into the familiar complacency of the past. He was wondering, "Have we really done enough? What will happen when the economy turns down again? Will we be able to pull off another death-defying stunt?" Schaefer was determined that Cat would never be caught flat-footed again, at least not on his watch.

In part, Schaefer's quiet determination to make a more lasting change was based on the fact that he was still the only person in the entire company responsible for its profitability. He understood that, not only was the competitive pressure on Cat likely to increase, but with the business model then in use, no one at Cat would bear responsibility for solving the problem except him. He realized that some of that pressure had to be felt by others in the company.

"WE HAVE MET THE ENEMY, AND THEY ARE US"

Schaefer stood atop an entrenched bureaucracy that was, in his words, "telling me what I want to hear, not what I need to know."[11] He began to understand the nature and extent of the problem by inviting a rotating group of middle managers to breakfast once a week, discovering in these informal discussions many issues that were more significant than what his senior management team was discussing in their formal meetings.

These breakfast sessions were so informative because the attendees understood Caterpillar's weaknesses but were not so entrenched in the current way of doing things that they wouldn't talk about them. As in many centralized organizations where authority is held by a small number of very senior executives, Cat's senior management had too much invested in the current organization to be expected to share their most serious concerns with the chairman.

Schaefer soon realized that he needed a task force to help him fix Cat, but that including senior managers on it would keep more junior managers from speaking their minds. So he excluded senior managers from the group and went one layer down. Schaefer asked each of his senior managers to provide a list of their best and brightest. When all the lists were combined, "we had about forty names, but there were one or two that I knew that didn't show up on these lists because they were real renegades—they were clear thinkers, they would 'upset the apple cart.'"[12] From this list and his own collection of "renegades," Schaefer chose about eight middle managers to form Caterpillar's first-ever Strategic Planning Committee, or SPC, that would help him chart Caterpillar's future.

Meeting for half a day each week, the SPC was charged with taking everything back to basics, figuring out where the company stood and where it was going. The review was not designed to look specifically for organizational problems: everything was on the table, and the debate ranged widely for the first few meetings. Schaefer remembers that "the first couple of meetings were pretty rough. The raw meat was on the table, stuff I never heard from the senior guys."[13] Glen Barton, who was on the committee, credits Schaefer with being tolerant enough to allow this kind of free-swinging, unguarded debate. "He wasn't defensive. He didn't come out and say, 'Well, you can't do that,' or 'That's not what we're here for.' He was more receptive to hearing what people had to say and what their frustrations were than trying to give specific direction as to where we might go."[14]

Meanwhile, the rest of the organization knew there was something going on, but frankly didn't expect much to come of it: "George Schaefer announced that he had selected a team of breakthrough thinkers, and he said, 'Within a year, we'll come back to you and tell you what we plan to do with the company.' [But] I don't think it gave anybody any sense of hope, because I don't think anybody perceived that we were going to make any change as radical as the reorganization of the company."[15]

Over time, however, it became increasingly clear to the SPC that Cat's problems were fundamentally organizational in nature, and that a major reorganization was needed. The SPC concluded that Cat was "just not getting the job done in terms of the final customer. We were too long to react, too long to get a price change, everything had to funnel through this hierarchy. Just slow. And sometimes, not very knowledgeable about what needed to be done."[16] And the SPC was beginning to develop some ideas about where the solution lay: "We did not have clear accountability. If we were better organized and more optimally organized, we would be more responsive, we would be more effective as an organization, we would be more competitive."[17]

Seven or eight months into the initiative, Schaefer concluded it was time to get the SPC's findings onto senior management's agenda. But that would be no small feat, given that the findings were not particularly complimentary to senior management, and the recommendations would in large part dismantle the organization that Cat's leaders had spent their careers building. So Schaefer introduced the ideas gradually, by first inviting Don Fites and Jim Wogsland, then president and executive vice president, respectively, to join the SPC. Schaefer recalls that "the first couple of meetings were really tough, because when [Fites and Wogsland] heard what we were thinking about, they said, 'You can't do this!' But as they got deeper into it and as they got exposed to the whole logic and soul-searching and experts' advice, they quickly came aboard. And once I got those two aboard, I knew I had it made, because I could bring the rest of them aboard. It was a tough road for a month there. I didn't want to get them to just *tell* me they were buying in, they had to buy in."

And buy in they did. In Fites's words, "We just couldn't live in this [G.O.–dominated] world. Even though we came up through Operations, we knew that the frustration level of the company was very high and we had to make these changes." In short order, Fites, as CEO, would lead the charge of implementing a new, reorganized Caterpillar.

A New Organizational Blueprint

While all four building blocks of Cat's organization would eventually be overhauled, Schaefer and Fites began with a massive structural revolution that shocked the firm out of its complacency, quickly taking the lead in creating a blueprint of the new organization. It moved accountability dramatically downward in the organization by reorganizing Caterpillar into "accountable" business units that would have P&L statements and be judged on divisional profitability.

Stunningly, the functional general offices that had only a day before been "kings," deciding everything, simply ceased to exist. Their talent and expertise, including engineering, pricing, and manufacturing, were parceled out to the new accountable units. The decision rights once held by the all-powerful functions were decentralized to the new accountable business units as well. The business units could now design their own products, develop their own manufacturing processes and schedules, and set their own prices. They did not need permission from anyone at headquarters.

Initially, the plan was to roll out the new organization gradually, piloting the accountable P&L idea in one business unit, and then broadening to others as the concept took hold. But that changed as senior management and the board saw that the only way to ensure Cat's people would indeed operate differently was to reorganize all at once, forcing people to wake up and realize that the future was about different relationships, a different structure, and a different way of doing business.

"And then," laughs George Schaefer today, "I retired!"

The Announcement: Shock and Awe

The new organization was a profound change for nearly everyone at Caterpillar. And the speed and certainty with which it was announced was every bit as surprising as the change itself. Jim Owens, who was a managing director in Indonesia at the time, recalls, "I got a phone call on January the fourth, my birthday, while I was on vacation at Squaw Valley. I was on my way back to Indonesia, and was told there would be a reorganization, and that I would be promoted to vice president and president of the Solar Business Unit, adding that I shouldn't tell anyone or say anything to anyone, that I should just be in Peoria on January twenty-eighth for my first council meeting. At that time everything would be explained to me.

"That was it. I asked if I could talk to the guy I was replacing, but was told not to talk to anybody. 'You show up in Peoria, and don't come early. The meeting is the morning of the twenty-eighth. You get here the night of the twenty-seventh.' I showed up on the day of the meeting, and nobody knew who was going to be there from the executive office!"

Almost overnight, the entire senior team changed. Owens recalls, "It was pretty abrupt. And when that shoe dropped, there was a massive announcement, five or six officer retirements, a total new team. This was a radical, 'Wow,' revolution." Many of the heads of the powerhouse functional divisions were demoted to division managers in the business units, working for someone else, and were now expected to serve the product and marketing managers that they used to impose rules upon. "All the metrics, all those flowcharts? Gone."[18]

Delegating Decision Rights

Through George Schaefer's thorough SPC and Don Fites's dramatic implementation, Caterpillar's new organization was founded steadfastly on a small number of core principles. Most fundamentally, business unit managers would have the decision rights to run their own businesses as they saw fit, without interference from headquarters. They could buy and sell inputs from one another at market-based transfer prices, or they could buy what they needed from outside suppliers. They could make their own pricing decisions, develop their own product designs, and create their own manufacturing and marketing plans.

But hand-in-hand with that authority, business units would be accountable for how well they used those decision rights, because they would be judged on the profitability and return on assets (ROA) in their divisions. If a division could not achieve 15 percent ROA or higher, it would face elimination.

In the new model, with business unit management making virtually all of the decisions, the role of headquarters was much different. First, since many of the decisions that were once made centrally had been delegated to the business units, headquarters could be much leaner, with fewer layers. Second, headquarters focused almost exclusively on setting goals and measuring performance for the business units, and in fact, that is how Fites spent nearly all of his day-to-day energies. He would hold regular meetings with each of his division vice presidents, keeping notes on what the managers said they would achieve in a spiral-bound notebook. At the next meeting, Fites would produce the notebook and review each manager's performance against the commitments made in the previous meeting: "You made a commitment, how are you doing on that commitment? It worked very well," recalls Fites. "Instead of having all this energy used internally, we focused on the endgame. What are the results we want?"

For a business unit manager, the two models produced starkly different behaviors: Consider the case of a plant manager in Switzerland before the reorganization. He is told by headquarters in Peoria to buy a particular machine from a certain supplier at a given price and to install it according to a predetermined layout in the factory. He is told to machine a part according to a drawing developed in Peoria, using a prescribed manufacturing process. When the resulting parts are defective, he calls Peoria, complaining about the design, the machine, the supplier. His behavior, naturally, is to assign blame, because the onus is on headquarters to fix the problem that they created with their design, their machine, their supplier.

But after the reorganization, the same manager is told by headquarters only to make a profit on the excavator product line. When the parts come off the line defective, there is no reason to call Peoria. Instead, he has to fix the problem himself, and he has all the levers to do so under his control—if the supplier is the problem, his purchasing group can find another. If the drawing is bad, his engineers can redesign it. The clear accountability of the new model forced people close to the problem to focus their attention on finding a solution instead of finger-pointing.

Teaching Fish to Swim

As in all heavily centralized organizations, very few managers in the old Cat had much general management experience. While centralized, siloed organizations often contain very deep functional talent, the focus on "doing what headquarters says to do" means that few managers get much experience with the broad range of problems encountered routinely by a general manager. For these organizations, moving to a more decentralized model would expose their talent weakness, which often keeps them from changing at all.

Cat was no exception—very few people in the company at the time of the reorganization had any previous experience in running anything resembling a business. What's worse, because Cat promoted almost exclusively from within, almost no one in middle or upper management had ever worked outside the company at all, let alone in a position of authority. They had all grown up inside the old, functional Cat, and knew well how to operate within the old silos, the silos that had just been obliterated in the reorganization. But several of them were being handed the keys to multibillion-dollar business units.

Newly created global product managers were running huge businesses with little or no formal training. "The most spectacular part of the job was that they really didn't know what they expected you to do. There weren't a whole lot of guidebooks. We were it, exceptionally overempowered. We could do what we thought was right. We could make informed decisions and we got tremendous support. And we were kings."[19]

Some couldn't manage the transition and the new autonomy, and had to be moved to positions with less authority. But others found the new decision rights invigorating, and were thrilled to see their first divisional P&L. AJ Rassi, who became the general manager of the Wheel Loader and Excavator division in Aurora, Illinois, shortly after the reorganization, recalls the first time he saw his divisional P&L: "I was so excited, because I was in a very profitable business unit and I could see that we were making a lot of money for this corporation. When we got those P&L statements, we had meetings every month and shared them with our top management people in the Aurora group. And, in our plant managers' meetings, we showed every plant, profit or not. Before, there was nothing."[20]

Others were less excited. When Jim Despain, who became vice president of the product division that Caterpillar was founded on, the track-type tractor, saw the first P&L of his professional career, he was shocked to learn that "we were losing a lot of money. And we had no idea how to fix it. [And this was the] first time we realized it, because the *company* was profitable, and we had the original product, the best product, the original plant, the most seasoned employees."[21] As AJ Rassi put it, "I joined the Caterpillar *Tractor* Company, and we're losing money on our *tractors*!"[22]

But resourceful, empowered managers eventually figured out how to run profitable businesses. The accountability and autonomy of the new model quickly unleashed a vast amount of entrepreneurial energy and general-management-like discipline from Cat's considerable talent pool, even though they had been trained and conditioned to think about their jobs completely differently. "People really started intensely looking at how they made money in their division. All of a sudden you've got all this energy focused on *my* division getting *my* costs down, and making the compromises that are needed.

"It also caused the big product plants to say, 'Hey, I'm an assembly plant and an engineering plant. What the hell am I doing cutting steel? I'll outsource this to Mexico at four dollars an hour versus us doing it at forty-five dollars an hour. I've got to worry about how I'm going to take ten million dollars, twenty million, fifty million dollars out of my cost structure this year, and the only way I can do this is to identify the stuff that clearly I shouldn't be doing.' That was really the catalyst to it. And it became evident very shortly afterward. People started putting together one-year and three-year plans, and it was almost embarrassing what people could come up with."[23]

Information in the New Organization

The reorganization to an accountable business unit model dramatically decentralized decision rights. At the same time, Caterpillar completely changed the information flows in the organization and the metrics used to measure performance. Return on Assets became the overall goal at Cat, because it was correct, simple, and straightforward to use, which was particularly important for the pragmatic engineers who were mostly now running the businesses at Cat.

Transfer Prices—The Unsung Information Heroes

To operate their businesses, division managers clearly had to have divisional P&Ls and balance sheets. But only a few of Caterpillar's divisions sell to outside customers; the rest lack any natural measure of revenue to use as the top line of their P&L. For the profit-center model to work, Cat needed to create a measure of revenue for the divisions that sold most of their products to other Cat divisions, so that those divisions would have a measure of profits for which they could be held accountable. These measures were provided through transfer prices, at which Caterpillar divisions "bought" and "sold" intermediate goods from one another.

It is easy to underestimate the importance of transfer prices—after all, they are tantamount to "trading wooden nickels," since they only move money from one division in the organization to another. However, because transfer prices enable organizations to re-create supply and demand economies inside their boundaries, they are the often-overlooked lynchpins that hold together decentralized organizations like Cat's accountable model.

Using market-based benchmarks, divisions would negotiate with one another to determine transfer prices. These negotiations were often contentious and protracted, and consumed a lot of management time and attention. But they were essential to making the new organization work properly. Jim Owens recalls a meeting of the administrative council two years after the reorganization in which "a large group of vice presidents from materials purchasing and the plants had gotten together and concluded that they were wasting a lot of time doing all these commercial negotiations over transfer prices.

"They came to the meeting and said 'we're too inward looking; we're wasting our time.' They went on and on, and they gave a little presentation about it. And Fites got up and said 'You don't understand. Half your cost is purchases from outside suppliers. US Steel didn't have any trouble whatsoever establishing those prices. So I want you to establish these things, and that's the way we're going to run the railroad. If you can't work that way, you can get another job.' That ended the debate rather succinctly."

As an economist and new CFO at the time, Owens recognized that the strength of the business unit structure was that it would highlight where in the organization the cost problems were, but could only do so if transfer prices were negotiated from market benchmarks, "so the losses showed up where the cost problems were. And if you lose that discipline, you've lost it. I was thrilled that [Fites] took that very staunch position."[24]

The Mother of All Accounting Challenges

Creating the new information and metrics that would underpin the new organization and ensure that it worked properly was no small feat. Entirely new metrics were required—what would constitute a division's P&L, what measures should be used, and how would they drive profitability while ensuring fit among all of Cat's internal divisions? They had to be developed quickly, but at the same time needed to be very specific and highly reliable.

Fites recalls the magnitude of the challenge. In about June of 1990, "I went to the accounting people, who have to take this huge thing now and divide it up so every division has its own balance sheet and P&L, and I said, 'How long will it take us?' Accounting said, 'We think we can be ready in three years.'

"And I said, 'I want every one of these divisions to budget this year on the basis of their new balance sheets and come up with a P&L. And Bob Gallagher, who was our comptroller—the blood drained from his face. I thought he was going to faint right on the spot! But you know what? They did it. And they did it well. We hardly ever had to make any changes in the balance sheets or the P&Ls. But that six months was probably one of the most incredible transitions that ever took place around here."[25]

Motivators in the New Organization

Cat's reorganization also involved an overhaul of the compensation plan, although, as Don Fites puts it, "the great motivator was survival—survival of the company, your personal survival as an important player, survival of this product that you love, that you designed, the survival of your plant." Nevertheless, financial incentive payments for the business units were provided, based on how much performance had improved over the year prior. Before the reorganization, individual bonuses were based on overall corporate performance rather than business unit objectives. After the reorganization, an employee could make anywhere from 7 to 45 percent additional salary per year based on meeting their business plan targets.

These incentives cascaded through the organization and helped the business units to focus on very tangible, measurable outcomes that line employees could affect. For example, one plant focused on meeting their delivery commitments: "We supplied all these little components, and we wanted to have the reputation of never missing a shipping date, because prime product plants just go berserk when you shut them down because you missed a shipping date. So our incentive plans were heavily skewed [toward meeting shipping dates]. And what happened was, we started meeting [our shipping dates without] expediting stuff all the time."[26]

Schaefer credits the compensation plan with generating buy-in for the change deep down in the organization. "We had a lot of trouble in the middle and lower ranks buying into these many changes. But if you'd tell them 'If you get your revenue up by ten percent, and you get your profit up by twenty percent, here's the amount of bonus you earn,' they bought into that in a hurry!"[27]

For top management, the compensation committee of Caterpillar's board set up a long-term incentive plan as well as short-term incentive plans for individual units. Under the short-term plan, managers in business units who outperform their ROA targets receive bonuses even if the company does not meet an overall target. But by far the larger incentive is provided by the long-term plan, under which Cat executives can earn bonuses when the company outperforms a peer group of about fifteen other companies on ROA and profitability growth targets. Glen Barton believes that the incentive plan has "caused people to work together and to recognize that the company is willing to reward them on the results of this."[28]

But Cat's timing was also fortuitous, and from 1993 to 1994, as the effects of the reorganization began to kick in at the same time as the economy started to recover, "the world started getting good. People started making their business plans, started getting a lot of incentive compensation, and they said, 'Hey this is a great reorganization!' And that was very good, because that success and the extra pay fixed in people's minds that this is a great thing to have done. People stopped fighting the change, and they embraced the change and said, 'This is great, we did the right thing, I'm happy we're doing this.'"[29]

The Turnaround

The resulting turnaround in Caterpillar's financial performance was nothing short of spectacular. After posting a $2.4 billion loss in 1992, Cat's profits turned positive in 1993 and reached a record $2 billion in 2004. Cat's revenues have nearly tripled since 1992, from $10.2 billion to $30.3 billion in 2004. The results showed not just in Cat's top and bottom lines, but in operational indicators as well. Immediately after the reorganization, Glen Barton estimates that the Construction and Mining Products division he was leading reduced head count in the product manager groups by roughly 30 percent, "simply because they were either redundant or they were doing things that we no longer had to do, and the decision-making process was simplified."[30] After "twisting the arm" of one of his divisions to bring him a long-range plan that would produce 20 percent ROA, Barton recalls that the division delivered more than 100 percent ROA one year, simply by taking out costs and head count. Over a longer period of time, Cat reduced its product development cycle to roughly thirty-six months from forty-eight to seventy-two months before the reorganization, and reduced its capital requirements, because assets were tied back to product profitability, and the businesses no longer sought massive capital investments to renew manufacturing operations for every product upgrade.

But the real story here is not Cat's financial or operating improvements. Instead, it is about how everyday behavior in this formerly Overmanaged organization changed, in the smallest corners of Cat's business, to be focused on the customer and profitability rather than on internal process and budget.

For example, Cat started developing products more in synch with what dealers and end customers wanted. Because each product business unit now had a full complement of functional talent in its new product introduction teams, and those teams were empowered to make all product-development decisions without requiring approval from any other source, they could act more quickly and responsively with more complete information. In 1995, Caterpillar introduced an updated version of its D9 tractor after just three years of development. The model was so successful that it captured 100 percent market share in North America in just two years. Komatsu withdrew from the market completely in the face of the D9R's overwhelming superiority in the customer's eyes.[31]

Another example of how Cat was able to respond more nimbly to its customers and its competitors was when Cat won an order for eight hundred pieces of road-maintenance equipment from the county governments in Vancouver, Canada. John Deere, one of Cat's main competitors, had offered a big discount and looked like they were going to win the bid. But Cat quickly assembled a very attractive lease program, creating an even better deal than Deere's, and won the entire purchase.

The district manager in Vancouver at the time remembers that such an approach would never have been possible in the old organization. "First of all, to do that, we had to do all kinds of creative marketing and merchandising programs, and bring in Cat Finance. It was a very comprehensive approach. Second, we had to be able to ship all that stuff in two months, so we essentially took the entire production capacity of the Decatur plant for two months and devoted it to this customer. That would never ever have happened before the reorganization. Nobody at that level would have ever had the authority to do something like that. Even to propose it would have taken a year to work through the old pricing G.O., and then to get the capacity allocated to do something that was so strategic was impossible."[32]

Another example shows the impact of providing the sales force with the tools and the information they needed to sell new products. At the time of the reorganization, Cat's hydraulic excavator product line had a gap in the middle, lacking a forty-ton excavator that was very important to the North American market. Finally, after several years of development, the product division launched a forty-ton excavator, the 345, with an unprecedented campaign. They conducted competitive analyses, and spent a million dollars developing a three-day hydraulic excavator training institute to arm the sales force with the tools they needed to sell the machines. The institute brought in competitive machines and displays, and hosted dinners and speakers for the sales force, and they ran it for three cycles. "It was unbelievably successful. We hit the ground, we taught salesmen how to sell for the first time in many, many years. And we literally went from a very, very low twenty percent share of market to almost thirty-eight percent overnight. In the first two years, the enterprise made over thirty-five million in incremental variable margin. No substitution [from our other products], we just took market share away from the competition."[33]

Examples of the more responsive, more profit-oriented Cat abound in its manufacturing operations as well. At Cat's plant in Mexico, "We started focusing on steel utilization. One square inch of steel, a half inch thick, costs about one dollar. We were throwing away about twenty-eight percent of all the steel we bought, selling it as scrap. But we found that, with our labor rates, we could take that scrap steel and we could cut little blocks out of it. When you look at heavy machinery, there are little steel blocks all over it—where something is tacked to the machine; a wire, a hose, a cylinder rod, and they're all about two-inch squares. We just started cutting those out of scrap and storing them in tubs, and when we got twenty tubs full, we'd send an e-mail to [the prime product plant in] Grenoble, France, and say, 'Hey we have twenty tubs of this part number, give us a purchase order.' And we'd sell it to them at half price. It's easy to motivate an organization to do stuff like that, to focus on the here and now. We had examples all over the shop there. One square inch was half the salary of a guy for an hour."[34]

Perhaps the most significant turnaround of any of Caterpillar's manufacturing operations took place in Cat's tractor plant in East Peoria. Jim Despain, who headed the division during the turnaround, commented on the power of decentralized decision rights in the reorganization at Cat: "When people feel accountable, they do wonderful things, if they really are accountable. I'll never forget, it was down in the fabrication buildings where all the really tough guys hang out, the welders.

"One of the more cooperative people down there was given some responsibility to look at saving money in the weld-repair area. We had this little red lens that you put on the eye of the welding robot so the robot can follow the weld route. And we burned those up pretty quickly, because the fire was hitting them with pellets all the time. These lenses were costing us sixty-two dollars apiece, and he found a way to make them in our own tool room here for six cents. Sixty-two dollars to six cents. And there were many other things the same way."[35]

On another occasion, an hourly welder on the production line stopped Despain on the plant floor and said, "'I want you to come over and see what the team's doing.' So I went over and I was so impressed, I said, 'Hey, if you don't mind, I want to bring a couple of group vice presidents down here to look at this.' And he said, 'No, I don't mind.' I said, 'What about this Friday?' He said, 'Well, I can't do it Friday, I'm going to Cleveland—I read in a welding magazine that they've got something they're trying out there and I want to go take a look at it to see if it would fit here.'

"I said, 'Well, that's wonderful! The next time I see your supervisor, I'm going to tell him that I really am impressed with him supporting these kinds of things for you guys.' And the guy says, 'Oh, I haven't told him yet.' And I thought, 'Here's an empowered person!'"[36]

Despain's division went from heavy losses in 1990 to significant profitability by 1995, and cut headcount from 4,500 to 2,000. "We never invested a dime in more technology, never did any outsourcing," he recalls. "We just changed the way people worked together. They were putting their own creativity into the opportunities they were provided. They forgot about themselves and started looking at the bigger picture."[37]

As Despain sees it, before the reorganization, "there were a lot of people who were being like they thought they had to be, based on what they had seen throughout their careers. And when we were really asking them to be themselves, it took a lot of pressure off of them. We had supervisors almost lined up to retire after thirty years, who talked about it openly—'We're going to get out of here in one year, four months, and thirty days' or whatever. And then we had the same people say they were going to stay as long as they could. We had people turn down promotions to stay here. Promotions!"[38]

A Resilient Organization

Caterpillar today looks somewhat different than it did when it was first reorganized, but the original principles of the organization are still intact: decentralization, profitability, market-based transfer prices, and accountability. And the basic architecture of the accountable business unit model has been unchanged since its first introduction in 1990. There are more and different business divisions now, as some have been eliminated because they couldn't perform (e.g., Agriculture, Lift Trucks), and some have been split into multiple divisions as they've succeeded and grown (e.g., Engines).

But the fact that Cat has operated and thrived using essentially the same organizational model it established fifteen years ago is testament to its resilience: at Cat, organization is not "flavor of the month"—Cat does not reorganize every few years, as many companies do, just to "shake things up." Such a concept would be anathema at Caterpillar.

Caterpillar today demonstrates all of the traits of a resilient organization. For example, in 2001, Cat showed the courage of its convictions when it announced it would use its revolutionary new Advanced Combustion Emissions Reduction Technology (ACERT) on its diesel engines to meet the EPA's increasingly strict standards for truck engine emissions. At the time, nearly every other diesel-engine manufacturer was touting cooled Exhaust Gas Recirculation (EGR) technology as the only way to meet the tougher standards. But Cat believed that EGR could be only a stopgap solution, and that ACERT was a better long-term solution. However, the decision essentially required Cat to "bet the farm" on the new technology, and abandon twenty years of research on other technologies, including EGR. What's more, Caterpillar had to pay "nonconformance penalties" on the first engines it sold after the stricter EPA standards went into effect, because the full ACERT solution wasn't ready yet. But today, Cat uses the technology in all its on-highway engines, where it is receiving an overwhelmingly positive customer response. Cat has also begun installing ACERT-equipped engines on its off-road equipment, and the two Cat engineers who developed the technology were named 2004 Inventors of the Year by the Intellectual Property Owners Association.[39]

As do all Resilient companies, Cat periodically moves the goal posts to keep stretching the boundaries of what it can achieve. Although many of the industries in which Cat competes are highly cyclical, after Cat's initial turnaround in 1993, the company upped the ante, seeking to prove that it could be profitable not only at the top of the business cycle, but at the bottom as well. Cat did, indeed, show a profit of more than $800 million in 2001, at the bottom of the latest recession, and then raised the bar: the next goal was to be "attractively profitable" at the top of the business cycle, which it achieved in 2004. The next objective is to be increasingly profitable at the bottom of each successive trough.

Cat's reorganization from the functional silos of G.O. to accountable business units was all about encouraging more "horizontal" thinking, another trait of Resilient organizations. Cat continues to build upon that horizontal emphasis when it develops its management talent, consciously moving leaders across business units, functional areas, and geographies through the course of their careers. After several years with the company, almost every manager at Cat has experience in two or three different business units. As a result, Cat has developed one of the deepest management benches in its industry. In fact, Cat's organizational structure, with many more-or-less complete businesses being run by essentially autonomous general managers, has "allowed us to identify people that are business leaders that we would not have probably uncovered as quickly," in Glen Barton's words. "People have emerged from this process very, very qualified, very capable of leading a business, and being a lot more than they probably could have ever realized in the old bureaucratic organization we were in."[40]

Cat has also institutionalized the practice of listening to the complainers. Having learned the power of listening to key voices in the organization from George Schaefer, every Caterpillar chairman since Schaefer has convened a Strategic Planning Committee to help him tackle the most important and challenging issues of his term as CEO.

And Caterpillar's businesses today routinely "self-correct," that is, change course without someone in the executive office prompting them to do it. As one senior manager describes it, "This organization is ready to pull the trigger on growth or cost reduction at a minute's notice, and we know where to do it. . . . We've seen that on the way up this time, where some groups are doing great and others aren't, and they pull the trigger without waiting for us to tell them. This year, we had a number of divisions that, among other things, canceled fourth-quarter conferences, and travel and entertainment even though we're having a record year. That never would have happened in the past because we'd be waiting for somebody from the executive office to say 'We've got to cut ten percent.' As we're going through this huge upturn, we have units actually doing that. What's happening is what's supposed to happen."[41]

Finally, like any truly Resilient organization, Cat refuses to rest on its laurels. Even the reorganized and resilient Caterpillar is not complacent, striving for improvement every day. In 2000, Glen Barton introduced a Six Sigma process-improvement program to the organization. Even though Cat implemented the program long after the Six Sigma "fad" of the late Eighties had faded, no company had ever seen Six Sigma succeed as quickly, extensively, or completely as Caterpillar.[42]

SUMMARY: MAKING IT HAPPEN

Caterpillar's story is evidence that any company, no matter how organizationally or competitively challenged, can change the course of its history. But the scale of such a transformation effort required is enormous, and the nature of its successful execution is not accidental. The precise changes required will of course depend on a company's specific circumstances and challenges. But Cat's journey from Overmanaged to Resilient organization contains some key elements of *how* the transformation was undertaken that are common across all successful organizational transformation efforts.

First and foremost, the thoughtfulness and thoroughness that went into understanding the organization's problems, and how to solve them, is a hallmark of Cat's transformation. George Schaefer intuitively understood where the truth was likely to lie when he populated his Strategic Planning Committee with contributors who would know and share the truth, rather than the conventional wisdom, about the organization. He encouraged free-swinging debate and listened without defensiveness, eventually accepting what had to have been a personally demoralizing message, rather than denying and ignoring it. And then he found and brought on board the right people to champion its implementation, even though he would not personally oversee it. Not surprisingly, ever since Schaefer developed the Strategic Planning Committee (SPC) idea, Cat chairmen have continued to convene similar SPCs periodically to help guide company strategy or develop major change initiatives.

Second, the reorganization plan and its implementation happened quickly, dramatically, and unequivocally. While senior management had thought for a brief time about rolling out the organizational change gradually, they quickly abandoned that plan when the board felt strongly that such an implementation would doom the change. So the reorganization that was publicly announced on January 26, 1990, was broad, comprehensive, and a tremendous shock to most within the Caterpillar system. As Jim Owens describes it, "This was a major, cataclysmic turn of events. It was like someone acquired the company. It was that dramatic."[43] The new organization was in many ways the polar opposite of what Caterpillar had been up until then: "Nothing central. Run away from it as far as you can go. I don't want you to think about anybody else's problems, you think about your own."[44]

Third, the resolve that the leadership, particularly Don Fites, demonstrated throughout the implementation was unshakeable, and his steadfastness was critical. While there were many small details of the new organization that were not perfect at the start, Fites resisted the temptation to continually revise and perfect the design in the early days of the new organization. In those first critical months, constantly announcing changes to the new organization would have undermined its credibility, causing people to think that they could wait until the rules were changed, and encouraging them to lobby for rule changes instead of getting on with life in the new organization. Fites's implementation of the new organization taught one senior manager at Cat today that "it is better to live consistently with something which is not perfect than to have something changing every day in a constant attempt to perfect it."[45]

Perhaps because of the enormous scope and tremendous speed of the change, no one in the organization thought (at least not for very long) that "this too shall pass." Instead, behavior began to change almost immediately, and within twelve to eighteen months of the announcement, the company was working in the new model. As Jim Owens recalls, "Within three years it was crystal clear that you could see a real renaissance occurring.

"This was a revolution that became a renaissance, a spectacular transformation of a kind of sluggish company into one that actually has entrepreneurial zeal. And that transition was very quick, because it was decisive, and it was complete, it was thorough, it was universal, worldwide, all at one time. It was a big leap off the board.

"I strongly believe if you get the right people in the right chairs, and let them know what their goals and objectives are and get out of the way, you'll get it done."[46]

THE RESEARCH BEHIND
THE BOOK

The research that forms the basis for this book is inspired by experience, underpinned by economic theory, and fueled by hard data. Our combined five decades of experience helping clients with organizational transformation issues has armed us with some robust perspectives on organizational dysfunction and its causes and remedies. This experience, informed by some path-breaking ideas on the economics of organizations helped us create an assessment tool called the *Org DNA Profiler*^{SM}.[1] Between December 2003 and January 2005, thirty thousand *Org DNA Profiler*^{SM} surveys were completed voluntarily by individuals who visited our Website, www.orgdna.com. In addition, more than fifteen-thousand profiles have been generated on client-specific Org DNA sites set up to facilitate work with both corporate and not-for-profit organizations. In these cases, we have set up a password-protected site for each client to collect and analyze employee input on organizational issues.[2]

Based on our experience, we have distilled seven basic organization types—some healthy, some unhealthy—that together describe the persistent patterns we've seen in corporate, government, nonprofit, and/or academic organizations. These profiles reflect different interactions between and among four organizational building blocks: decision rights, information, motivators, and structure.

These four building blocks and the way they combine and recombine describe the unique attributes of any organization and predict its ability to execute effectively and deliver results. Like the four nucleotides that comprise human DNA, they determine the inherent nature of an organizational entity. So we've dubbed this approach Organizational DNA or Org DNA. We are not the first to use the metaphor; we are merely the first to use it in this manner.

We debuted this framework in November of 2003 when we published an article entitled "The Four Bases of Organizational DNA" in *strategy+business*, Booz Allen Hamilton's quarterly general business publication. The article generated a tremendous response, and on December 8, 2003, Booz Allen launched the Website www.orgdna.com, containing more information about Org DNA and offering visitors the opportunity to complete a nineteen-question online survey on the organizations they worked in (see Figure A.1).

A kind of "personality test" for organizations, this Web-based assessment tool provides visitors immediate gratification, enabling them to identify the DNA profile of their own organizations

FIGURE A.1—*ORG DNA PROFILER^SM*: NINETEEN QUESTIONS GROUPED BY BUILDING BLOCK

		Potential Responses	
STRUCTURE	1. At the middle management level, the average number of direct reports is...	5 or more	4 or fewer
	2. Promotions include lateral moves (from one position to another on the same level in the hierarchy)	Agree	Disagree
	3. "Fast track" employees here can expect promotions...	Every 3 years or more	Less than every 3 years
DECISION RIGHTS	4. The culture of this organization can best be described as...	"Persuade & Cajole"	"Command and Control"
	5. Important strategic and operational decisions are quickly translated into action	Agree	Disagree
	6. The primary role of corporate staff here is to...	Audit the Business Units	Support the Business Units
	7. Managers above me in the hierarchy "get their hands dirty" by getting involved in operating decisions	Frequently	Rarely
	8. Once made, decisions are often "second-guessed"	Agree	Disagree
	9. Everyone has a good idea of decisions/actions for which he or she is responsible	Agree	Disagree
INFORMATION	10. Overall this firm deals successfully with discontinuous change in the competitive environment	Agree	Disagree
	11. Important information about our competitive environment gets to headquarters quickly	Agree	Disagree
	12. Field/line employees usually have the information they need to understand the bottom line impact of their day-to-day choices	Agree	Disagree
	13. We rarely send conflicting messages to the marketplace	Agree	Disagree
	14. Information flows freely across organizational boundaries	Agree	Disagree
	15. Line management has access to the metrics they need to measure the key drivers of their business	Agree	Disagree
MOTIVATORS	16. If the firm has a bad year, but a particular division has a good year, the division head would still get a bonus	Agree	Disagree
	17. Besides pay, many other things motivate individuals to do a good job	Agree	Disagree
	18. The individual performance appraisal process differentiates among high, adequate, and low performers	Agree	Disagree
	19. The ability to deliver on performance commitments strongly influences career advancement and compensation	Agree	Disagree

Note: An alternative Mission-Oriented profile is available.

in as little as five minutes (see "The Seven Types" section following). After answering the nineteen questions, respondents receive a "diagnosis" of their organization and links to additional reading materials about the issues relevant to their particular situations, as well as proposed remedies.

In addition to the nineteen core questions, the *Org DNA Profiler*[SM] asks respondents for some demographic information (e.g., their organization's size and industry, their own level and department in the organization). We use these data to categorize responses and identify differences across industries, functions, management levels, and the like. When we create a custom site for a particular client, we tailor the demographic questions to establish the comparison groups that are most relevant to that client's situation (e.g., what division/location a respondent works in, whether he or she came from an acquired entity). On both the public site and the company-specific sites, individual responses are strictly anonymous; no names—company or individual—are requested or revealed. The data collected are used only for analysis and comparison purposes.

The *Org DNA Profiler*[SM] distills years of experience and research on how companies organize and perform, and gives visitors an easy shortcut to finding more information about the organizational issues and remedies most relevant to their particular situation. Visitors to the site will find an array of downloadable articles on the concept of Organizational DNA and organizing to achieve results, written not just by the two of us, but also by many of our colleagues at Booz Allen Hamilton.

The concept and findings of the *Org DNA Profiler*[SM] appeal to so many people precisely because they are so accessible; people "get" the DNA metaphor and the notion that their organization has a distinct "personality" that can be used to predict its behavior or explain its shortcomings. The idea of Organizational DNA transcends pat prescriptions based on culture (which can be too touchy-feely for some) or structure (which can be perceived as too mechanistic). Organizational DNA is multidimensional and takes into account multiple variables that, together, explain results. It feels right to people inside organizations, who notice how familiar factors combine to produce the same results, time after time. Now, they can isolate those factors, recognize where they are malfunctioning, and do something about it.

Moreover, the DNA metaphor effectively conveys the danger of tinkering with any one element—say, structure—in isolation. A change to any one building block is likely to combine with the other three in ways that are not intended, and may set the organization back rather than moving it forward. The framework we've developed tries to take all of the building blocks' interactions into account, so that the consequences and results of interventions become more predictable.

Beyond furnishing a framework that makes intuitive sense to people living in organizations, Organizational DNA provides practical, tangible, and actionable remedies for the variety of organizational ills that compromise results. And that's the greatest benefit of this research. The patterns and common themes that emerge from our growing database shed light on lessons learned and fixes that are transferable to organizations of the same type.

The data collected by the *Org DNA Profiler*[SM] cuts a wide swath across industries, geographies, and organizations. Represented are twenty-three industries—from banking to transportation to energy—and more than ten internal departments/functions (Human Resources, Information Technology, Legal, etc.). We also have data related to position or level within the company (e.g., top management, corporate staff, etc.).

With the addition of a "country" field in April of 2004, we began capturing location information, and now have profiles submitted from more than one hundred different countries. The Website has been translated into twelve different languages, including German, Japanese, and Chinese. The data collected by the *Org DNA Profiler*[SM] are from an extraordinarily broad cross-section of global organizations, a robust dataset from which to draw conclusions.

Because we continue to collect responses as new individuals visit the site and complete profiles, we periodically update the research results to reflect the addition of new data. To download the latest results, visit www.orgdna.com.

THE SEVEN TYPES

The nineteen questions in the *Org DNA Profiler*^{SM} are organized around the four building blocks: decision rights, information, motivators, and structure. Based on an individual's responses to these questions, his or her organization is classified as one of seven "types."

Based on the nature of each of the four DNA building blocks and the way they integrate with the others, most organizations fall into one of these seven categories. But not every company will generate one of these seven profiles—some responses indicate elements of more than one profile, and are categorized as "inconclusive." Moreover, not every individual in a given company will generate the same profile. While there is generally a predominant type, each organization is a mosaic of different perspectives and profiles. Indeed, these varying vantage points help us to isolate and identify the right set of remedies.

ORG DNA PROFILER^{SM} DEMOGRAPHIC DATA

Responses in the main data set come from companies of all sizes in a wide variety of industries and represent every function and every level in the corporate hierarchy (see Figures A.2 and A.3).

BREAKDOWN BY TYPE: MOST PEOPLE SEE THEIR ORGANIZATIONS AS UNHEALTHY

More than half of the thirty thousand respondents who've completed surveys as of this printing describe their organizations as "unhealthy"

FIGURE A.2—SURVEY RESPONSES BY COMPANY SIZE

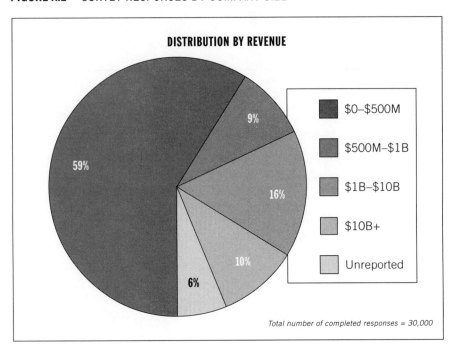

FIGURE A.3—SURVEY RESPONSES BY FUNCTION AND LEVEL

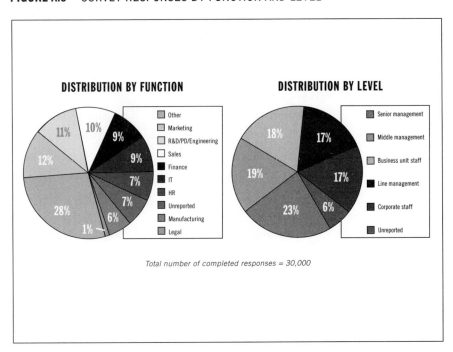

FIGURE A.4—ORGANIZATIONAL DNA PROFILE[SM] DISTRIBUTION

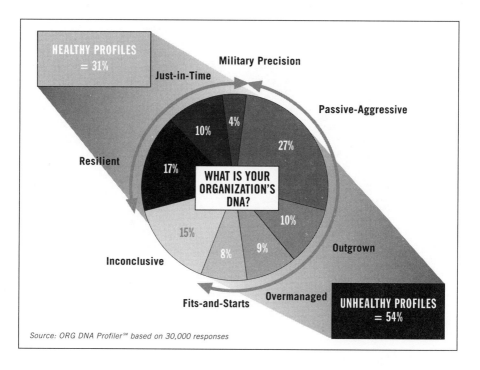

Source: ORG DNA Profiler[SM] based on 30,000 responses

(i.e., Passive-Aggressive, Fits-and-Starts, Outgrown, or Overmanaged). That's almost twice as many as describe their organizations as "healthy" (i.e., Resilient, Military Precision, Just-in-Time).

As Figure A.4 shows, Passive-Aggressive is the most prevalent organizational type, with 27 percent of respondents generating that profile. Ten percent describe their organization as Outgrown, nine percent as Overmanaged, and eight percent as Fits-and-Starts. Only 17 percent of respondents describe their organizations as Resilient.

PROFILES BY COMPANY SIZE: ORGANIZATIONAL DNA CHANGES AS COMPANIES GROW

While our data are cross-sectional—not time-series—they suggest that healthy growth is the exception, not the rule (see Figure A.5).

FIGURE A.5—PROFILES BY COMPANY SIZE: Healthy Growth Is Difficult

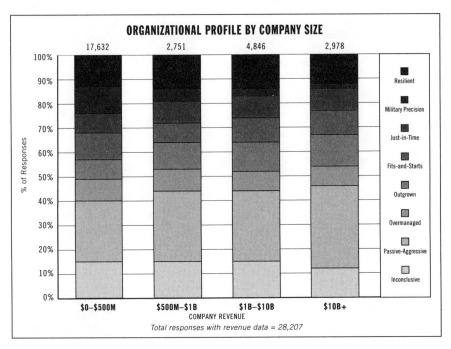

Specifically, by breaking down profile distribution by organization size (in terms of revenues), we can infer that companies migrate through certain stages as they grow. From these observations, we can posit that DNA *does* evolve as organizations adapt to growth and changes in the competitive environment.

Step 1: $0–$500 Million. Responses from small companies (in terms of annual revenues) are more likely than those of larger firms to result in healthy (Resilient, Military Precision, or Just-in-Time) profiles. These types of organizations are effective at execution.

This finding is intuitive as small companies tend to be younger and therefore may be more attuned to and aligned behind the vision and strategy of a founder who is still involved in the business. Moreover, their small size allows them to adapt more quickly and nimbly to external market shifts.

Step 2: $500 Million–$1 Billion. As firms cross the $500 million threshold, many seem to address their growing coordination challenges by centralizing authority in a strong senior team that drives the business. Not surprisingly, the Military Precision profile peaks in this revenue segment. We also see a significant increase in Outgrown profiles, suggesting that many firms in this size range become slow and unwieldy because of a badly centralized business model.

The data indicate that most of the increase in Military Precision, Outgrown, and Passive-Aggressive profiles in this size range comes at the expense of the Resilient and Just-in-Time categories. It appears that, as firms grow, many begin to lose the ability to execute and adapt.

Step 3: $1 Billion–$10 Billion. Once past the $1 billion mark, organizations become too large and complex to be run effectively by a small senior team via command-and-control mechanisms. Companies are thus forced to decentralize. Given that the proportion of Fits-and-Starts profiles increases in this revenue range, it appears that the transition to a decentralized organizational model often goes badly. Local managers may be given the authority to make decisions, but not the incentives or information to choose well.

Passive-Aggressive profiles also continue to increase as companies move through this size category. Incoherent and uncoordinated structures and processes create inertia, confusion, and ultimately a failure to execute.

Step 4: >$10 Billion. Above $10 billion in revenue, the proportion of healthy profiles (Resilient, Military Precision, and Just-in-Time) in the mix shrinks still further, suggesting that as companies grow larger, they are increasingly difficult to run effectively. Passive-Aggressive is the most prevalent profile in companies of this size.

PROFITABILITY BY PROFILE: WHERE THERE'S HEALTH, THERE ARE PROFITS

After the *Org DNA Profiler*^{SM} had been online for a few months, we added a question on relative profitability to confirm that our assumptions regarding health did indeed correlate with some financial measure of success. We asked respondents to indicate whether their companies were more profitable than their industry's average, less profitable, about the same, or unknown/inapplicable.

Not surprisingly, visitors whose responses result in one of the three healthy types (i.e., Resilient, Just-in-Time, Military Precision) are more likely to report better-than-average profitability (see Figure A.6).

However, organizational health alone does not deliver results. To win, firms need a sound strategy in addition to impeccable execution. This explains why, even among Resilient organiza-

FIGURE A.6—PROFIT LEVEL BY ORGANIZATIONAL PROFILE

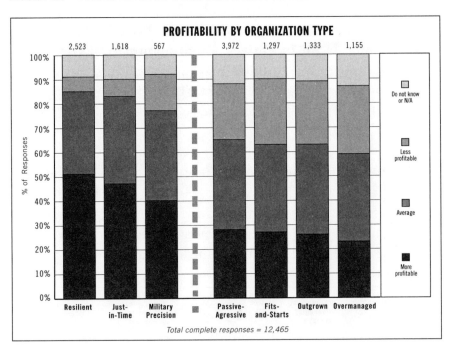

tions, 6 percent describe themselves as *less* profitable than the industry average. They may be healthy enough to execute well, but they may be executing the wrong strategy!

PROFILES BY LEVEL: ALTITUDE DETERMINES ATTITUDE

The *Org DNA Profiler^SM* has generated interest at every level: 23 percent of respondents identify themselves as senior management, 19 percent as middle management, 18 percent as business unit staff, 17 percent as line management, and 17 percent as corporate staff.

Our survey results indicate sharp differences in perception, however, between upper management and less senior groups, suggesting a fundamental disconnect between senior executives and the rest of their organization. Specifically, senior managers are consistently more optimistic in their assessment of organizational health (see Figure A.7).

FIGURE A.7—PROFILES BY LEVEL: Altitude Determines Attitude

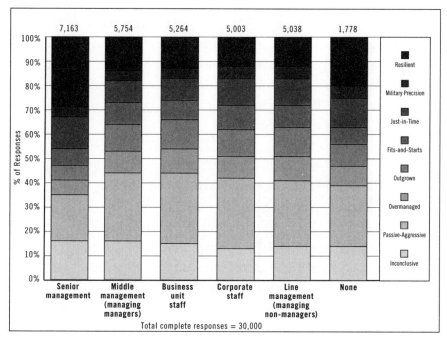

More than any other group in the organization, senior executives in our survey saw their firms as one of the healthy types: Resilient, Just-in-Time, or Military Precision. In fact, a senior manager completing the survey is more likely to get a healthy result than an unhealthy one. The opposite is true for any other level of respondent.

Digging deeper into individual question responses shows that senior management's positive bias persists across nearly all questions. Most strikingly, senior managers are far more likely to agree with the statement that "important competitive information gets to headquarters quickly" than are others in the organization. Given the yawning gap between their perception of their organization's effectiveness and that of every group that reports to them, one might question how well informed these executives really are.

Question-level analysis also shows widespread agreement among business unit and corporate staff, as well as line and middle managers, that "decisions are often second-guessed" in their organizations. But there appears to be a disparity in views regarding the role of corporate staff. Business unit staff believe that, in their companies, "the primary role of corporate staff is to audit the business units." Corporate staff, however, see their role as supporting the business units, a view senior management overwhelmingly supports. This reveals a basic disconnect between what corporate thinks it is providing, and how its services are perceived by the business units. These differences in perception can lead to significant organizational dysfunction.

PROFILES BY REGION: GLOBAL DISTINCTIONS EMERGE

Since we began asking respondents what country they were from, we have received roughly twenty thousand completed surveys, which reveal significant differences across regions.

For one, twice as many identified Europeans have taken the survey as identified Americans, and their responses, overall, tend to be much healthier (see Figure A.8). This finding holds across

FIGURE A.8—EUROPEAN PROFILES ARE SIGNIFICANTLY HEALTHIER

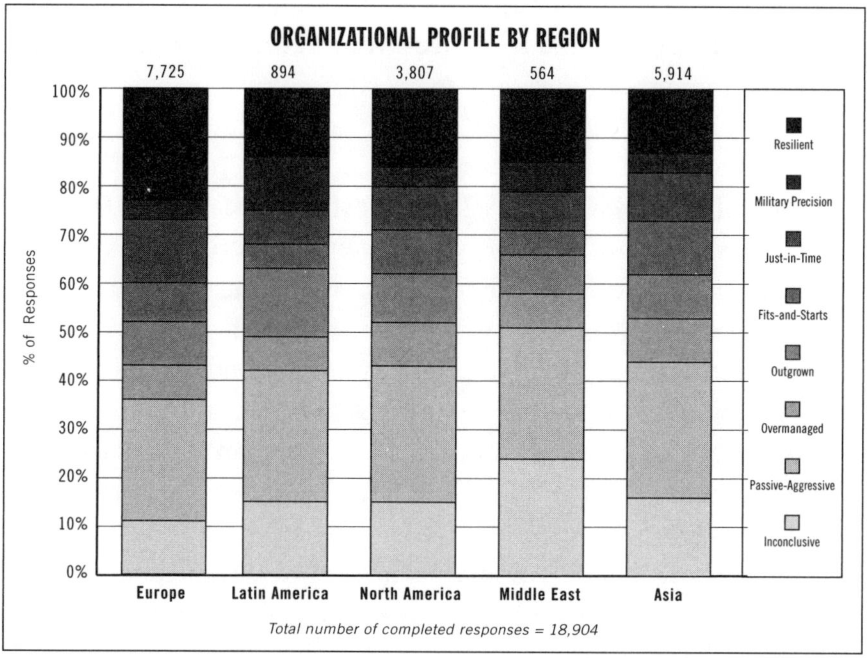

ORGANIZATIONAL PROFILE BY REGION

revenue segments and management/staff levels, despite the fact that North American respondents are, on average, more senior and therefore, one might have expected, more optimistic in their assessments.

At the heart of this discrepancy are strikingly different views within European and American companies on information flows and horizontal career movement. Europeans are much more likely than Americans to agree that "important information reaches headquarters quickly" and that "promotions include lateral moves." Economic and cultural differences certainly play a role in shaping perspectives, but we can hypothesize that American organizations do a less effective job of moving information to where it needs to go because they lack the formal communication channels and informal networks that managers often build as they move horizontally through an organization.

Other regional distinctions have also become apparent. For

example, Japanese respondents are much more likely to report Passive-Aggressive profiles than either their North American or European counterparts, and responses from Latin America generate the highest incidence of Outgrown profiles.

INDUSTRY DISTINCTIONS: SIZE AND ENVIRONMENT DO MATTER

Looking across the entire data set, the five industries with the highest proportion of unhealthy organizational types are (in descending order): utilities, health care, energy, autos and components, and technology hardware (see Figure A.9). The "healthiest" industries are real estate, food/beverage/tobacco, consumer packaged goods, commercial service and supplies, retail, hotels/restaurants/leisure, and food/beverage/tobacco.

It's easy to take a cursory look at these findings and conclude

FIGURE A.9—PROFILE DISTRIBUTIONS VARY BY INDUSTRY

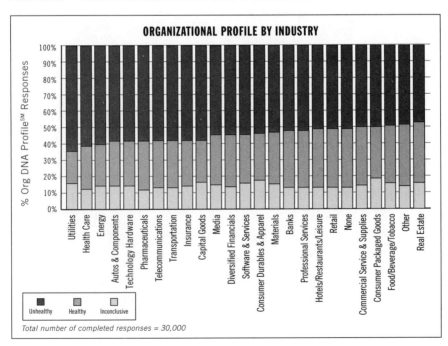

that size is the determining factor. In general, smaller companies tend to be healthier, and utilities, on average, are larger than real estate firms. But when we compare profiles by industry for companies in the same revenue segment, we see that utilities is still in the bottom quartile . . . in all four revenue segments. Health care, capital goods, and energy companies are among the bottom six industries in three out of four revenue segments. We can speculate that these laggards survive because they compete in regulated and/or capital-intensive industries. High barriers to entry likely protect unhealthy organizations from failure. In contrast, healthy profiles are dispersed among a wider set of openly competitive industries.

So, there it is: an intuitive idea grounded in decades of experience and a basic understanding of organizational economics becomes a unique organizational assessment tool and guide for how to get healthy and stay that way. For more information about the *Org DNA Profiler*[SM]—both research and remedies—we encourage you to visit www.orgdna.com to get the latest updates.

NOTES

1. A Tale of Two Managers

1. By "organization," we refer to any working unit—be it company, government agency, not-for-profit, university . . . or any division, committee, region, or functional unit therein.

2. Eighty-five percent of all organizations fall into one of the seven types. The remaining 15 percent generate an "inconclusive" result, meaning they track to more than one profile or display uncommon patterns, the exception rather than the rule.

3. As of December 2004, more than thirty thousand individuals have visited the site and completed profiles. Respondents come from companies of all sizes in a wide variety of industries and represent every function and every level in the corporate hierarchy. Their responses (and the thousands more we continue to collect) prompt a number of general observations about the health of most organizations. (For a more detailed analysis of our research findings, please consult "The Research Behind the Book," or visit www.orgdna.com.)

4. Of course, the more people within an organization that take the survey, the richer the analysis and the more targeted the set of remedies. The truth is, a colleague may experience a different organization than you do, and that is important information in developing a comprehensive sense of the enterprise and where it's working and breaking down. Most organizations are a mosaic of different types; the more employees you ask, the clearer the picture that results.

5. To diagnose your organization, go to www.orgdna.com and complete the *Org DNA Profiler*^{SM}.

6. *Org DNA Profiler*^{SM} research findings are discussed in greater detail in "The Research Behind the Book."

2. The Four Building Blocks

1. Ranjay Gulati, Gary Neilson, and David Kletter, "Organizing for Success in the 21st Century: The Relationship-Centric Organization," Kellogg School of Management at Northwestern University and Booz Allen Hamilton, March 2002.

3. The Passive-Aggressive Organization

1. More than a quarter of the thirty thousand individual respondents who have completed the *Org DNA Profiler*^{SM} survey describe their companies as Passive-Aggressive.
2. Of "Passive-Aggressive" respondents, 75 percent agree that "once made, decisions are often second-guessed." Only 27 percent "have a good idea of decisions/actions for which he or she is responsible."

   Only 23 percent of field/line employees in Passive-Aggressive organizations "have the information they need to understand the bottom-line impact of their day-to-day choices," and only 20 percent say "information flows freely across organizational boundaries."
3. Only 33 percent of Passive-Aggressive respondents feel their firms "deal successfully with discontinuous change in their competitive environment."
4. Personal interview with John Thompson, chairman, president, and CEO of Symantec Corporation, Cupertino, Calif., September 16, 2004.
5. Only 42 percent of Passive-Aggressive respondents agree with the statement "We rarely send conflicting messages to the marketplace" (versus 78 percent among "healthy" organizations).
6. Less than half of those who describe their organizations as Passive-Aggressive agree that the "individual performance appraisal process differentiates among high, adequate, and low performers." Only 41 percent believe that "the ability to de-

liver on performance commitments strongly influences career advancement and compensation."

7. New Horizons Medical System is a representative model of an organization we have encountered many times in our management consulting work. In fact, the quotes in this story are real. In this composite case, New Horizons is a multifacility medical group employing more than three thousand physicians, nurses, and other medical support personnel through six physician groups and ten medical centers in the Northeastern United States. It recently merged with another medical system in Pennsylvania. It also provides health insurance to high-risk populations through a wholly owned subsidiary. An executive team of one hundred people manages New Horizons.

4. The Fits-and-Starts Organization

1. Only 23 percent of Fits-and-Starts respondents "have a good idea of the decisions/actions for which he or she is responsible," far below the average of 78 percent for healthy profiles.

2. Not surprisingly, only 26 percent of those who generated a Fits-and-Starts profile on the *Org DNA Profiler*^{SM} report that the managers above them "regularly get involved in operating decisions," as compared to 71 percent for healthy organization types.

3. Of Fits-and-Starts respondents, 60 percent concede that their organizations frequently send conflicting messages to the marketplace, as compared to an average of 14 percent among healthy organizations.

4. Respondents agree that "important information reaches headquarters quickly" less than half the time at Fits-and-Starts organizations (47 percent), versus 84 percent, on average, for healthy organizations according to *Org DNA Profiler*^{SM} results.

5. Employees of Fits-and-Starts companies are half as likely to be promoted or compensated based on their performance than are employees of Resilient firms according to our *Org DNA Profiler*^{SM} data (44 percent Fits-and-Starts vs. 85 percent for healthy, 94 percent for Resilient).

6. Personal interview with Ken Freeman, former chairman and CEO, Quest Diagnostics, New York, N.Y., July 8, 2004.

7. Personal interview with Surya Mohapatra, PhD, chairman and CEO, Quest Diagnostics, Lyndhurst, N.J., July 26, 2004.

5. The Outgrown Organization

1. Wayne G. Broehl, Jr. *Cargill: Trading the World's Grain* (Hanover, N.H.: University Press of New England, 1992).

2. Personal interview with Jim Haymaker, VP of strategy and business development, Cargill, Inc., Minneapolis, Minn., September 17, 2004.

3. Only 7 percent of Outgrown respondents agree that "information flows freely across organization boundaries."

4. Only a third of Outgrown respondents believe that "information about our competitive environment gets to headquarters quickly."

5. Fully three-quarters of Outgrown respondents do not think that their firm "deals successfully with discontinuous change in the competitive environment."

6. Telephone interview with David Murray, chairman and CEO, Commonwealth Bank of Australia, September 29, 2004.

7. Of those who describe their organization as Outgrown, 79 percent agree that Corporate's primary role is "to audit the business unit," as compared to 23 percent among healthy organizations. And 91 percent feel decisions are often "second-guessed" (versus 37 percent).

8. Christopher A. Bartlett, "Microsoft: Competing on Talent (A)" (Boston: Harvard Business School Publishing, July 25, 2001), p. 5.

9. Donald N. Sull, "Why Good Companies Go Bad," *Harvard Business Review*, July 1, 1999, p. 42.

10. Alison Smith, "Laura Ashley's Floral Patterns Produce Budding Profits," *Financial Times*, May 28, 2001, p. 20. David Hoare, former CEO, finally closed five of seven Welsh factories.

11. Laura Ashley and Marianne Brun-Rovet, "Laura Ashley Tries to Get Back to Black," *Financial Times*, March 15, 2003, p. 14.

12. Helene Cooper, "Fashion: The Struggle to Mend Laura Ashley," *Wall Street Journal*, November 6, 1997, p. B1.

6. The Overmanaged Organization

1. Of all seven profile types, Overmanaged organizations are most likely (58 percent) to report that they are "less profitable than their competitors."
2. *Org DNA Profiler*SM respondents who describe their organizations as Overmanaged report more unhealthy behaviors than do other profiles.
3. Only 24 percent of Overmanaged respondents agree that their firm "deals successfully with discontinuous change." That compares to 90 percent, on average, among healthy profiles.
4. Of Overmanaged respondents, 68 percent *disagree* that "important information about our competitive environment gets to headquarters quickly," the most pessimistic take on this issue of any of the seven profiles.
5. Seventy-six percent of Overmanaged respondents report that "the primary role of corporate staff here is to *audit* the business units."
6. A staggering 92 percent of Overmanaged organization dwellers agree with the statement "Once made, decisions are often second-guessed," as compared to an average 37 percent among healthy-organization respondents.
7. Only 32 percent of Overmanaged respondents believe that "the ability to deliver on performance commitments strongly influences career advancement and compensation."
8. Only 33 percent of Overmanaged respondents feel that "line management has access to the metrics they need to measure the key drivers of their business."
9. Roughly 70 percent of Overmanaged profiles disagree with the statement "We rarely send conflicting messages to the marketplace."
10. Personal interview with Cyrus Freidheim, former chairman and CEO, Chiquita Brands International, Chicago, August 16, 2004.

7. The Just-in-Time Organization

1. Relative to Resilient organizations, Just-in-Time firms fall short on many of the measures you might expect. They are low on "lateral promotions" (54 percent vs. 72 percent), high on "second-guessing" (55 percent vs. 26 percent), and low on "informed field employees" (46 percent vs. 85 percent).
2. Personal interview with Tim Shriver, former chairman and CEO, Special Olympics, Washington, D.C., August 24, 2004.
3. Telephone interview with P.V. Kannan, founder and CEO, 24/7 Customer, October 26, 2004.
4. Personal interview with P.V. Kannan, founder and CEO, 24/7 Customer, Bangalore, India, July 26, 2004.
5. The World Games took place in Dublin, Ireland, in 2003, and will take place in Nagano, Japan, in 2005 and Shanghai, China, in 2007.
6. The Healthy Athletes initiative is designed to help Special Olympics athletes improve their health and fitness, leading to enhanced sports experience and improved well-being. It encompasses these disciplines: Fit Feet, FUNfitness, Health Promotion, Health Hearing, Opening Eyes, and Special Smiles.

8. The Military Precision Organization

1. Personal interview with Jim Keyes, president and CEO, 7-Eleven Inc., Dallas, Tex., November 12, 2004.
2. Only 23 percent of Military Precision respondents agree with the statement "Overall, this firm deals successfully with discontinuous change in the competitive environment."
3. Only 41 percent of respondents who describe their organization as Military Precision agree that "once made, decisions are second-guessed" (compared to 77 percent for unhealthy profiles).
4. Over two-thirds of Military Precision respondents agree that their organization "rarely sends conflicting messages to the marketplace."

5. Roughly three in four Military Precision respondents agree that "the ability to deliver on performance commitments strongly influences career advancement and compensation.

6. David B. Bell and Hal Hogan, "7-Eleven, Inc." (Boston: Harvard Business School Publishing, January 27, 2004), p. 17.

7. Harvard case study.

8. Personal interview with Stan Bromley, regional vice president, Four Seasons Hotels and Resorts, San Francisco, Calif., December 14, 2004.

9. The Resilient Organization

1. Fred Smith, "How I Delivered the Goods," www.fortune.com; "Innovators Hall of Fame," www.fortune.com/fortune/fsb/specials/innovators/smith.html.

2. Personal interview with Bill Cahill, corporate vice president, Human Relations, FedEx Corporate, Memphis, Tenn., December 12, 2004.

3. Telephone interview with Carlos Ghosn, president and CEO, Nissan Motor Co. Ltd., November 11, 2004.

4. Fred Smith.

5. *Keiretsu* is a consortia of loosely affiliated companies with business relationships that dominate the industrial landscape in Japan.

6. *Total Shareholder Return* as Procter & Gamble defines it is "the rate of return a business generates over a given period of time as a function of its beginning value, the interim cash flow it generates, and its end value."

7. Personal interview with Clayton Daley, CFO, Procter & Gamble, Cincinnati, Ohio, July 19, 2004.

8. Fred Smith.

9. Fred Smith.

10. Carlos Ghosn, "Saving the Business Without Losing the Company," *Harvard Business Review*, January 2002, pp. 37–45.

11. Ibid.

12. Fred Smith.

10. Caterpillar's Journey to Resilience

1. In-person interview with George Schaefer, retired chairman and CEO of Caterpillar Inc., Peoria, Il., October 20, 2004.
2. In-person interview with Glen Barton, retired chairman and CEO of Caterpillar Inc., Peoria, Il., October 20, 2004.
3. In-person interview with Stu Levenick, group president of Caterpillar Inc., Peoria, Il., November 24, 2004. In the mid- to late 1980s, Levenick was an assistant manager in the product source planning group.
4. In-person interview with Don Fites, retired chairman and CEO of Caterpillar Inc., Peoria, Il., October 18, 2004.
5. In-person interview with Steve Wunning, group president of Caterpillar Inc., Peoria, Il., November 12, 2004. In the mid- to late 1980s, Wunning was in Cat's logistics business.
6. In-person interview with Gerry Shaheen, group president of Caterpillar Inc., Peoria, Il., November 12, 2004. In the mid- to late 1980s, Shaheen was a regional manager in the North American sales group.
7. In-person interview with Jim Owens, chairman and CEO of Caterpillar Inc., Peoria, Il., November 11, 2004.
8. Levenick interview.
9. In-person interview with Gerard Vittecoq, group president of Caterpillar Inc., Peoria, Il., November 19, 2004. In the mid- to late 1980s, Vittecoq was a junior manager in the marketing organization.
10. Shaheen interview.
11. Schaefer interview.
12. Schaefer interview.
13. Schaefer interview.
14. Barton interview.
15. In-person interview with Jim Despain, retired general manager of the Tractor division, Caterpillar Inc., Peoria, Il., November 19, 2004.
16. Schaefer interview.

17. Barton interview.
18. Owens interview.
19. In-person interview with Dan Murphy, VP of Global Purchasing, Caterpillar Inc., Peoria, Il., November 19, 2004. In the reorganization, Murphy was appointed global product manager for the Hydraulic Excavator product line.
20. In-person interview with AJ Rassi, retired vice president of Human Services and Purchasing, Caterpillar Inc., Peoria, Il., November 19, 2004. Rassi headed the Wheel Loader and Excavator product division after the reorganization.
21. Despain interview.
22. Rassi interview.
23. Telephone interview with John Pfeffer, October 13, 2004. Pfeffer, now retired, was a plant manager in Mexico after the reorganization.
24. Owens interview.
25. Fites interview.
26. Pfeffer interview.
27. Schaefer interview.
28. Barton interview.
29. Pfeffer interview.
30. Barton interview.
31. Telephone interview with Mark Johnson, Caterpillar Corporate Public Affairs, March 4, 2005. The D9R matched Komatsu's horsepower but had the advantage of differential steering, a feature that Cat knew customers loved on their smaller tractors, and introduced on the D9 that year.
32. Levenick interview.
33. Murphy interview.
34. Pfeffer interview.
35. Despain interview.
36. Despain interview.
37. Despain interview.
38. Despain interview.
39. Caterpillar 2004 Annual Report.

40. Barton interview.

41. In-person interview with Doug Oberhelman, group president of Caterpillar Inc., Peoria, Il., November 17, 2004.

42. Caterpillar 2003 Annual Report, p. 16.

43. Owens interview.

44. Oberhelman interview.

45. Vittecoq interview.

46. Owens interview.

The Research Behind the Book

1. See, for example, Michael Jensen and William Meckling, "Specific and General Knowledge and Organizational Structure," *Journal of Applied Corporate Finance,* Vol. 8, No. 2, Summer 1995.

2. The research findings in this epilogue are based only on the data collected through the public site www.orgdna.com.

ACKNOWLEDGMENTS

Results is the product of the hard work, creativity, and insights of many talented people. While our names appear on the cover, we could not have written this book without the help and support of so many others.

Our clients in more than 300 companies have stretched our thinking and always kept us excited about our work. For more than fifty years between us, it has been a privilege to serve these leaders in business, government, and other organizations who provided the foundation of our ideas about achieving results. We especially want to thank the individuals and organizations who told their stories in *Results*: Jim Haymaker, Bob Lumpkins, Greg Page, and Warren Staley of Cargill; Glen Barton, Don Fites, Jim Owens, and George Schaefer from Caterpillar; Cyrus Freidheim of Chiquita; David Murray from Commonwealth Bank; Bill Cahill at FedEx; Stan Bromley of Four Seasons Hotels; Clayt Daley from Procter & Gamble; Carlos Ghosn and Pascal Martin at Nissan; Ken Freeman and Surya Mohapatra of Quest Diagnostics; Jim Keyes from 7-Eleven; Tim Shriver at Special Olympics; John Thompson of Symantec; and P.V. Kannan of 24/7 Customer. Their experiences brought the concepts in this book to life.

Our partners at Booz Allen Hamilton are extraordinary professionals and colleagues. Special thanks to those who reached out with us to encourage others to tell their stories in this book, especially DeAnne Aguirre, Gary Ahlquist, Paul Branstad, Andrew Clyde, Vinay Couto, Paul Kocourek, Decio Mendes, Jan Miecznikowski, Les Moeller, Mark Moran, Dermot Shorten, and Eric Spiegel. The management team at Booz Allen Hamilton, including Ralph Shrader, Dan Lewis, Cesare Mainardi, and Marie Lerch, provided support and resources throughout the process. Randall Rothenberg inspired and encouraged us to take on this project, and provided unmatched creativity in the earliest stages of structuring the story. Our technical team of Peter Hahn and Randy Johnson helped us launch the research, and Michael Bulger and Emma van Rooyen helped us communicate the messages.

A special acknowledgment and thank-you is owed to Karen Van Nuys. Karen was instrumental in developing the Org DNA framework and web-based profiler, she was a peer in contributing content and reviewing drafts, and could always be counted on to ensure the integrity of the ideas and analysis underpinning our work.

We were blessed by working with the exceptionally talented Tara Owen, a master writer and storyteller who translated our consultant-speak into stories that people would want to read. Tara brought the words to life and rearranged several months of her life during the process.

Our book support team of Vicki Anderson, Gretchen Hall, Anamika Singhal, Ilona Steffen, and Brenda Williams kept us on track and in sync throughout the process. Laura Brown assisted us in the early stages of the development of the book.

Jim Levine, our literary agent, helped focus the book and provided equal doses of optimism and realism.

Our editor at Crown Business, John Mahaney, was a constant source of creative, thoughtful, and constructive advice, and was instrumental in giving *Results* a voice that would resonate for everyone in an organization, not just the senior managers. His guidance about structure, flow, and messages vastly improved the final product.

Finally, no acknowledgments would be complete without heartfelt thanks to our wives, Trudy Havens and Lynne Pasternack; and our children, Eric and Lindsay Neilson and Joanne, Laura, and Dan Pasternack. They put up with late-night and weekend work, phone calls at odd hours and during vacations, and our inability to relax for several months. Their support means more to us than we could ever measure.

Gary L. Neilson and Bruce A. Pasternack

INDEX

accounting, Cat and, 253–54
Armstrong, Lance, 207
Ashley, Laura, 105

Ball, Jeff, 57–58, 60–62
Barton, Glen, 238–39, 245, 255-56, 261–62
Booz Allen Hamilton, 266–67
bouncing back from adversity, 212, 223–25
Bromley, Stan, 197, 202, 205–6
bureaucratic layering, 135–36, 139–40, 144–45
burnout, 2, 80
   and Just-in-Time organizations, 9, 158, 166–67

Cahill, Bill, 214–15, 220–22, 225, 227–28, 230–32, 234–35
Caliber System, The, 215
Cargill Incorporated, 97–100, 123–26
   blank slate look at itself by, 100, 109
   decision-making at, 99–100, 102–3, 110, 113–15, 118–20
   entrepreneurship at, 99, 109-10, 123, 125–26
   information flow at, 102
   key behaviors identified by, 118–19
   leadership cultivated at, 123–24
   in professionalizing manage-ment model, 118–20
   in refocusing headquarters on helm, 111–13

Caterpillar Inc. (Cat), 236–64
   characteristics of, 237–55, 258–64
   financial problems of, 237, 242–43, 255, 259
   financial turnaround of, 255–60
   new organizational blueprint of, 246–47
   as Overmanaged organization, 238–44, 256–57, 259, 262
   on Road to Resilience, 212, 244–59, 262–64
chains of command, 190–93
Chiquita Brands International, 137–43
   decision-making at, 137–40
   information flows at, 137, 139-41
   motivators at, 139, 141–42
   structure of, 137–40
commitment, commitments:
   Cat and, 249, 254
   and Just-in-Time organizations, 174–75
   Resilient organizations and, 215–17, 234, 236
Commonwealth Bank of Aus-tralia, 103–4, 110, 120–23
   decision-making at, 116–17
   leadership cultivated at, 121- 23
   in professionalizing manage-ment model, 120–21
   workarounds at, 106, 116–17
communication, communica-tions, 239, 277
   cascading of, 198–99

communication, communications
(*continued*)
  and Fits-and-Starts organiza-
    tions, 77, 86, 92–95
  and Just-in-Time organizations,
    160, 168, 182
  Military Precision organizations
    and, 187, 189, 198–99, 202–3
  organizational DNA building
    blocks and, 27, 29, 36
  Outgrown organizations and,
    99, 115, 122
  Overmanaged organizations
    and, 146, 148, 239
  Passive-Aggressive organiza-
    tions and, 49, 53, 60, 68
  Resilient organizations and,
    214, 216, 228, 233
competition, competitors, com-
  petitiveness, 3
  Cat and, 240, 242–44, 246, 256-
    57, 260, 262
  and Fits-and-Starts organiza-
    tions, 73–75, 78, 80
  and Just-in-Time organizations,
    9, 153–54, 159–60, 167, 172-
    73, 178–79, 184
  Military Precision organiza-
    tions and, 188, 190–92, 195,
    198, 206, 208–9
  organizational DNA building
    blocks and, 15, 27–29, 37,
    41–42
  Org DNA Profiler[SM] and, 272,
    276, 279
  Outgrown organizations and,
    98, 100, 102–3, 106, 108,
    116–17, 120, 122–23, 127
  Overmanaged organizations
    and, 129–32, 135, 145, 151,
    240, 242–44
  Passive-Aggressive organizations
    and, 45, 47, 51, 54, 59, 70
  Resilient organizations and, 10,

211, 217, 223–24, 227, 235,
  260
complaints, 230–32, 261
consistency, 190, 195–98, 206,
  209, 211
Corning Clinical Labs, 80–83, 85,
  89
corporate cultures:
  Cat and, 240, 250, 264
  controlled chaos and, 158–61
  and Fits-and-Starts organiza-
    tions, 71–72, 77, 92
  and Just-in-Time organizations,
    158–61, 175, 179
  Military Precision organiza-
    tions and, 201–2, 208
  organizational DNA building
    blocks and, 33–35, 38–41
  Outgrown organizations and,
    99, 102–3, 112–13, 118,
    121–22, 124–25, 127
  Overmanaged organizations
    and, 134, 136–38, 240
  Passive-Aggressive organiza-
    tions and, 45, 47, 53
  Resilient organizations and,
    212, 215–17, 221–22
courage of convictions, 219–23,
  260
creativity, 120, 200, 213–15
  Cat and, 257, 259
  and Fits-and-Starts organiza-
    tions, 72, 74–75, 94
  and Just-in-Time organizations,
    9, 153, 158, 179
  Overmanaged organizations
    and, 134, 136
customers, 7
  Cat and, 237–39, 243, 246, 252,
    256–57, 260
  and Fits-and-Starts organiza-
    tions, 72–74, 77, 81–82, 86,
    89, 92–93, 95
  and Just-in-Time organizations,

157, 159, 162, 164–66, 172, 176, 179–80

Military Precision organizations and, 188–91, 193–97, 200–202, 206–9

organizational DNA building blocks and, 15, 17, 19–23, 25, 28–29, 37–38

Outgrown organizations and, 98, 101–2, 105, 107–10, 112, 114–17, 119, 124, 126

Overmanaged organizations and, 129, 134, 140, 142–43, 147–48, 150–51, 239, 243

Passive-Aggressive organizations and, 49–50, 52–55, 59, 63, 65–66, 68

Resilient organizations and, 214–15, 220–21, 224, 226–27, 230–32, 260

Daley, Clayton, 223–24, 229, 235

decisions, decision-making, decision-makers, decision rights, 1, 4–8

bottlenecked, 136–37, 140, 241–42

Cat and, 237–43, 246–50, 252, 256, 258, 260

centralization of, 24–25, 81, 85, 91, 133, 188–89, 240

charting road maps for, 60

corporate hierarchy and, 135

decentralization of, 25, 76, 252, 258

delegation of, 145–47, 248–49

and Fits-and-Starts organizations, 18–19, 71, 75–76, 78–79, 81–82, 84–85, 87–93, 96

and Just-in-Time organizations, 157–58, 160, 162, 167–68, 170–73, 175, 183

making them stick, 65–66

Military Precision organizations and, 18, 188–93, 202–5, 210

organizational DNA and, 6–7, 10, 16–26, 29–30, 33–34, 36–37, 39–41

Org DNA Profiler^SM and, 265–66, 268–69, 273, 276

Outgrown organizations and, 8, 97, 99–104, 106, 108–11, 113–21, 126

Overmanaged organizations and, 129–40, 143–51, 190, 238–43

Passive-Aggressive organizations and, 43, 45–46, 49–51, 56–60, 62, 64–66, 68

and power of individuals, 4–5

pushing them out and measuring results, 113–15

Resilient organizations and, 212, 215–16, 219–23, 231, 260

shopping for, 50

single-point, 87–88

turf wars over, 56–57

defensive memos, 53–55

Despain, Jim, 251, 258–59

discipline, 229, 253

balancing entrepreneurial spirit with, 179–83

institutionalizing of, 170–74

and Just-in-Time organizations, 170–74, 179–83

Military Precision organizations and, 189–92, 196–98

entrepreneurs, entrepreneurship, 189

balancing management discipline with, 179–83

Cat and, 241, 251, 264

and Fits-and-Starts organizations, 8, 71, 75, 77, 187

and Just-in-Time organizations, 164, 169, 173, 179–83

entrepreneurs, entrepreneurship
    (*continued*)
  Outgrown organizations and,
    99–100, 108–10, 123, 125–27
  reigniting torch of, 108–10
executives:
  Cat and, 238–56, 258, 261–64
  and comparisons between man-
    agers, 1, 3, 5
  as deciders vs. presiders, 90–91
  and Fits-and-Starts organizations,
    19, 72, 74–75, 77–96, 187
  and Just-in-Time organizations,
    156–57, 159–66, 168–84
  Military Precision organiza-
    tions and, 185–89, 191–209
  organizational DNA building
    blocks and, 15, 19–21, 24,
    27–32, 35, 37–38, 41
  Org DNA Profiler^{SM} and, 273,
    275–77
  Outgrown organizations and,
    97–103, 105–17, 120–22, 125
  Overmanaged organizations
    and, 130–43, 145–50, 238–44
  Passive-Aggressive organiza-
    tions and, 7, 44–58, 61, 63–70
  and refocusing headquarters on
    helm, 108, 111–13
  Resilient organizations and,
    214–36, 261–62
  see also leaders, leadership

FedEx Corporation, 230–35
  in bouncing back from adver-
    sity, 225
  in entertaining inconceivable,
    213–15
  horizontal thinking at, 227–28
  in listening to complaints,
    230–32
  motivators at, 233–35
  in showing courage of its con-
    victions, 220–23

Fites, Don, 240–41, 246–49,
    253–54, 263
Fits-and-Starts organizations,
    11–12, 40, 71–96
  characteristics of, 8, 12, 18–20,
    71, 75–80, 91–93, 187–88,
    201, 274
  and organizational DNA,
    18–20, 82, 84
  and *Org DNA Profiler*, 271,
    273–75, 277
  and Quest Diagnostics, 80–90
  remedies for, 90–96
  and Southland, 187–88, 201, 206
Flying Tigers, 214, 225
founders, 134, 206, 272
fingerprints of, 104–5
  and Just-in-Time organizations,
    159–60, 162–63, 165, 172,
    181–82
  Outgrown organizations and,
    98, 102, 104–5, 107–8, 111,
    121, 125–27
  Resilient organizations and,
    213, 220, 225, 232–33
"Four Bases of Organizational
    DNA, The" (Neilson and
    Pasternack), 266
Four Seasons Hotels and Resorts:
  consistency at, 197
  feedback loops at, 202
  leadership at, 205–6
Freeman, Ken, 80–86, 89
Freidheim, Cyrus, 137–43
frequent losses, 76–77

Gallagher, Bob, 253–54
Gates, Bill, 104
Ghosn, Carlos, 216–19, 222–23,
    226–27, 230, 235–36

Haymaker, Jim, 98–100, 102,
    110–15, 118–20, 123–25
horizontal thinking, 225–28, 261

individuals, power of, 4–5, 17
information, information flow,
    15–33
  Bermuda Triangle of, 51–52
  as black box, 85–86
  brainpower tapping and, 175–79
  bridging trust gap with, 147–48
  Cat and, 237–41, 244, 246–48,
    250, 252–53, 256–57
  centralization of, 189, 240
  decentralization of, 101–4,
    133
  and Fits-and-Starts organiza-
    tions, 19, 71, 76, 79, 81,
    84–86, 91, 94, 96
  and Just-in-Time organizations,
    154–57, 159–60, 167–68,
    171–80, 182–83
  Military Precision organiza-
    tions and, 18, 188–89, 192,
    199–201, 204, 206
  organizational DNA and, 6–7,
    10, 16–33, 36–41
  Org DNA Profiler*SM* and,
    265–66, 268–69, 276–77
  Outgrown organizations and,
    101–4, 108–9, 113, 115–18,
    120–21
  Overmanaged organizations
    and, 79, 129, 133–37, 139–41,
    143, 145–49, 239–41
  Passive-Aggressive organiza-
    tions and, 43, 45–46, 50–52,
    56–62, 65–68, 70
  quagmires of, 79
  Resilient organizations and,
    212, 215, 218–19, 224,
    226–28, 231
  surfeit of, 57–58
  timely and efficient access to,
    66–68
integration, 101, 163, 239, 269
  and Fits-and-Starts organiza-
    tions, 75, 81, 87, 95

organizational DNA building
    blocks and, 40–42
  Passive-Aggressive organiza-
    tions and, 56, 59, 62–63
  Resilient organizations and,
    212, 214, 229
internal dissent, 46–50, 78

John Deere, 256
Just-in-Time organizations, 11–12,
    40, 153–84
  characteristics of, 9, 12, 190,
    153, 157–68, 274
  and Org DNA Profiler*SM*,
    271–77
  and Special Olympics, 159–61,
    165–70, 172–74, 176–79,
    181–84
  treatments for, 170–83
  and 24/7 Customer, 161–65,
    171–72, 175, 179–81

Kannan, P. V., 161–65, 171–72,
    175, 179–81
Keyes, Jim, 186–89, 191–93, 198-
    201, 203–4, 206–8
Komatsu, 240, 242–43, 256

Lafley, A. G., 224, 235
leaders, leadership:
  Cat and, 238, 263
  development of, 121–24,
    148–51, 203–6
  and Fits-and-Starts organiza-
    tions, 77–78, 82, 84–90
  and Just-in-Time organizations,
    160, 168, 170, 172–74, 176–77
  Military Precision organiza-
    tions and, 185–87, 203–6
  Outgrown organizations and,
    103, 108, 110–15, 119–24,
    126
  Overmanaged organizations
    and, 139, 148–51

leaders, leadership: *(continued)*
  Resilient organizations and,
    217, 220, 224, 231, 235
  see also executives
lean operations, 190, 193–95

managers, management, 13
  Cat and, 237, 239–42, 244–45,
    248–52, 255–59, 261
  centralization of, 101–2, 104–5,
    109, 111, 114
  command-and-control model of,
    101, 132–35, 137, 148–49, 151
  comparisons between, 1–7,
    32–34
  and Fits-and-Starts organizations,
    19–20, 73–77, 79–83, 85–94
  and Just-in-Time organizations,
    154, 158, 161–63, 170–77,
    179–83
  mavericks meeting, 161–63,
    179–80
  Military Precision organiztions
    and, 9, 18, 101, 185–92,
    194–200, 202–9
  organizational DNA and, 6–7,
    15–36, 38–41
  Org DNA Profiler^{SM} and, 267,
    273, 275–77
  Outgrown organizations and,
    99–100, 102–8, 110–12,
    117–21, 126–27
  Passive-Aggressive organiza-
    tions and, 43–55, 57–61, 63–69
  professionalizing model for,
    117–21
  Resilient organizations and,
    212, 216–17, 221–22, 224,
    226–29, 231–34, 261
  senior, *see* executives
  see also Overmanaged organi-
    zations
manufacturing:
  Cat and, 238–40, 243, 247–49,
    256–58, 260

organizational DNA building
    blocks and, 22–26, 37
  Outgrown organizations and,
    98, 105
  Overmanaged organizations
    and, 144, 239–40, 243
  Passive-Aggressive organiza-
    tions and, 67–68
  Resilient organizations and,
    218, 260
markets, marketing, 1–2, 272
  Cat and, 237–43, 248, 252–53,
    256–57, 259
  and Fits-and-Starts organiza-
    tions, 71–72, 74–79, 83, 87,
    89, 92, 94
  and Just-in-Time organizations,
    158, 164, 179, 183
  Military Precision organiza-
    tions and, 185–87, 190–91,
    196, 201, 206–7, 209
  organizational DNA building
    blocks and, 22, 24, 30–32, 37,
    41
  Outgrown organizations and,
    97–98, 103, 106–7, 109–10,
    114–17, 119–20, 123, 125
  Overmanaged organizations
    and, 130, 132–36, 138, 143,
    145–46, 148, 151, 238–43
  Passive-Aggressive organiza-
    tions and, 43–48, 50–52, 54,
    59, 61–63, 66–68
  Resilient organizations and, 10,
    211, 213, 215–17, 219,
    221–25, 228–29, 232, 235, 259
mavericks:
  Cat and, 245
  and Just-in-Time organizations,
    161–63, 176, 179–80
Micek, Ernie, 100, 113
Military Precision organizations,
    40, 185–210
  characteristics of, 9, 12, 18,
    101, 185, 189–97, 210, 274

Four Seasons and, 197, 202,
  205–6
Org DNA Profiler^{SM} and,
  271–77
7-Eleven and, 186–89, 191–93,
  196, 198–208
treatments for, 197–210
Mohapatra, Surya, 82, 86–90
motives, motivation, motivators, 4
Cat and, 237–39, 246–48, 250,
  254–55, 258–59
for collective endeavor, 95
and Fits-and-Starts organizations, 19, 71, 79–80, 84, 86,
  92–93, 95–96
and Just-in-Time organizations,
  153, 156, 160, 167–69, 175,
  180–83
Military Precision organizations and, 190, 194, 204
mixed-message, 52–53, 58
organizational DNA and, 6–7,
  10, 16–21, 29–41
Org DNA Profiler^{SM} and,
  265–66, 268–69, 277
Outgrown organizations and,
  103, 105, 108, 112–13, 118,
  121–23, 127
Overmanaged organizations
  and, 129–30, 132, 136,
  139–43, 148–50, 239
Passive-Aggressive organizations and, 43, 46, 50, 52–53,
  56, 58–59, 61, 63, 67–70
randomness of, 79–80
Resilient organizations and,
  211–12, 216–18, 220, 222–24,
  226, 233–35
Murray, David, 103–4, 106, 110,
  116–17, 120–22

Nagarajan, S. "Nags," 162, 172
New Horizons Medical System,
  55–62
Nissan Motor Co. Ltd., 216–19

culture of commitment and accountability at, 216–17
goal setting at, 217–19, 222
horizontal thinking at, 226–27
in refusing to rest on its laurels,
  235–36
as self-correcting, 229–30
in showing courage of its convictions, 222–23

organizational DNA:
building blocks of, 6–7, 10,
  15–42, 46, 62–63, 76, 84, 113,
  167–68, 183, 212, 218, 228,
  237–38, 246–47, 265, 268–69
Cat and, 237–38, 242,
  246–47
and Fits-and-Starts organizations, 18–20, 82, 84
and Just-in-Time organizations,
  167–68, 170
Outgrown organizations and,
  99, 113
Overmanaged organizations
  and, 143, 242
Passive-Aggressive organizations and, 62–64
Resilient organizations and,
  212, 218, 223, 228
organizations:
brainpower of, 175–79
flexibility of, 10, 100, 102, 173,
  179, 194, 209–11
health of, 11–13, 18, 24, 41, 85,
  90, 97, 108, 126–27, 139, 143,
  157, 167, 169–70, 175, 182,
  197, 200, 211, 223, 236,
  269–76, 278–79
Org DNA Profiler^{SM}, 10–12, 135,
  265–79
company size and, 270–73
demographic data and, 267, 269
and function and level of respondents, 270, 275–76
global distinctions and, 276–78

Org DNA Profiler^(SM) *(continued)*
  industry distinctions and,
    278–79
  on organization distribution,
    271
  profitability and, 274–75
  questions in, 266–67, 269
Outgrown organizations, 40,
    97–127
  Cargill and, 97–100, 102–3,
    109–15, 118–20, 123–26
  characteristics of, 8, 12, 77, 97,
    100–108, 133, 274
  and Commonwealth Bank of
    Australia, 103–4, 106, 110,
    116–17, 120–23
  Org DNA Profiler^(SM) and, 271,
    273–75, 277–78
  remedies for, 108–24, 127
outsiders, 61, 63–64, 110
Overmanaged organizations, 40,
    129–51
  Cat and, 238–44, 256–57, 259,
    262
  characteristics of, 8, 12, 77, 79,
    129–30, 132–38, 150–51, 190,
    238–44, 256–57, 259, 262,
    274
  Chiquita Brands and, 137–43
  Org DNA Profiler^(SM) and, 135,
    271, 274–75, 277
  remedies for, 143–51
Owens, Jim, 241, 247–48, 252–53,
    263–64

Passive-Aggressive organizations,
    11–12, 40, 43–70
  characteristics of, 7, 12, 43,
    45–55, 62, 274
  New Horizons and, 55–62
  Org DNA Profiler^(SM) and, 271,
    273–75, 277–78
  remedies for, 62–70
  Symantec and, 48–50, 53,
    63–66, 69–70

Pennsylvania Medical Center,
    56–57
performance evaluations, 118
  Cat and, 248–49
  and Fits-and-Starts organiza-
    tions, 79–80, 93, 95
  and Just-in-Time organizations,
    165–66, 178, 182, 184
  organizational DNA building
    blocks and, 34–36
  Overmanaged organizations
    and, 136, 149
  Passive-Aggressive organiza-
    tions and, 51–52, 68–70
  Resilient organizations and,
    224, 231–34
plans, planning, 94
  Cat and, 245, 248, 251, 255,
    261–63
  and Just-in-Time organizations,
    174, 177–78, 181
  Military Precision organiza-
    tions and, 188, 191, 206–8
  organizational DNA building
    blocks and, 22–25, 27, 30–31,
    34
  Overmanaged organizations
    and, 130–31
  Passive-Aggressive organiza-
    tions and, 48, 54, 58, 66
  Resilient organizations and,
    213–20, 222, 226, 231, 236, 261
Poissant, Genevieve, 55
price, prices, pricing, 59, 191
  Cat and, 238–43, 246–48,
    252–53, 257–59
  organizational DNA building
    blocks and, 21–22, 30
  Outgrown organizations and,
    99, 105, 111, 120–21
  Overmanaged organizations
    and, 134, 239–43
  transfer, 252–53, 259
Procter & Gamble (P&G), 142,
    223–24, 229, 235

products, production, productivity,
    1–3
  Cat and, 238–43, 247–52,
    254–58, 260
  and Fits-and-Starts organiza-
    tions, 76, 78, 81, 95
  and Just-in-Time organizations,
    164–66, 172, 180, 182
  Military Precision organiza-
    tions and, 186–89, 191,
    194–97, 199–202, 204–9
  organizational DNA building
    blocks and, 15–16, 20–24, 27,
    37–39
  Outgrown organizations and,
    98–99, 102, 104, 106–7, 109,
    111–12, 114–17, 120, 126
  Overmanaged organizations
    and, 134, 139–44, 148, 239–43
  Passive-Aggressive organiza-
    tions and, 44–46, 48–55,
    62–63, 65–68, 70
  Resilient organizations and,
    213–16, 218–20, 222–27,
    229–30, 232, 235, 260
profit, profits, profitability, 13, 23,
    30
  Cat and, 237–41, 243–44,
    247–57, 259–61
  and Fits-and-Starts organiza-
    tions, 72–73, 78, 81, 85, 91,
    93–95, 274
  and Just-in-Time organizations,
    171, 180, 274
  Military Precision organiza-
    tions and, 187, 202, 205, 274
  Org DNA Profiler^SM and,
    274–75
  Outgrown organizations and,
    106–7, 115, 274
  Overmanaged organizations
    and, 133, 139–40, 142, 147,
    150, 238–41, 243–44, 274
  Passive-Aggressive organiza-
    tions and, 58–59, 69, 274

  Resilient organizations and, 9,
    211, 214, 216, 218, 220–21,
    224, 227–28, 234, 259–61, 274

Quest Diagnostics, 80–90

Rassi, AJ, 250–51
reinvented wheels, 155, 164–65,
    168, 176
Resilience, resiliency, 42, 151
  definition of, 223
  and Just-in-Time organizations,
    183–84
  Military Precision organiza-
    tions and, 209–10
  Road to, 11–13, 212, 244–59,
    262–64
  Special Olympics and, 183–84
Resilient organizations, 40,
    209–64
  Cat and, 212, 238, 244–64
  characteristics of, 9–10, 12,
    209–36, 259–62, 274
  FedEx and, 213–15, 220–23,
    225, 227–28, 230–35
  Nissan and, 216–19, 222–23,
    226–27, 229–30, 235–36
  Org DNA Profiler^SM and,
    271–77
  and P&G, 223–24, 229, 235
  Quest Diagnostics and, 89–90
responsibility, responsibilities:
  assigning of, 92–93
  Cat and, 240–42, 244, 246–49,
    251, 258–59, 261
  and Fits-and-Starts organiza-
    tions, 73, 80, 85, 88, 90,
    92–93
  institutionalizing of, 170–74
  and Just-in-Time organizations,
    158–59, 168, 170–74, 176,
    181–82
  Military Precision organiza-
    tions and, 186, 190–91, 201,
    204, 206

responsibility, responsibilities:
    (continued)
    organizational DNA building
        blocks and, 24–26, 30, 32
    Outgrown organizations and,
        100–101, 107, 114–15,
        118–19, 122, 124–25
    Overmanaged organizations
        and, 130–31, 134, 136,
        138–40, 142, 144, 146–51,
        240–42, 244
    Passive-Aggressive organiza-
        tions and, 45–46, 56, 59–60,
        65
    Resilient organizations and,
        215–17, 219, 223, 227,
        229–30, 259, 261
resting on one's laurels, 235–36,
    262
restructuring, *see* structure, re-
    structuring

sales, salespeople, 1, 180
    Cat and, 238–39, 241, 243, 248,
        252, 257–58
    and Fits-and-Starts organiza-
        tions, 73, 81, 86, 88, 92
    Military Precision organiza-
        tions and, 186–87, 192,
        199–201, 204–5, 207
    organizational DNA building
        blocks and, 15, 22, 25, 37–38
    Outgrown organizations and, 8,
        97, 102–6, 116, 120–21, 124
    Overmanaged organizations
        and, 140, 144–50, 239, 241,
        243
    Passive-Aggressive organiza-
        tions and, 44, 48, 50, 65, 67
    Resilient organizations and,
        223–24, 227–30, 232
Schaefer, George, 238–48, 254,
    261–63
Schmidt, Larry, 55, 61
self-correcting, 228–30, 261–62

7-Eleven, 186–89, 198–208
    chain of command at, 191–93
    communication at, 189,
        198–99, 203
    consistency at, 196
    feedback loops at, 200–202,
        205
    information flow at, 199–201,
        204, 206
    leadership at, 186–87, 203–5
    planning at, 191, 206–8
shadow staffs, 39–41
Shriver, Eunice Kennedy, 159–60,
    165, 181–82
Shriver, Tim, 159–60, 165–66,
    168–70, 172–74, 176–78,
    181–84
signposts, 93–94
Smith, Fred, 213, 220, 225,
    232–33
Sony Music, 199
Southland Corporation, 187–88,
    201, 206
Special Olympics, 165–70, 181–84
    accountability and discipline
        at, 172–74
    balancing entrepreneurial spirit
        with management discipline
        at, 181–83
    corporate culture of, 159–61
    decision-making at, 160,
        167–68, 173, 183
    firefighting burnout at, 166–67
    information flows at, 160,
        167–68, 173–74, 176–79,
        182–83
    motivators at, 160, 167–69,
        182–83
    reinvented wheels at, 165–66,
        168
    structure of, 160, 167–69,
        173–74, 177, 181–83
    tapping brainpower at, 176–79
structure, restructuring:
    Cat and, 237–38, 245–50,

252–64
and Fits-and-Starts organizations, 84, 88–89, 96, 187–88
flattening organization and, 143–45
horizontally and vertically reinforced, 88–89
and Just-in-Time organizations, 9, 153, 160, 163–64, 167–69, 172–74, 177, 179, 181–83
Military Precision organizations and, 188, 191–92, 198, 200
organizational DNA and, 6–7, 10, 15–21, 30, 36–41
Org DNA Profiler^{SM} and, 265–69, 273
Outgrown organizations and, 113–14, 120, 125
Overmanaged organizations and, 132–33, 135–40, 143–45, 147, 149–50
Passive-Aggressive organizations and, 46, 56, 59, 61–62, 66
Resilient organizations and, 212, 224, 259–62

scattered vs. synergistic, 56
shadow staffs and, 39–41
Symantec Corporation, 53, 63–66
internal dissent at, 48–50
making decisions stick at, 65–66
ringing bell curve at, 69–70

Thomas, Don, 200–201
Thompson, John, 48–50, 53, 63–66, 69–70, 206
transfer prices, 252–53, 259
trust, 147–48, 202, 220
24/7 Customer, 161–65
accountability and discipline at, 171–72
balancing entrepreneurial spirit with management discipline at, 179–81
mavericks vs. managers at, 161–63, 179–80
reinforcing promises at, 175
reinvented wheels at, 164–65

Wogsland, Jim, 246
workarounds, 24, 105–7, 115–17

ABOUT THE AUTHORS

Gary L. Neilson is a senior vice president of Booz Allen Hamilton in Chicago, having been with the firm since 1980. He is a member of Booz Allen's board of directors and operating council, and has served as the managing partner of the Chicago office.

As the global leader for the firm's service offering on organizations and people, Gary works with Fortune 1000 companies on issues of business model transformation, organization model design, organization restructuring, and major change initiatives. He serves clients across all industries, including consumer products, retail, utilities, transportation, automotive, health, industrials, banking, and insurance. In his 25 years with the firm, he has served more than 250 companies and public sector institutions on organization matters.

Gary leads the global Booz Allen team that developed the Org DNA ideas and deploys the related "Organizing for Results" service offering, helping companies diagnose and solve the issues associated with ineffective organizations and strategy implementation. The team's research base includes more than 50,000 Org DNA profiles from more than 100 countries. Gary has authored or coauthored more than 25 articles on organization design and transformation, and has appeared on CNBC's *Power Lunch* and ABC's *World News This Morning*.

Gary has an MBA in finance from Columbia, where he received the Wall Street Journal Award for overall academic excellence in finance. He also holds a B.S. in accounting from King's College, where he earned the S. Idris Ley Memorial Award for the highest academic achievement in his graduating class.

Bruce A. Pasternack is president and CEO of Special Olympics, which provides year-round sports training and athletic competition for almost two million children and adults with intellectual disabilities in more than 50 countries, based in Washington, D.C. Prior to joining Special Olympics, Bruce was a senior vice president and managing partner of Booz Allen Hamilton in San Francisco, having been with the firm since 1978. There, he founded and led the organization and strategic leadership practice, helping clients solve their organization, business model transformation, leadership, and governance issues. Bruce also served as managing partner of the firm's global energy, chemicals, and pharmaceuticals practice, and as a member of Booz Allen's board of directors and operating council.

Bruce coauthored *The Centerless Corporation,* and has written more than twenty-five articles related to organization and leadership. His article *Yellow Light Leadership* appeared in the *Wall Street Journal* in 2003. Bruce also led Booz Allen's worldwide study with the World Economic Forum on how companies build the organizational capacity for leadership and renewal, which was reported on in Davos, Switzerland, and in *Strategy+Business.* He has appeared on CNBC, CNN, CBS, and NPR.

Prior to joining Booz Allen, Bruce was Associate Administrator for Policy and Program Evaluation at the Federal Energy Administration, responsible for energy policy development and coordination in the executive branch, and served as principal staff to the President's Energy Resources Council. He also worked at the President's Council on Environmental Quality in the executive office of the president, and at General Electric Company. Bruce holds engineering and operations research degrees from The Cooper Union and University of Pennsylvania, respectively. He serves on the board of trustees of The Cooper Union, and has served on the board of directors of Special Olympics and the Advisory Council of Stanford's Graduate School of Business, the Advisory Board for the University of Southern California's Center for Effective Organizations, the Bay Area Council's board of directors, and the Western Regional Advisory Board of Catalyst.